YOUR PERSONALITY

and How to Live with It

YOUR PERSONALITY

and How to Live with It

GREGORY G. YOUNG, M.D.

New York *1978* ATHENEUM / SMI

Library of Congress Cataloging in Publication Data

Young, Gregory G
  Your personality and how to live with it.
    1. Personality. 2. Typology (Psychology)

I. Title.
BF698.Y59   1978   155.2'64   78-55423
ISBN 0-689-10918-0

Copyright © 1978 by Gregory G. Young, M.D.
Published simultaneously in Canada by McClelland and Stewart, Ltd.
Designed by Kathleen Carey
Composition by Kingsport Press, Inc., Kingsport, Tennessee
Printed and bound by Fairfield Graphics, Fairfield, Pennsylvania
First Edition

Contents

v

YOUR PERSONALITY

and How to Live with It

Know thyself.
ORACLE OF DELPHI

An Introduction to Personality Style

"HEY! THAT'S ME!"

Yes, indeed. This book is about you and your personality style. After reading it carefully, you will be able to recognize yourself and perhaps others close to you: spouse and good friends, parents and children, brothers and sisters, and even a few colleagues and co-workers. You should also come to know and understand more clearly why you do many of the things that you do in the ways that you do them. You should be able to appreciate why you experience certain feelings and emotions and to understand why you differ from others in attitudes and actions. You should know more fully and consciously how you behave, and what you can expect of yourself. And if all this happens, you should find yourself enjoying yourself and others—and all of life—much more fully and contentedly.

Our first task is to be sure that you understand what we mean by "personality." It has nothing to do with those affectations and mannerisms acquired in charm schools and self-improvement courses, or from watching television's pop heroes and heroines. Those are fads and fashions that come and go. *Personality* is a word that signifies the

3

personal traits and patterns of behavior that are unique to the individual. You experience these traits and patterns of behavior as your own; others observe them directly or through your communication with them. Personality includes attitudes, modes of thought, feelings, impulses, strivings, actions, responses to opportunity and stress, and everyday modes of interacting with others. When these elements of personality are expressed in a characteristically repeated and dynamic combination, we have what I call a *personality style*.

Personality is unique to each individual. Personality style is shared with others who repeatedly display the same characteristic and dynamic combination of traits and behavior patterns. Personality style is evident in the things that we do and the ways that we do them again and again in the same recurring fashion. Given like situations in the same or similar environment, persons of the same personality style have a tendency to respond in a relatively consistent and recurring pattern. This is what I mean by personality style. I am not speaking of personal habits—repeated mannerisms such as the way you brush your teeth or the ritualistic way you always drink your Scotch with a splash of water. I am speaking of those recurring responses such as your good feeling when the boss says "Good morning," or your competitive urge every time you step up to the first tee, or your fear of flying, or your resistance to job relocation even when it would mean a promotion and salary increase. These recurring attitudes and dispositions and behavior patterns constitute personality style.

Each style has its individual purpose, yet it has an effect on and is altered by its environment. Each style can experience happiness and pleasure as well as tension and despair. An awareness of personality styles can help you understand why there are various opportunities and dangers that occur at particular times in your progress through life. One personality style may be influenced greatly by graduation from school or by the death of a parent; another might be positively or negatively influenced by a compliment or by success. Each style displays different kinds of skills and coping strategies and opportunities for investment of emotional energies. Thus the better you know your own personality style, its identifying traits and characteristic strengths and weaknesses, the more you can know what to expect of yourself as you move through life.

I cannot emphasize too strongly the need for and the potential

4

value of your recognizing and responding to your personality strivings. This might be a basic definition of health. When you are able to look at the positive, constructive aspects of your personality style, you have certain options and alternatives open to you, as well as a frame of reference to explain your meaning, value, and humanity. You can be more aware of feelings of tension, helplessness, and meaninglessness. And you will be able to deal with them more appropriately. In short, by knowing yourself better, you can better deal with both your strengths and your weaknesses.

THE TWELVE PERSONALITY STYLES

So far as I have been able to determine, there are twelve identifiable personality styles. Why twelve and not thirteen, or three, or three million? I don't know. What I do know is that since I first began to recognize separate styles in my psychiatric practice, I have encountered only twelve distinct styles. There may be more, but so far in my experience with diagnostic interviews and treatment of many hundreds of people, only twelve styles have surfaced. Together with my staff and the personnel of several hospitals, I have identified these same dozen styles again and again, in persons of all ages and of both sexes, of all races and ethnic backgrounds, of all economic and educational levels, and in all degrees of illness and health.

Some people feel that their individuality is threatened when they are first exposed to the concept of personality style. They fear that in our highly compartmentalized and computerized culture, this is just another indication of the diminished individual. Not at all. If anything, a clear understanding of the concept of personality style is liberating. It helps us to see ourselves as being more unique. It enhances our individuality as we learn to appreciate more fully those things about us that are alike *and* those that are distinguishing. Through the concept of personality style we recognize new depths in each personality. We appreciate more distinct and available resources in each person. Much is enriched, nothing is lost. Each of us becomes more recognizably a unique person when we can describe the many ways that proclaim our common human sameness *and* our distinguishing characteristics—height, weight, color of hair, eyes and complexion, blood type, interests, abilities, values, tastes, experiences, occupations, and skills. And now personality style. Each distinguishing factor gives every one of us distinctive features that contribute to individual identity. Now we can each say, and mean it: "If you know yourself, you don't have to be everything to everybody."

And yet it is also true that the more we discover about our sameness, the more we are attracted by what we share in common with others. Our sense of community, so necessary to the human condition, is solidified and intensified by common experiences and shared feelings. It is nice to know that in Manhattan and Miami, Moscow and Madrid, there are other human beings who share our strengths and weaknesses and our feelings, who tend to react under stress as we do, who behave in like situations in much the same way that we do. The more we discover about our shared characteristic behavior, the less our ignorance of each other and the fewer our fears and prejudices.

Too often we hear generalizations expressed that simply aren't true. Item: "All Americans are aggressive and competitive." *Some* Americans are, but many more are not. "All politicians are power-hungry and manipulative." Some few may be, but others are idealistic lawmakers, or conscientious representatives of the people, or responsive administrators in public service. Many stereotypes and clichés crumble when we know and properly apply the concept of personality style. In categorizing people, we need to be very careful and open to the breadth and range of human potential made evident through the proper understanding of the dynamics of all personality styles.

It is true that a given culture may promote a particular personality style as the norm in terms of the needs and climate of the times. Nineteenth-century Western culture, for example, placed great emphasis on being right and proceeding forcefully, thus accenting the style of the Determined Personality. The youth movement of the 1960s focused on independence, individuality, and high standards of institutional morality, qualities that match the style of the Idealistic Personality. But here we need to note a danger. A cultural climate or a particular environment may so demand conformity to a certain style that it tends to inhibit free development and expression of other styles. It may even be punitive.

This can even happen in the home where a more dominant parent demands that a child conform to a style that is not his own, thus expecting him to behave inappropriately in terms of his own personality style. Then, too, simply because such a parent seems powerful

culture

and attractive, the child may attempt to pattern himself after that parent—or after an authoritative teacher or other appealing adult. A frustrated child is certain, and neurosis is likely. When the home, or any other environment, insists on lock-step conformity to a solitary style of behavior, it becomes a factory for neurosis.

One of the more interesting experiences in group therapy and family therapy is to observe how sympathetic and generous persons of the same personality style are toward each other—without even being aware of sharing the same personality style and what that means. They are simply aware of each other. Empathy and concern always surface, as do basic insights into problems and how they might be resolved.

How does this recognition come about? Each personality style has its own "currency." The Ambitious Personality, for example, places much emphasis upon competing and winning. Another Ambitious Personality will pick up on the striving and the aggressiveness; but, being outside the subjective moment, he can more objectively evaluate and recommend and thus can help the other a great deal. The same experience of recognition can and does happen anywhere. It is no accident that we often hear casual comments such as, "Bill is just like his father." Bill doesn't look a bit like his father; he looks like his mother. But Bill's expressed attitude and his actions very much resemble his father's characteristic ways of looking at things and doing things. "Oh," you say, "Bill learned all that from his father." True, Bill did learn many things from his father. But, more importantly, Bill inherited a *personality style* from his father. His father may have been particularly influential as a very good model of how someone with that style might use it to good advantage. But Bill and his father were both *born* with a comparable disposition to see things and do things in characteristically repeated ways consistent with their shared personality style.

You may have had an experience like this: "I don't know why, but you remind me so much of this buddy I had in the navy twenty years ago." Or you may have said: "Alice's new husband is so much like her first husband—and, come to think of it, her second husband, too." It is no coincidence that Alice's husbands are all so much alike, or that you are attracted to two very like buddies twenty years apart. These casual comparisons are really the concept of personality style at work in the world.

Once you understand the essential concept and what you can

expect of a given personality style, you can go beyond casual comparisons to a much deeper understanding of and appreciation for the behavior of others with whom you live, work, and play.

PERSONALITY STYLE IS INHERITED

How do you come by your personality style? As I noted in the example of Bill above, you are born with a fixed personality style inherited from *one* of your parents, not from both. Constituted with your own personality style, you project your own life goals, purposes, plans, and approaches in a characteristic, consistent way. And this one, basic same personality style endures recognizably throughout your life. It is as much a part of you as the color of your eyes, the patterns of your fingerprints. You utilize this personality style in everything you do—waking or sleeping, pondering the fate of the world, arguing prices with the grocer, working or playing, making love, seeking a pay raise.

From infancy on through life you can either use this personality style to your advantage and comfort in your progress, or you can struggle against it with great stress and anxiety. Each personality must progress through the different stages of development in its own particular way, meeting its own needs and problems, responding to opportunities and crises with its own particular strengths and vulnerabilities. Each personality has early experiences that influence later perceptions, even when these earlier experiences are not recalled consciously. So the more and the earlier you know about how you function within the organization of your own personality style, the greater your opportunity to live progressively in a fulfilling and contented manner.

Since personality is inherited from one parent only, the probability of two styles coexisting in the same family is high. The need is great that both styles be recognized, understood, and appreciated. Otherwise communication and interaction can be difficult, and the peace and harmony of the family disrupted. We have to learn to appreciate the differences, encourage openness, practice patience and understanding. We have to become more accepting of others, and this is first learned—or not learned—in the family.

Understanding begins with the two parents of differing per-

8

sonality styles learning to adapt to each other. Courtship may have greatly facilitated this process of adaptation, but with their own progress through life, parents will need to adapt continually—to the births of children, to sicknesses, to ways of handling finances, to mobility, to the growth of their children into adulthood, to middle-age and beyond. All the while they are interacting and adapting to each other, their children are learning how to be aware of and to appreciate all the likenesses and differences between themselves and their parents, themselves and their siblings. This process carries on into all of life as they make friends, enter school, grow, and face the business of living. The mutual awareness and regard, the quality of values, the tolerances for different values and styles, the mode of communicating and coping demonstrated by parents influence children immediately and all through life. So, understanding and insight into personality style are important throughout the early years as well as later.

RECOGNIZING PERSONALITY STYLES

As you read the chapters on the twelve personality styles, be attentive to the language. As much as possible, I have used the language of individuals representing each style, as they have told me their wishes, dreams, early recollections, their problems, successes, strengths, and vulnerabilities. What I know of personality style is derived from listening carefully to my patients and their relatives: they are my teachers. Even the descriptive titles of the styles come from them. "Patient," "Determined," "Adaptable" are the terms that they use repeatedly to characterize themselves. Each word succinctly summarizes some essential disposition of a style. The Patient Personality is characteristically patient, the Determined Personality readily admits to a tenacious pursuit of goals, and the Adaptable Personality will talk of adapting to the standards of others. So you will find it helpful to pay close attention to the language. The recurrence of key words—as well as repeated themes and dominant thought patterns—may trigger a spark of recognition.

The description of each personality style is based largely on actual case and personal histories. The names, of course, are not those of my patients, and the circumstances and details presented here have been altered sufficiently to make personal recognition impossible. But the situations, the interactions, the expression of feelings, and the characteristic behavior are very real and true and quite typical of my patients and others who share the style depicted.

Most of the material presented pertains to adult life, although early childhood recollections are given for each personality style and a brief account of progress through the various stages of life is sketched. Emphasis is given to strengths and vulnerabilities—which quite often are one and the same—and to the coincidence of opportunity and crisis within the same situation. Typical stresses are described as they affect choices of partners, occupation, relationships, and recreation. Life-changing events are exemplified, as are the usual ways of handling difficult situations such as death, illness, divorce, or retirement.

Each personality style will view all occasions and situations differently, and the alternatives open to the individual will vary from style to style. Here clear recognition of a person's own style is critical: a crossing of styles in solving problems can create emotional disaster —real harm can be done. Within the concept of personality style the folk axiom is true: "One man's meat is another man's poison." So be very careful about identifying yourself—and others—with a given personality style until you have read through *all* the styles described here. Recognition of your own style means that consistently you have identified with typical statements, patterns of behavior, strengths and weaknesses. And be just as careful in identifying others. There are real dangers in relating to others—particularly children—on the basis of wrong identification of style.

A cautionary comment needs to be made about traits and symptoms and the language that describes them. You may read the description of the Patient Personality as giving, generous, patient, tolerant, security-minded, and then say to yourself, "I'm all of those, but that doesn't sound like me." And you would probably be right in both conclusions. Most of us are giving, generous, patient, and so on, just as all of us get angry and feel anxious at times. Any personality style has sufficient room for abuse of drugs and alcohol, just as all of us can feel the desire to cry or get angry or be unfaithful.

What distinguishes personality styles is the dynamic combination of traits and patterns of behavior as they occur *repeatedly*. So when I speak of the Patient Personality as generous, this trait and corresponding behavior are constantly and emphatically evident and characteristic. Beware of isolating on a single trait or descriptive word unless that trait or word is given specific focus in the general discussion of the personality style. In that case, the discussion itself should make clear the given emphasis.

THE ESSENTIAL DETERMINANT

Each personality style has what I call its *essential element* or basic operating principle. This is that style's primary orientation or fundamental attitude in encountering other people and the environment. This essential determinant is a dynamic disposition to respond in a characteristic pattern, so it is the key to understanding as well as recognizing a particular personality style. You will note in reading the description of the personality styles that these essential elements surface often, and the reason is that they help greatly in explaining the actions and interactions of the individuals exemplifying each style. The determinants are sometimes expressed and highlighted by a key phrase involving the word "urge"—for example, the "urge for the ultimate," or the "ultimate urge," when dealing with the Influencing Personality; the "urge to give," or the "giving urge," with the Patient Personality.

Here is a basic rule to remember as you read through the description of personality styles: *The essential element of any personality style provides the individual with his greatest strength and his greatest weakness.* This means that each new situation that arises can be either an opportunity or a crisis. For example, the essential determinant of the Patient Personality, as I have indicated, is the "giving urge," the great emphasis that personality places on being tolerant and giving in order to avoid being vulnerable. This is a truly great strength. Society benefits greatly from the Patient Personalities who are constantly responding to other people's needs through giving and doing. But, as you will note when you read the chapter on the Patient Personality, a person of that style can render others helpless with his incessant giving and doing. More, the Patient Personality can "give" himself into a frenzy of generosity that finally prompts him to want to bolt the door, disconnect the phone, and hide from everyone. Or he can give and give until he bankrupts himself. It happens. Here you see the coincidence of opportunity and crisis and the pivotal option of strength or weakness.

ENVIRONMENTAL INFLUENCES

No one lives in isolation. Each of us exists within an environment made up of all the physical things that surround us: our social and economic circumstances, a political structure, a media climate, a culture, and other people. All of these factors influence our lives and development. Our environment nurtures us, supports us, threatens us, comforts us, gives us pleasure, limits us, worries us, responds to us, accepts us, rejects us. Most of us live most of the time in a particular scaled-down environment of familiar places and people, and it is in this sense that we usually use the word "environment" here.

Each personality style tends to view the same environment differently, according to the vantage point of his own essential determinant. The Patient Personality, again, sees the environment as demanding, the Persistent Personality sees it as providing, and the Sensitive Personality views it with caution as possibly threatening. The environment is always there to be reckoned with. Each personality style relates and behaves on the basis of his perception of the environment —his reality—and on the basis of how he feels about himself. If his attitude toward himself and environment is both healthy and realistic, he can expect to interact optimally, drawing what he needs from the environment while also contributing to it. Mutuality and reciprocity govern his interactions and make it possible for him to form relationships. Equilibrium is maintained in all transactions.

The healthy person can be said to have strength. By "strength" I mean an individual's ability to assess his personality assets and capabilities and life opportunities realistically and then respond decisively to whatever situation confronts him. Part of this process, of course, involves an awareness of the ability and potency of others in the environment and realistically appraising them. Too often in my practice of psychiatry I see the individual who has stripped himself of authority, surrendering it to someone or something else in the environment. I often hear a patient in group therapy tell of a situation in which he feels helpless and powerless, only to have another member of the group comment, "You sure give the boss a lot of power." The boss could equally well be a spouse, a friend, or a mother-in-law, or it could be the total environment.

The person without a sense of his own strength feels not only helpless but rejected or unworthy or wounded. You could describe this person as unrealistic, immature, or unhealthy; he simply isn't able to function with full energy; he cannot respond fully to opportunity. And, more often than not, he constantly suffers anxiety, which can be defined as a pervading sense of feeling trapped, scattered, and powerless. Commentators recently have begun to describe our age as an age of anxiety—overwhelmed and powerless, apathetic and alienated, by an environment that presents mass culture, mass produced by the mass media. It needn't be that way—you don't have to experience "dispersion anxiety." The person who knows his own personality style, its assets, capabilities and opportunities, also is aware that he possesses strength, and the environment is then an invitation to an optimal exercise of that strength.

The healthy person also is aware that limitations to his exercise of power are imposed from within as well as from without. Each of us has a repertoire of motor skills, capabilities, aptitudes, intelligence, interests, and so on. However, the environment imposes certain limits upon all of these. The healthy person tends continuously to test both the limits imposed by the environment and the limiting factors of his own person and personality style. He probes for the outer boundaries in a continuing process that goes on from birth to death. At each new stage of development he learns new skills and expands his limitations while also testing the perimeters of his environment. This is how he grows and matures. Thus he learns to walk, ride a bicycle, dance, milk a cow, carve a statue, invent a better mousetrap. Or he learns that he cannot ride a bicycle or carve a statue. Fine. Then he is free to try dancing or inventing the mousetrap.

Limits too often are viewed negatively. We need to recognize their positive value, which is to describe opportunity. For example, we cannot fly by defying gravity, but we can fly at enormous speeds and at great altitudes by *accepting* and *applying* the law of gravity. Limits free us from attempting the impossible so that we can do what is possible. Each new situation that we encounter presents a new problem, and so often the healthy person finds that a problem is nothing more than an unexplored opportunity. By recognizing and accepting limits, we are free to pursue opportunity. Or, to say it another way, freedom can be defined as the pursuit of opportunity while fully accepting the limits encountered. Freedom is as much an internal attitude as it is a set of political or economic or cultural conditions. Freedom is the art of the possible.

What have limits, problems, opportunity, and freedom to do with the concept of personality style? Quite a bit. The person who recognizes his personality style also recognizes that he is most truly himself when he accepts the freedom, opportunity, and limits of his particular style. The Anticipating Personality, for instance, would be working against his own style if he accepted a position that involved frequent relocation and ever-changing work situations. The Ambitious Personality, on the other hand, would thrive on the challenge of meeting a variety of changing work situations. A Determined Personality might accept the alternative of jail if that were to be threatened as the result, say, of his efforts to organize hospital workers. He would consider this an exercise in freedom and an opportunity to publicize his cause, whereas a $40,000-a-year position promoting cosmetics might seem confining and purposeless. Yet the Accomplishing Personality might be delighted with the promotional opportunity to put on a dazzling campaign.

Freedom, opportunity, probing for the outer limits: all this supposes some reasonable risk. But risk we must if we are ever to use our capabilities, exercise our talents, and realize some of our goals. The greatest risk is to risk nothing, to pursue no opportunities, never to know our potential. We remain less than mature, frustrated, unhealthy, stunted, unfulfilled. The healthy personality is open to reasonable risk, free to be what he can be.

HEALTH AND MATURITY

"Health" has many meanings, from "feelin' good" to "optimal functioning of the organism." Essentially it means openness, flexibility, feeling, interacting, loving, caring, sharing, and much, much more. The healthy person can be expected to handle stress, conflict, crisis. He doesn't avoid stress because he can't. Stress happens in life; it is unavoidable and it has to be met. The healthy person is aware of his ideas, strivings, and the implications of his behavior. And he knows that others have their own ideas, strivings, feelings, and patterns of behavior. And he can say with the French, *"Vive la différence!"* He enjoys the mix. He attempts to interact productively and constructively with the world and its people. The healthy person is secure. He knows himself; he is at ease with himself. He is compassionate; he can suffer with others. He is capable of developing his own value system, of reaching out for new ideas and fresh concepts and insights. He is able to reach out to acknowledge, support, and give love to others. He accepts love and support. The healthy person is able to use his talents and acquired skills for his own gratification and in service to the world around him. He is able to make choices, even hard choices that involve risk. He is able to grow in his personal capabilities and social responsibilities. He cares.

"Mature" is used here interchangeably with "healthy." "Maturity" and "mature" have a physiological and chronological meaning, but I won't use them in that sense. A person is mature at any age if he is open to the exercise of his capabilities and strengths as they exist at his stage of development and within the norms of his own personality style. His progress is measured not on a composite scale of all the other children in the family, classroom, or neighborhood or by the company handbook for young executives, but by his own response to opportunity to grow and reach out.

A strong word of warning. Parents today are offered a wealth of assistance in parenting. But so often the material assumes a universal and interchangeable child. And that is a dangerous assumption that could do harm. Remember, each personality style has its own essence, its own strengths and weaknesses. So what is healthy and mature behavior for one personality style might not suit another. A non-like parent might expect the child to behave in a manner wholly inappropriate to the child's personality style. For example, the Influencing mother who expects her Adaptable daughter to be the take-charge organizer of scouting events is asking that child to go against her own style. Or the Accomplishing father who expects his Sensitive son to sing for adult company is placing him in a stressful situation. Always remember that the rules of encouraging, disciplining, supporting, and correcting must be relative to personality style.

The same rule of relativity applies in so many areas of giving direction to others. One of the great slogans of the 1960s was "Get involved." It is still good advice. But "getting involved" means something different for each personality style. For the Influencing

Personality it means relating to others in an open and receptive way while avoiding the urge to control the situation or the relationship. For the Sensitive Personality it means trusting self and others and being open to relationships. For the Determined Personality, it means communicating purpose and goals openly in dealing with others. For the Perceptive Personality it means maintaining contact rather than retreating into independence. Good health supposes getting involved in a general sense, but the *mode* of involvement varies with personality style.

The *Alternatives and Options* proposed at the end of each chapter reflect, again, the relative nature of appropriate responses. Alternatives are always appropriate to the individual personality style. They suggest better ways of handling stressful situations and of breaking usual patterns of inappropriate reactions and feelings. The real value of the alternatives is that they help us to realize we needn't be locked into a single, habitual, and often debilitating way of viewing situations and of responding. Developing a clear understanding of the alternatives and learning that genuine choices are open to us are steps toward better health and greater freedom.

THE QUESTIONS THEY ASK

Whenever I discuss personality styles with professional groups interested in the concept, I am asked questions reflecting concern for its effect on existing relationships, and its implementation by the individual. Since these questions are important and so frequently asked, I will answer them here:

Q. *Can a person have more than one personality style?*

A. No. Each of us has his personality style as a unique and distinguishable component of his total being. It is singular and identifiable at a very early age, and it persists as such throughout life.

Q. *Can a personality style be changed to another style?*

A. Again, no. A person can change his mannerisms, his habits, but not his personality style. True, we can all change *within* our own styles, but we cannot cross over to another style. The French have a saying: "The more things change, the more they remain the same." So it is with personality styles. We don't really change our style but we do grow within it. The more you know yourself and what you can expect of yourself, the more you can use the knowledge of your own style to be your true self, the real you. Your personality grows, adapts, develops, and matures as you move through life. Or it doesn't. Either way, the essential core of your personality, functioning within the perimeters of your style, remains the same.

Q. *What if I don't like my personality style?*

A. But you will. All of us fear the unknown. So the solution to the problem is to get to know your personality style. Every style displays great worth, offers enormous opportunities and real strengths. The more you know yourself and your opportunities, the more you will like who you are and what you can be. And so will others. Plato said it very well some 2,400 years ago: "I must first know myself, as the Delphian inscription says; to be curious about that which is not my concern while I am still in ignorance of my own self would be ridiculous."

Q. *Isn't the concept of personality style too complicated and sophisticated for anyone who isn't a psychologist or psychiatrist?*

A. Not at all. Most of us have the basic tools and experience to understand and to use this concept. Nothing is more typically human than our curiosity about ourselves and others. Wherever we are and whatever else we are doing, we tend to make observations and to speculate about what other people are like, what we are like. This process helps us to get in touch with our own feelings and behavior and to know what we feel about others as we interact with them. The concept of personality style only broadens and enhances this process. With a little help from our friends, each of us can pursue a more accurate knowledge of himself and others so that he can live more freely and openly, more productively and contentedly, more intimately and maturely. We are all equipped to do it; we can all know ourselves much better. And it's nice to know.

I

The Adaptable Personality

THE ADAPTABLE PERSONALITY is a person who looks on life as a celebration and every day as a movable feast. He or she is aware of and attuned to others, communicative and responsive, affable and considerate, rarely overly aggressive and seldom destructively competitive. The Adaptable Personality has an eye for the fashionable, senses what is current and appropriate, delights in a broad range of interests. He or she makes friends easily, blends well into almost any environment, has a festive flair for the dramatic and the eventful. This is the person who reacts openly to the presence, moods, and good qualities that others display. He or she can laugh when you laugh, weep when you weep, get excited by your ideas, share silence comfortably, admire your successes, soften your defeats. The Adaptable Personality, in sum, is a friend for all seasons.

When the Accomplishing Personality does his dazzling best, who applauds? The Adaptable Personality, delighted to share in the excitement. Who warmly congratulates the Ambitious Personality as he steps into the winner's circle? His Adaptable opponent. Who is attentive to the end when the Influencing Personality tells his tale? The Adaptable listener.

However, should the Adaptable Personality have to decide whether to listen to the Influencing story, or to play opposite the Ambitious challenger, or to watch the Accomplishing performer, he can falter. Decisions—having to choose—are the agony of the Adaptable Personality's life. "No decision is a decision," is an aphorism that aptly suits the Adaptable Personality faced with a choice. Rather than pursue the decision, he lets the decision pursue him. This Hamlet-like hesitancy, however, is not always what it seems to be. The Adaptable Personality often forms a tentative decision, but, his confidence on the low side, hesitates to voice it. Instead, he invites others into the process, soliciting other points of view, sampling various attitudes and proposed solutions. He is shopping for consensus. Thus "What do you think?" is usual to his conversation, as are "It seems to me . . ." and "I may be wrong but I think . . ." The forum is always open. Friends praise him for his flexibility, but others find his approach vexing and indecisive.

THE URGE TO CONFORM

The term "adaptable" describes so well the prevailing attitude of this personality style. The Adaptable Personality wants to share in whatever the environment offers. This is what we call the *conforming urge.* The Adaptable Personality is easily met and comfortable to be with. He exudes a rather optimistic aura that suggests that all is well with the world. Others readily welcome his company. He is unpretentious, deferential, disarming—even a bit on the humble side, tending at times to minimize his own role or importance, but usually in such a jovial manner that his charm is enhanced. Thus the Adaptable Personality makes a great dinner companion, a marvelous fourth at bridge, a warm and affectionate friend. The Adaptable Personality tends to accept others as they are, to encourage the best of what they have to offer, and to delight in the ideas and opinions that others find so easy to share with him. He always seems to be the right person to introduce the after-dinner speaker. He will set the stage with an expectant manner and only enhance the message to come, never competing with it or detracting from it. Asking the Adaptable woman for a date is always comfortable.

The element essential to understanding Adaptable Personalities is this: they are alert to and want to share in the thoughts, attitudes, feelings, and behavior of everyone around them.

They are attractive to others because of their openness and their capacity to be interested in a wide assortment of ideas and activities. If someone shouts, "Everyone into the pool!" in plunges the Adaptable Personality, feeling wet and wonderful. If touch football is the game, the Adaptable Personality plays, but never too aggressively. If someone suggests cutting chemistry, the Adaptable classmate is ready. Whether the call is for tennis or Tennyson, the Adaptable Personality responds enthusiastically. If motorcycles are the vehicle in vogue, he rides tall in the saddle, perhaps commenting: "It's almost part of me. My body moves with the bike." If her sorority sisters are knitting, she purls too. If the trend is to lighter beer, he drinks light. He or she will experiment with you in eating squid or snails, sit with you through a dull movie, rub your tired neck, laugh at your corny jokes, go Dutch treat, wait for your phone call, soothe your hurt feelings. He or she wants to go where you go, do what you do, hear what you have to say, like what you like, share what you feel. As one young Adaptable woman comments: "I usually go right along with whatever everyone else does." And she says it with such a warm, disarming smile that "whatever" sounds like exactly the right thing to do. Quite simply, the Adaptable Personality adapts so well.

THE AVID LISTENER

Adaptable Personalities are naturally inquisitive. Often at work or in a social setting, the Adaptable Personality is the attentive listener who is alert to the full scope and range of conversation, picking up the varying opinions and divergent attitudes. He is not prone to interrupt or interject a dissenting point of view. He doesn't challenge unless invited. He is ever intent on listening; this is his preferred way of learning. But should he be invited to express his opinion, the Adaptable Personality usually will seek a middle position or a compromise. He has an admirable knack for harmonizing the seemingly irreconcilable, for settling disputes, for arbitrating differences. Thus he functions well as moderator or negotiator. And when the situation is strained, he has a way of defusing the tension; his remarks are gentle and jovial, disarming and never personal—unless he directs them

20

toward himself. His spirit of optimism, his quest for high standards of conduct and decency set a tone that can lift the level of argument toward purpose and compromise. But praise him for his facility for reconciling differences and he blushes and stammers. He is surprised that others find him so helpful and capable: "Who? Me?" he is likely to exclaim. He seems constitutionally incapable of assessing his great value to friends and family and working associates.

Even when he suffers personal defeat, the Adaptable Personality tends to find some small light in the darkness. He remains the gentle peacemaker, the blessed optimist. If he is passed over for an expected promotion, he might be genuinely relieved not to have to assume the greater burden, even though perhaps disappointed. He might react by taking a long vacation—he dearly loves to travel—or by simply visiting good friends or by taking a long walk in the woods. But first he would congratulate the newly promoted co-worker; he is never the sorry loser crushed by defeat. And he might even surprise everyone by urging support for the person promoted over him. He is ever gracious, ever adaptable.

Now consider the opposite situation. The Adaptable salesman is offered the position of sales manager. The company president expects an immediate response, and perhaps enthusiasm. Instead, the Adaptable salesman smiles graciously but humbly, looking a bit bewildered. He asks for a day or two to consider. He wants time to reflect. Is he *really* the best choice? Can he handle the added responsibility? What will the other salesmen think? What will his wife say? After some temporizing, he decides to accept. But he wants to discuss the promotion with his wife, who wants to know how much of a raise goes with it. Now the Adaptable candidate is confused. Is he worth more money? Confidence sags. If he were the right man, why didn't the president simply tell him he was the new sales manager? Of course, he accepts two days later, as he first was inclined to do. But he asks if the president is really *sure* he is the man for the position. The president nods, although perhaps by now he's a little unsure of his own decision.

This pattern is typical of the Adaptable Personality when faced with the need to make a decision. First, he reacts with surprise, then, if the situation involves some pressure or stress, might come some panic. Always prone to totter on the low side of confidence, he will go shopping for other points of view, other perspectives. But dissenting or divergent opinions or considerations can cause his confidence to dip even further. Eventually he will sift and sort advice offered into something approaching consensus. Then he will move ahead toward positive resolve. But his vacillation and hesitancy, tinged with self-depreciating asides and much humility, bewilder and bother those around him, especially those who feel that they have tried to further his interest. And they might be annoyed when he doesn't follow the advice given.

If pressed too hard for an immediate decision, the Adaptable Personality may fluster and become irritable, even angry. Or he may fall apart. Either reaction is a stalling mechanism. Whatever the tactic, he is trying to gain time while he probes for consensus. He needs time to maneuver others to offer opinions, plans, direction.

THE GRAND STRATEGY

It would be fair to say that the Adaptable Personality is a masterful strategist who knows how to arrange for others to arrange his life. However, his seeming dependency on others is often an artful illusion. What he is actually doing is deftly maneuvering others, consciously or not—and usually it is not a conscious effort—to support him in his quest for the ideal role or the proper conduct in a given situation. The Adaptable Personality manages to rule by being ruled, to possess by being possessed. He seldom volunteers for a role or responsibility; he is quite capable of arranging for others to "draft" him for that role. And if he is accused of being overly dependent, or of relying too much on the input of others, he may not mind, because "dependency" is not a dirty word in his lexicon. As one Adaptable Personality remarked: "It doesn't bother me. People aren't really telling me what to do or doing it for me. They're telling me that *I* can do it. They're urging me."

His maneuverability is also grand strategy for not making waves. While the Adaptable Personality may vex and frustrate those from whom he seeks advice and consent, he rarely alienates them in the process. He is much too gracious, too flexible and open, too likable. And all that charming reticence is seductive. Others find themselves quite willing to help, and they always seem to come back for more.

The facility with which the Adaptable Personality is able to alter his viewpoints and to adopt new standards is another example of his

22

artful ability to be flexible and open. The young college student who readily espoused liberal causes on campus may surface five years after graduation as a full-blown conservative in the suburbs. The young Adaptable woman who sang in the church choir and was a member of the student council may run off at nineteen to join a commune in the wilderness. This shift in positions and ideals is neither fickle nor feckless. Remember, for the Adaptable Personality, life is a continual quest for the right environment and the right ideals. He is an open person who avidly absorbs and keenly responds to whatever ideas and information are current in the environment. He tends to interact freely and comfortably with many contrasting groups.

The Adaptable Personality can truly appreciate values in seeming opposition. Thus he will attempt to reconcile the irreconcilable. The Adaptable Personality wishes always to merge with the environment, to belong, to espouse the values of whatever or whoever is significant in the world around him. And all the while he is sincere and dedicated in his probing, honest in his viewpoint—while always remaining open to change and to a fresh perspective in his ongoing search for what is right and good. Once he finds those roles and ideals that he believes right for himself and purposeful for others, he is able to fulfill them with all his might. But until he finds them, he is always in danger of being too aware and too alert too much of the time. He may try to respond to so many different wishes and inclinations, always so tantalizing and exciting, that he sometimes permits himself to be pulled in too many directions, losing his own center of identity.

The search for self, the quest for identity, ideals, and a purposeful role in life, takes the Adaptable Personality into a wide and varying series of directions. He can have a high interest in his ancestors and genealogy. He wants to identify with the right school or the right club, the right company in his field, or the right neighborhood, and he will be impressed by those people who have found this "right" sort of identification. In fact, he can be so impressed at times that he can overrespond to superficiality or shallowness, becoming embarrassed when he realizes that he has been a little too impetuous. In short, he can be gullible and naïve. But he is quite capable of correcting the fault, moving on to a more substantial environment or group, because he is a very mobile person. His inquisitive nature prompts him to enjoy the exotic, so he is a willing tourist and traveler. And here again his keenness in observing and listening makes his wandering exciting and enriching. Those who accompany him or meet him along the way will generally find him exciting and enriching.

VULNERABILITIES AND CRISES

So long as things are going well, so long as all channels of life and interests are moving in more or less converging lines, the Adaptable Personality finds life exhilarating and rewarding. But, as noted earlier, he can find himself attempting to respond to too many influences, even influences in conflict. He can be too responsive to the opinions and positions of others, avoiding taking a stand or sorting out direction for himself. He can too easily arrange for others to make his decisions. He can too readily adopt the standards of others, lacking confidence in his own observations, judgments, and values. Flexibility is in danger of degenerating into indecision. Pursuing so many interests and so much excitement can lead to vacillation and a commitment to nothing. He can temporize until the moment of opportunity is lost. He can be so flirtatious and seductive in his interest in others, so friendly and interested in making them comfortable, that, at last, he himself is in danger of being seduced—intellectually or physically.

He can, like the chameleon, take on the colors of many different environments, but in doing so he runs the risk of subverting his own identity and individuality, and with them his sense of confidence and self-direction. In drawing sustenance from the environment, he is tempted to gorge himself, always eager to sample each new fad and fashion, idea and opinion. The overindulging Adaptable Personality can become too gracious, too easily captivated, too self-doubting, too entrapped by his own arranged dependencies. He can fear being alone so much that he is easily overcome. He floats along on the currents of ideas, opinions, advice, standards, and suggestions, sighing as he goes, "Ah, destiny." Once again he has decided not to decide.

Because the less mature Adaptable Personality, lacking confidence in his own judgments, is prone to adopt the standards of others too readily, he runs the risk of giving too much power to others. Anna, a young patient of mine, spent most of her life submitting to the standards set for her by the significant people in her life—first her father, then her sorority mother, then her work supervisor, then her roommate, and finally her fiancé. Shifting from one set of standards to another wasn't always easy. In the background always were earlier values, especially those of her family. But as each new situation arose, Anna felt it necessary to conform, so low was her level of confidence on leaving home, where her father ruled unchallenged. The power—or much of it—that she once had given her father finally settled onto Mark, the young man to whom she became engaged.

Anna had gone to college despite her father's objection; a college education, he said, was wasted on a woman. It took Anna many nights of agonizing and soliciting other advice before she decided to go to college over her father's objection. She was generally liked in college, managing to be invited into a sorority where she mixed well. She also joined a dramatics club, even though she was fretful about joining. And she dated frequently. Her grades were good, although not high. When she did receive two A's one semester, she was disappointed that her father didn't react with any show of interest.

After finishing college, Anna began teaching, and she did well. The children loved her gentle yet enthusiastic style, and she was especially effective in using dramatic devices such as role-playing and improvised skits. Her principal and peers all recognized her as a very fine teacher and found her a charming member of the group. But, typically, Anna never felt that she really deserved their praise and recognition. "Oh, I think I'm capable," she would say, "but I usually don't give myself much credit."

Anna moved away from home after her first year of teaching, sharing an apartment with a former college friend who was a rather assertive and opinionated individual. Before long, Anna was miserable. Her roommate was forever criticizing the style of the couch, the color scheme, the lamps, the art hangings on the walls—all furnishings belonging to Anna. "Much too garish," her roommate would say. Anna, although she knew that her taste was good, would retreat to her bedroom to weep.

When Anna met Mark, she was delighted. He was a rather good-looking sales engineer, garrulous, forceful, and assertive. Mark told Anna that she looked wonderful in black, so she began to acquire a wardrobe dominantly black. He was politically active, so she began to attend lectures on politics and joined the Young Republicans. Mark liked gourmet food and good wines, so Anna enrolled in a gourmet cooking class, and she began to run up a tab at an exclusive wine shop. She would also visit Mark's mother to learn to cook his favorite dish, even though she abhorred the smell of garlic. And because Anna was so likable and charming, so responsive, Mark's mother thoroughly enjoyed teaching Anna.

Mark was a very affectionate person, and, of course, Anna was responsive. In time, Mark began to urge her to take weekend trips with him. After some wrestling with her conscience, she did. But whenever she entered a motel with Mark, she felt that everyone, clerk and guests alike—and her parents too—would know, and she would blush uncomfortably. Anna loved those tender moments when Mark just held her and spoke lovingly to her. But he was also passionate and aggressive, and he liked to experiment. Anna did not, and, worse, she discovered that she was frigid. Not wanting to disappoint Mark, she pretended orgasm. Even after marriage—and after she had converted to his faith, not from conviction but to please Mark so that he would continue to give her direction—Anna found no joy in their sexual activity. In fact, she found it more and more a chore, often nerve-racking.

A BETTER RESPONSE

Sarah is another Adaptable young woman whose background is a little different from Anna's and whose level of confidence and her use of her Adaptable characteristics are quite different. So too her relationship with her father, to whom she was always close and whose positive support she could expect. Sarah's father encouraged her to go to nursing school and she did. He was paying the bill and he put great value on grades, so she worked hard to make good ones, even though they meant little to her personally. But she did want her father's continuing support and encouragement.

After Sarah had worked a year in nursing in a large urban hospital—which she found exciting with so many things happening around her—a large decision came up. Jim, the young man with whom she had been going, was transferred to a town six hundred miles away. "At first, I couldn't decide what to do. Jim wanted me to join him there, but I didn't know if it would be the right thing to do." Sarah did decide to join him: "I was so proud of having made a decision." That was before she sought assurance from her friends, some of whom thought it wasn't such a good idea. However, when she sought the

opinion of her parents, she found that her father supported her original decision to join Jim. Thus assured, Sarah quit her job, packed her
belongings, and left town. She moved in with Jim, a little hesitantly
because she felt that her mother, a religious woman, would object.
Once again, her father—"I depend on him a lot"—was able to smooth
things at home. And, still mindful of her father's wishes, Sarah began
looking around for a position in a hospital, feeling that she still
wanted his support. Even at a distance, he continued to be a significant
person in her life.

Meanwhile, Sarah would have liked to marry Jim. But he kept
urging her to wait until they had some money saved and until his
position at work improved. Even though marriage was very desirable
to Sarah—she could then be sure that Jim would be a permanent influence in her life—she was willing to wait: "All I need is the reassurance that he cares." Sarah always needs to hear that others care or
that they will continue to support her. "I'm always worried that they
don't care when they don't tell me. One of the worst things that can
happen is for people not to like me, or for me to do something that
they would consider wrong." But Sarah is so adaptable and so charming that it is difficult to imagine anyone not liking her or what she
does. And since conforming comes so naturally to Sarah, there is little
chance that she might do what friends or family might find offensive.

GROWING UP ADAPTABLE

The Adaptable child is usually described by parents and teachers as a
quiet and lovable youngster who will accept direction and correction.
Parents speak affectionately of him, noting that he is a child whom you
can talk to and "reach." He is aware of his surroundings very early,
responsive to things happening in his environment. He is also an
early talker.

The Adaptable child is usually close to his parents, but especially
to one parent, readily assimilating the values and interests of that
parent. As he grows and becomes more aware of the environment, he
sensitively picks up any tension or nervousness displayed by his parents, and becomes upset when they are upset. But he is also a very
consoling child, overtly responding with hugs and kisses. He responds
to heavy-handed correction with some show of frustration and fear of

disapproval. He very much wants to please, and his expression of desire for direction and fear of disapproval is a pattern that endures throughout his future development and living pattern.

Still, as his motor mechanisms and awareness of the environment improve, he begins to probe the world outside the home. Around age four or five, he is the child who has a tendency to disappear from the home or even to run away because there is just so much that interests and awes him about the larger world. Already he is displaying his roaming tendency—a tendency that will continue throughout life. And if the outside world isn't available to him, he may invent his own world and people it with imaginary friends.

Entry into the educational process is exciting for the Adaptable child—less for its academic appeal than for its human content. Teachers find that they thoroughly enjoy this child, even though he isn't too interested in doing well in school, unless grades come easily or are important to the standard-setting parent. The Adaptable child is attentive and excited when the teacher tells stories of foreign countries or customs, or of those personal experiences that relate to life; but the hard-core curriculum, homework, and reading assignments offer few thrills.

The Adaptable child usually communicates well. In fact, he talks often in class, sometimes too much. And, curiously, he is often a poor speller, which may have something to do with his lifelong preference for learning by listening rather than by reading. Since the Adaptable child enjoys being with people and blends well socially, he is delighted to be with other children, doing what they do, sharing in all the adventures of childhood. He will not, however, push himself into a leadership role: that would be too aggressive. He is sought after because of his very agreeable ways, his love of excitement, and his rather tantalizing way of hanging back just enough to be attractive. He will enjoy a role in the Christmas play—where invariably he is cast as an angel—and costuming for Halloween. When he feels frustrated by needing direction or being faced with decision, his eyes have a tendency to tear up, which might prompt good-natured jibes or "Baby!" from classmates. Like behavior at home might provoke a sibling's taunt of "Momma's boy." But the remarks are more a matter of teasing and not harsh ridicule. The Adaptable child normally maintains good relations with siblings as he does with friends and peers.

28

The Adaptable child is so responsive and pleasant that parents, especially the same-style parent, tend to be too permissive with the child and overly indulgent. It would be better if the same-style parent in particular were to encourage organized activities, like scouting, so that the child would learn early to accept structure in life. One other point: this is the child who shows rather early in his school years that he cannot say no to his friends. Most of the time it will all be good clean fun, but there are mischievous moments that the Adaptable child cannot resist—for example, that first clandestine puff on a cigarette because his friends are doing it. He will go along with the crowd unless the proposed activity repulses him or is in complete opposition to the standards of the significant person in his life, such as the dominant parent.

ADOLESCENT REBELLION

The teenage years can be stormy. The Adaptable adolescent may find himself rebelling. The girl of thirteen or fourteen, long the cooperative and pleasant child, suddenly may sass her surprised mother. One who did recalls, "I was being a tough kid. But then I came around when Mom slapped me." Reflecting a moment, she smiles, then comments: "It's hard to believe. I could never do that now."

What happens is that the Adaptable Personality, having gone along with the directions of others, especially of parents, suddenly becomes aware of himself and the possibility of setting his own standards. He yearns for greater confidence. He doesn't want to be so dependent on others. He begins to test himself and his adequacy—but in a protective circle of friends whom he trusts. And the rebellion against parental standards is never so vigorous that he alienates his parents or disavows their standards.

Soon he settles down to a pleasant blend of conforming to the direction offered by his teenage friends and teachers while keeping parental direction available. School becomes even more important in his life, especially when he senses how capable and recognized he can be. He can be more interested in what happens after school than during school. He becomes avidly interested in motorcycles and cars; he desires as much mobility as he can afford. He is friendly, cheery, gets along with everyone. He is involved in dramatics, student government, social clubs, any number of extracurricular activities such as cheer-leading or band. He avoids tight little cliques, preferring to move in a wide range of friends, but always the "right" crowd. The high school years, for the Adaptable adolescent, are very good years.

As graduation nears, the less confident Adaptable teenager may begin to feel the pressure of looking ahead to the time when he will be expected to assume greater direction over his life. This may explain why Adaptable Personalities tend to marry earlier than other personality styles—as early as seventeen and often with pregnancies (they also tend to divorce earlier).

The escape routes from the pressures to make decisions about the future are many. A young man may find himself in bed with a woman closer to his mother's age than his own, and may even accept money or gifts from her. On the other hand, a young woman who has heard her mother say, again and again, "A nice girl never has sex until marriage," very well may remain a virgin until marriage—and, symbolically, after marriage, at least as far as openness to orgasm is concerned. This happens because shifting from one source of direction to another is uneasy and confusing for the immature and unsure Adaptable Personality. Sometimes it is simply a matter of appeasing a parent so that he or she will continue to give guidance. A young man close to his attorney father, for example, may disregard his strong interest in social work as he tries hard to develop an interest in law school.

Operating from a low level of confidence, and always shy of making hard choices, the Adaptable Personality is a late starter who can be trapped early in a situation that has overtaken him. He may defer initiating his own direction in life until twenty-five, thirty-five, or forty. But once he makes that choice, however late, he will move forward decisively.

The college years are largely a replay of the high school years. The Adaptable Personality moves enthusiastically into a wide range of social activities. Only now his poise and social grace are more evident and more appreciated. His sense of what is "right"—the right crowd, the right fraternity or sorority, the right way of dressing, the right topics of conversation, and so on and on—is keen and well-informed and improving daily. His grades may be rather ordinary: he finds the ski weekend more interesting and exciting than a weekend of study. But his likable personality is building social ties that may be useful in later years for promoting his career.

30

COURTSHIP AND MARRIAGE

The Adaptable Personality is drawn to people who are physically attractive, socially appealing, assured and assertive, stimulating and exciting. If a person comes from the "right" background, or displays a certain degree of affluence, it would not go unnoticed by the Adaptable Personality, although it would not be a primary consideration. Forcefulness—the other person's ability to give direction and offer support—would be more significant. In marriage, the Adaptable spouse would be content to accept the lead of a capable partner who has definite ideas and knows what he or she wants; the Adaptable spouse responds to the inclinations of that partner and would permit him or her to set the standards. The mature Adaptable spouse's willingness to yield would set a tone in marriage and home life that would be productive and contagious, soothing and settling, for the entire family. He or she might be glorified as the unselfish parent who has so much to offer, who is so responsive to the children as well as to the spouse.

For the less mature Adaptable Personality, marriage and parenthood may not be that simple and serene; rather, it might be anguishing. He or she would have a tendency to be too dependent too much of the time; too clinging, too indecisive, too tearful. And there is often frigidity in the unsure Adaptable woman and impotency in the male. Interest might drift from the demands and duties of home life to the easier and more exciting social scene, whether it be morning coffee with the neighbors or the cocktail party circuit. Parental direction of the children would be evaded or left to the more directive parent. Rather than assess and arrest the tendency to drift, and to avoid confronting the need to assume greater direction over his or her own life and the lives of the children, the Adaptable Personality might join a little-theater group, or turn to drink, or enter into an affair (usually begun innocently in a coquettish flirtation). Or, the insecure Adaptable Personality might simply wilt in a pile of tear-soaked tissues. The choice of response—or lack of it—is a matter of opportunity: whatever is easiest and most available.

Learning to be resolute and more self-directed can be most productive and liberating for the Adaptable Personality. One Adaptable woman tells of being very content to let her resourceful and assertive husband make all the decisions and assume all responsibility in their marriage. After some time in therapy, she began to recognize that she, too, had many good ideas and values to offer. At first, her husband found the emerging flow of her ideas uncomfortable. But the more he listened and observed, the more he appreciated what she contributed. "It's much better now," she says, "more like two persons who have differing ideas, different interests, making different decisions. The mix is better. It's been a lot more exciting for both of us. I now have my own ideas and I feel confident to express them." When they purchased a new home, her mother-in-law, a professional decorator and a very vigorous woman, offered to help select furniture, drapes, and color schemes. "I let her know in a nice way that I would rather she wait. I told her I would rather she come to see it when the house was finished." She was able to handle her mother-in-law in an adroit, tactful way without offending. In the end, everyone, including the mother-in-law, was pleased with the finished house. And the Adaptable wife was pleased with herself, although properly modest when she was praised.

WORK AND CAREER

As I noted earlier, the Adaptable Personality can have a late start in seeking and finding the working situation most suited to his interests and talents. Sometimes a situation is thrust upon him: he tends to pursue a job or career that a parent or other significant person urges. Other times he will simply leave the situation open and flexible without the need to make a decision or to act assertively. Either way, the Adaptable Personality may have a tendency to change jobs or careers as opportunities present themselves. Even so, he will be diligent and responsible, efficient and purposeful at whatever he is doing, blending in with the tone and atmosphere of the working environment. Because of his openness to the ideas and opinions of others, and his keen interest and enthusiasm, he will be well received by co-workers and superiors. His ability to soften disputes and to summarize varying points of view, coupled with his willingness to yield, will make him persuasive in all sorts of confrontations and conferences. And, despite the fact that he tends to be a nine-to-five worker who seldom takes the job home, he will be marked as promotable, promising.

His co-workers will find every reason to enjoy the company of the Adaptable Personality. He is good-natured and jovial, genuinely nonaggressive, non-competitive, and therefore non-threatening. His naïveté and gullibility may make him the object of occasional joshing or practical jokes, but he will take it well, and enjoys the camaraderie it involves. Usually he will be well liked by everyone. The only person possibly not satisfied with his efforts may be the Adaptable Personality himself, because he always tends to diminish his importance or his contribution. However, even his tendency to give an embarrassed response to praise would endear him to others. He would be appreciated for his kindness, tact, and encouragement of others. He is the kind of a person whom his co-workers would invite for a drink after work, and he is the kind who would almost always join them.

The Adaptable Personality would make an excellent salesman, contract negotiator, actor, news commentator, clergyman, moderator, teacher, politician, or social worker. Any position involving travel would appeal, as would any position that would use to advantage his high verbal communications skills.

Retirement would pose no problem for the Adaptable Personality; in fact, he might welcome it as an opportunity to pursue the many interests and activities that he finds so attractive. He could be expected to enjoy the shade in his back lawn for long hours, going fishing, playing tennis, chatting with old friends about anything or nothing, taking that long-awaited trip to Paris that has intrigued him since his student days. He would love the luxury of leisure, feeling no pressure to do anything but what he wants. The rocking chair and the front porch were invented for the Adaptable retiree.

ALTERNATIVES AND OPTIONS

The Adaptable Personality, as discussed, is a very sociable person who is also open, flexible, gentle, optimistic, and interested in a broad range of ideas and activities. But he is also prone to vacillation, reticence, and indecision. His humility is ingratiating, but it can slide into self-depreciation. His urge is to conform, which while it makes him attract, also limits his self-direction. He is inquisitive and impressionable, sometimes gullible, and sometimes on the edge of becoming a dilettante. His reluctance is admired by friends but is annoying to others. His life is a quest after noble standards and high purpose, but he is in danger of missing opportunity. He seeks direction but tends to misunderstand support as criticism. He loves nice things but sometimes mistakes the glitter for substance. His bright optimism can tempt him to overromanticize people and relationships, only to be disappointed or disillusioned when they turn out to be less than he had hoped for. His soliciting advice and opinion can build consensus, but it can also degenerate into dependency.

To enhance his strengths so that they do not become weaknesses, the Adaptable Personality needs to be conscious of his behavior patterns and prevailing attitudes. He needs to rely more on his own resources and less on the advice and consent of others. In sum, he needs to "toughen up," to conform less, and to decide more. If you are an Adaptive Personality, here are some ways you can do that:

• Be aware that you often seek guidance to the point of arranging for others to set standards for you. Be more independent. Listen when others tell you: "You can do it. You know what to do." You really *do*.
• Irritability and tears will not resolve problems and conflicts. Act rather than react.
• Once you have made a decision, carry it out. Don't shop around for other points of view. Just *do* it.
• Substitute "I've decided to" for "I have to" when compulsively seeking guidance from others.
• Fantasize ways of becoming more independent. Explore the possibilities of being more assertive.
• Test what you can do for yourself rather than planning what others can do for you.
• Quit looking over your shoulder for the significant standard-setter in your life. Look straight ahead, set your own standards. Friends and family and co-workers are not a supermarket of opinions and standards; they are people who care about you, love you, believe in your ability to determine your own course of action.
• Listen to praise and compliments. Don't brush them off; don't minimize them with an offhand joke. People are telling you that you are capable.
• Stop seeing yourself as neglected and selfish or not good enough. Start letting yourself be more decisive and resolute.
• Consider that your fear of being alone is only another statement about your lack of confidence. Your capabilities are part of *you*, not part of the crowd.
• Reluctance is only a ploy to seduce others into making your decisions or giving you direction.

• Roots are important, but an excessive interest in the family tree may reveal more sap than substance. You need to identify with yourself as a substantial person.

• "Looking good" is nice, but here too you are mistaking appearance for substance. You are much more than a mannequin on display. You are an individual, a unique person of value and competence.

• Learn to say "no" and really mean it.

• Stand your own ground. Become aware of what *you* want. Know what *you* stand for.

• Once you develop more confidence, you will appreciate yourself much more. Your great social awareness will not diminish; it will be enhanced because you will be more adaptable—but with all your resources available to you.

• Genuine flexibility means being able to give a little and to take a little—but with enough self-assurance that you know that giving and receiving are a matter of choice, not submission.

• Take chances. Test what happens when you let your own desires be known. You'll gain confidence, which leads to further risks, further success, further confidence.

• You don't have to be sweet all the time. People won't desert you for having your own opinions and your own standards.

• Explore freedom—freedom to be yourself, to love and to be loved on your own merits, to share while retaining your sense of individuality and independence.

• Be close but not clinging. Speak up. Relax. These kinds of behavior are truly adaptability in action.

• Do things without the significant other holding your hand.

• Quit sending out the message, "Don't expect too much of me." Wouldn't it be a nice change to say, "Look out! Here I come!"

• The greatest assurance is self-assurance.

• Work on being the right person rather than seeking the right environment, or the right job, or the right crowd.

• Deciding not to decide is a poor decision.

• Your declaration of independence would be to make choices and then to act on them freely. When that happens, you truly have something fine and wonderful to celebrate with all those people who love you so much: a feast of freedom. But to have freedom you must choose freedom. So choose. And then celebrate.

II

Winning isn't everything.
It's the only thing.
VINCENT
LOMBARDI

The Ambitious
Personality

THE AMBITIOUS PERSONALITY is just that: ambitious. He welcomes challenge, and he competes willingly and willfully. He is sometimes openly aggressive. More often he is cautious as he moves purposefully toward the goal that he has set for himself. Achieving that goal—winning—is all-important. But when setbacks come, the healthy Ambitious Personality can shrug, then move on to another challenge, this one perhaps a little more reasonable and attainable. When he finds that he cannot win, he compromises: a compromise is better than a loss. He works hard, and he plays hard—fully committed, full of purpose and drive. Whatever he is doing, he is striving to win, to move ahead—if at all possible, to the top.

The Ambitious Personality is sociable and affable. But social moments are interludes; he is soon back to the task. And, while he works well within the group, he is forever urging others to move ahead toward whatever goal they are seeking. Those around him usually view him as a winner, and when they say so he is pleased. He likes to be told that he is getting the job done, that he does it well, that he is very good—perhaps the best—at what he does, whether it is baking bread or teaching school, selling computers or playing golf. When he hears the compliments and experiences the kudos, the healthy Ambitious Personality can savor the good feeling of having done well. Then he moves on to the next challenge. There is always another goal ahead.

"Ambitious," "challenging," "competing," "comparing": these terms fairly well describe all Ambitious Personalities. So do "cautious," "careful," "deliberate," and "diligent." But such words are relative. Ambitions come large and small, in low as well as in high places. Challenges and competition can be arranged in the recreation room as well as in the executive suite. They vary according to values, opportunities, training, talent, and temperament. One Ambitious Personality's meat is another's poison. The healthy Ambitious Personality may plan and evaluate in a situation where a less healthy counterpart might plunge without looking. One knows when to quit while he is winning; the other can't quit until he has lost everything.

One Ambitious Personality may strive to be president of the corporation, another captain of the bowling team. One nurse may work toward being the best nurse on the floor, another toward becoming the supervisor of nursing of the entire hospital. The draftsman new to the engineering department prudently knows he is not equipped to challenge the chief of engineering for his position. But he might find it exhilarating to test him at chess. And useful. Given his skill at the game, the chessboard might be his route to becoming head draftsman.

Consciously or unconsciously, whether openly and assertively or ever so subtly and cautiously, the Ambitious Personality is moving ahead, striving to achieve some goal he set for himself.

THE RATING URGE

Aren't most of us to some degree ambitious? Aren't we all assertive? Don't most of us have goals that we strive to achieve? Of course. And we all love to win. Competing and achieving are prized virtues in our society—but not as the dominant, all-defining style of behavior. Most of us will rise to a challenge, given an appropriate challenge at an appropriate time. Most of us compete. But most of us do so within limits. Some of us would settle for a four-day work week. Most of us enjoy relaxed moments away from the routine of striving and challenging and competing. We like to pause to savor success, to polish the trophy, or simply to putter in the garden and to smell the roses. Some of us like to have a beer in front of the television set while we watch others compete. Most of us can enjoy the game of golf for the exercise, the fresh air, and the nineteenth hole.

Not the Ambitious Personality. For him, the trophy displayed in the family room isn't simply an ornament: it's evidence of the challenge accepted, the contest won—recognition for having been the best. He doesn't play golf for the fresh air and the fellowship on the fairway or in the clubhouse; he plays to win. And when the Ambitious Personality isn't winning, he is plotting new ways to do so—a system for handicapping the horse races, a strategy for promotion, a sales scheme. His quiet way of relaxing is to watch a favorite television program: the one in which the aggressive detective always triumphs over the master criminal.

The Ambitious Personality views all of life as a challenge. To be human is to compete. And the only way to play the game is to win. As the late football coach Vincent Lombardi commented, "Winning isn't everything. It's the only thing." And every Ambitious Personality knows it. The essential element that distinguishes the Ambitious Personality from all other personality styles is the tremendous emphasis he places on achievement. And to achieve, one must have goals. You can't, however, rate the players without a scorecard. So the Ambitious Personality, fixed on achieving and always feeling competitive, tends to score himself and others at everything. We call it the *rating urge* —the urge to rate and to be rated. It goes on constantly. "Mirror, mirror on the wall, who is the fairest of them all?" Who is the best dancer on the floor, the greenest thumb on the block, the best backhand on the tennis court, the top salesman on the force, the fastest gun in the West? If the Ambitious Personality is not the best, the quickest, the top, the first, it isn't that he hasn't tried: he is *always* trying. But if he is a hair slower or a bit less skilled or a rung below the top, he feels anxious and frustrated. Then he rates himself low, or suspects that others are rating him low. If he is feeling sufficiently good about himself, he can wait for a better day. If he is not, he might kick the dog.

The healthier he is, the less the Ambitious Personality fears or needs rating. He can come back to the same challenge or the same

38

task with vigor and purpose, or move on to another that is more appropriate. But he will always have some goal in mind, always be willing to sweat, sacrifice, and suffer—*whatever* is required. He will miss a meal, work all sorts of late hours, study hard, practice often, drive an older car, skip buying theater tickets as he strives toward his goal. When he achieves his goal, he wants it to show. Then he treats himself to a steak dinner, buys the new car, moves up in the suburbs. All these visible signs of success draw good ratings. Thus every achievement is an opportunity for a doubly good rating: one for the success, another for the sign of success.

The rating urge is projected into all sorts of situations. She likes to be seen with the captain of the football team: that rates a good score. He drives a Corvette: that rates well on a date. She dresses smartly, even a bit seductively: she is inviting a favorable rating. He loses at golf but buys two rounds of drinks in the clubhouse: he is trying to buy a good rating to offset a low rating. His sales lead for the month and his report is submitted promptly—clean, clear, complete: the sales manager scores him a solid rating on two counts. He brings his wife flowers, guaranteeing himself a favorable rating as the thoughtful husband. He buys himself a new suit after receiving a salary increase: he is rating himself favorably. The quest is to be forever rated well, first, or best.

DISPLACEMENT

Unfortunately, keeping score constantly can be counterproductive. The Ambitious golfer is bound to miss an occasional putt. The Ambitious college girl isn't always invited into one of the better-rated sororities. Sales can slip, or the Ambitious salesman can accidentally spill his drink on the boss's wife. No one wins all of the time at everything. Low scores and poor ratings sooner or later come to all of us. The steady Ambitious Personality knows this, and while he might mumble a moment to himself, he can tally the occasional low score with his more frequent high marks to accept his cumulative rating as positive. More, he can adjust his perspective, learn from his mistakes, and move on. Next time out, he will take a few moments before the game to practice his putting. He will plan his month's calls more carefully, allotting more time to prime prospects. Certainly he will walk a wider path past the boss's wife at the next company party. But the less sure Ambitious Personality may respond by displacing the blame for his poor ratings. He will claim that someone coughed as he putted. The competition is paying kickbacks. The boss's wife bumped his arm. It is always someone else's fault. The Ambitious Personality, especially under stress, is nimble with excuses, artful in displacing responsibility for things gone wrong. If in dealing with a person you find that he or she manages always to be right while you always seem to be wrong, think Ambitious Personality.

I often notice this tendency to displace when an Ambitious Personality comes to me for help. Let's suppose he wants to discuss an affair he has been having for the past six months. Why does he come to me *now*? What else was happening six months ago? He tells me that about the same time the affair began his company began a reorganization after a merger with another company; there were duplications at the same supervisory level; his position might be in jeopardy. Here is the displacement. He wants to discuss an affair when the problem that truly concerns him is his endangered career. He is switching emphasis. If his career goes sour, he can always blame the affair. This is his insurance policy against having to accept the bitter fact that he didn't compete well in a most important situation.

In like manner, the working mother can always excuse her late arrival for work on having to get her children off to school. The young baseball player can blame his poor season on the manager for having switched him from right field to left. The poor student can always claim that he couldn't do his studies because his roommate always had the stereo on.

The Ambitious Personality finds many good uses for displacement. As any Ambitious salesman will tell you, "You sell the sizzle, not the steak." The Ambitious careerist benefits greatly when he tapers off a heavy workload in becoming aware of "how much I am missing of family life." This is the sizzle. The steak is his coincident awareness that he isn't really going to make it to the top of the corporate structure. The young lawyer defeated for city council suddenly realizes that his practice might have suffered had he won. Sometimes displacements take the form of an insurance policy going into a goal-oriented situation. The aspirant has alternative Plan B tucked in the back of his mind as he initiates Plan A. He has prudently arranged to avoid the frustration of defeat or a no-win situation. The healthy Ambitious

Personality is the one who is ready to accept a reasonable alternative, a viable option. He is like the young man who knows he isn't the best dancer on the floor—but who is going to notice (or give him a poor rating) when he's dancing with the best-looking girl on campus?

OVERPLAYING THE RATING GAME

Moving through life with a scoreboard on your back, always waiting for the next rating to flash on, can be a terrible burden. And that is the way the less effective, less sure Ambitious Personality behaves. Sooner or later the rating game becomes a losing game. If his goal is unreasonable or his plans inflexible, he is going to run up a series of low scores—even zeros. Then he is in danger of driving himself into depression. Still, the unsure, striving, struggling Ambitious Personality has to keep up the game, competing and comparing scores and ratings, even when sharing would be far more productive. Alternatively, he loses sight of his goal by running after easy wins that give him a false sense of achievement. Sometimes he may even begin to play the game with a stacked deck: desperate, he may resort to shading the rules or trampling on the competition. Worse, he projects his own tactics and hostility onto the opposition, and sometimes onto the world at large. Or he may leap and lunge after indiscriminate challenges just out of reach. When he loses, as he so often must, all he can say is: "I got screwed."

The healthy and more flexible Ambitious Personality, on the other hand, can alter his goal, adjust his sights, abandon an unproductive enterprise, or relax to enjoy the triumph when his goal is realized. Not the unhealthy Ambitious Personality. He will burn out trying or go down in flaming defeat. Frustrated and sometimes filled with anger after trying and trying and *trying,* the unsure Ambitious Personality sags. All that is left is his fear that he hasn't rated well— and he is right—and the fear that someone might have gotten hurt, himself or the competition. All that he feels is guilt. Then he may choose to withdraw completely, a choice that is counterproductive and defeating. He would be far better off totally re-evaluating his goals and challenges, and his tactics for achieving them.

The competition and the rating game really never end for the troubled and neurotic Ambitious Personality. He not only rates himself: he constantly rates everyone else—usually with a low score so that he can avoid scoring himself low. The wife never seems to measure up, nor the kids, nor the boss, nor the bridge partner, nor the bartender, nor his therapist. No one. Of course, he's displacing. Meanwhile, the fun of playing is lost. Victory is no longer sweet. Friends and fellow workers and other players, feeling all that hot aggression, shy away from him, alienated.

When things are going bad, he no longer knows a win from a loss. He feels guilty when he wins, inferior when he loses. Still, the need to achieve, to compete, to be rated remains strong. The driven Ambitious Personality may step on a toe or two as he strides toward the winner's circle, muttering all the way: "Get them before they get you." And should he be complimented, he doesn't particularly appreciate it; he feels too guilty. Should he lose, don't try to soften his defeat with gentle humor: that smacks too much of a low rating, and the guilt grows and grows.

At times like these, it would be better for the tense Ambitious Personality to try to relax, to consciously appreciate that he should rate himself well simply for having made the effort, for having worked hard in trying to achieve his goal. He would benefit greatly by viewing the effort itself as a symbolic victory. Next time out, he should examine each opportunity and challenge more carefully before acting, letting his natural caution work for him. By giving more time to planning, he might find it easier to refrain from inappropriate strivings and to rise above petty jealousies. That way he would avoid overly aggressive competition. He could relax, throw away the scorecard, and stop to smell the roses. Otherwise, he is back to the pitfall of indiscriminate challenges, the rough-and-tumble tactics, the gray clouds of guilt. The rating meter begins to click, and he is off again. Or else he backs off from large segments of life. He might, for example, have a healthy urge to give a party for friends and co-workers, but, fearing that his might not be rated party-of-the-month, he gives no party at all, brooding away a lonesome weekend.

What is happening inside the distressed Ambitious Personality? He is fearing that unless he is constantly achieving, he is nothing, no one. Unless he is triumphing constantly, he is simply not acceptable— if not to others, certainly to himself. He sees the whole world made in his image and likeness: competitive, aggressive, hostile—a bruising, battering battlefield of combat and combatants. Wherever he goes, he keeps an ear open for the fluttering wings of invisible vultures, those covert competitors whom he fears are hovering everywhere: in the executive dining room, in the hiring hall, at the card table, on the freeway, in the singles bar, over the back fence—everywhere.

The healthy Ambitious Personality can have many of these same feelings and urges in moments of stress. But he is more likely to recognize his aggressive feelings and to respond much more flexibly. He has learned to step back long enough to evaluate the situation; he will try consciously to make decisions based on assessment of the real situation, the facts, not on his feelings of competitiveness and aggressiveness. He avoids indiscriminate challenges and easy wins. He keeps sight of his true goals. He know what he wants to achieve—success—and he knows the difference between winning and losing. But he can accept an occasional loss because he knows that winning is a matter of attitude as well as of deed, a matter of having made a genuine effort. True, he enjoys recognition and praise and all the symbols of success, but they don't consume him or foster guilt feelings. He believes in sharing the winner's circle with colleagues and co-workers, because he knows he would be lonesome without them.

GROWING UP AMBITIOUS

In infancy, the Ambitious child seems content with himself, able to entertain himself with a pacifier, blanket, or whatever crib toys are available. However, he is always interested in something new. By age three or four, he is showing some assertiveness, perhaps a little aggressiveness, but at the same time he always seems to be smiling. At this age—three or four—the child is also demonstrating definite sex-role identification. This is because, unlike other personality styles, sexual identification is quite important to the development of the Ambitious child. He or she can be confused unless given sex-appropriate stimuli. The preschool boy benefits by being given a football or baseball and bat; the girl, frilly things, dolls, stuffed toys.

The Ambitious child has no trouble entering into school life. He plunges in, thoroughly enjoying the interaction with other children, and he is interested in pleasing parents and teachers and soliciting their response. Ratings, though not consciously regarded as such, are gladly received. The small pat on the back, praise for a good report card, or any form of encouragement propels the Ambitious child into trying a wider range of activities, usually in a deliberate and purposeful way. Always he is showing the winning instinct. He demonstrates an early interest in aggressive activities and in dramatics and role-playing—whatever offers an opportunity for competing or for achieving prestige or status. Status—a very favorable rating that is clear and recognizable not only to the Ambitious Personality but to everyone—remains important all through life.

The first year or so of schooling can have an important bearing on the direction of the Ambitious child's development. His feelings about succeeding or failing are very much influenced by family, school, and society's reactions and points of emphasis. Thus the child's healthy attitude toward schooling and his achievements can be deflected if his successes and failures aren't handled well. He can become the class nuisance or the giggler—his way of winning the competition for attention. He can also be troublesome at home if he finds it hard to compete with a sibling who is given attention for being good.

The early school years are also the time of close identification with the parent of the same sex. I noted earlier how important a clear sex-role identification is to the Ambitious child, and it now shows in the child's liking to wear the parent's clothes, in imitating his or her habits and mannerisms, likes and dislikes. It is all reinforced by the Ambitious child's flair for dramatics; but as long as Dad's best tie isn't worn in a mudball fight—or Mom's best bra in front of the neighbors —parents need to be tolerant, and, if possible, they might give the child a good-rating smile. And that shouldn't be difficult; the Ambitious child is lovable, and his zest for life is delightful to behold.

By age eight or nine the Ambitious child is beginning to focus his interest on specific areas, and here again he needs parental approval and encouragement. Boys can be attracted to fire-fighters and police officers, while girls show a lively interest in nursing, teaching, and home decoration. In the future it will be interesting to observe how Ambitious girls respond to opportunities as sexual discrimination breaks down. Considering the Ambitious Personality's spirit of competition, assertiveness, and ability to plan, this personality style could well provide leadership in opening new fields to women.

The Ambitious child at eight or nine is interested in the good rating that can be achieved not only in the classroom but in extra-curricular activities, sports, and hobbies. He is beginning to show

44

more openly his inclination to want to do better than others. He may want to dress a bit better than other children in the neighborhood or school, may make a strong effort to be part of a particular team or class or neighborhood group—the right crowd merits a good rating. But, perhaps due to his normally cautious approach to goals and his tendency to displace, he doesn't want to be the leader out front. He would rather be the second in command who has the ear of the leader, so if anything goes wrong, the Ambitious "advisor" can always point to the leader as the one who failed.

The Ambitious child needs to know that his competitiveness and his enthusiastic interest in so many areas are good and healthy and praiseworthy. He genuinely deserves and needs whatever good ratings he merits through his efforts. He needs praise for successes, even praise for having made the effort when he fails. Conversely, lack of recognition, indifference, or negative reaction—perceived as a poor rating— can lead to negative displacement or destructive sublimation. The Ambitious parent especially needs to be aware of the effects of his or her responses to the child's interests and achievements. The father who is a frustrated athlete, for example, can be so demanding and so critical in his comments that his son reads nothing but negative ratings. He may quit, even when interested greatly, or he may become overly aggressive. And should someone be accidentally injured because of his aggressiveness, the Ambitious child very likely will experience a strong sense of guilt. He easily develops a fear that his aggressiveness can result in harm to himself or to others—a fear that he can carry all through life—and he can also feel guilty when he believes that he hasn't worked hard enough to merit a good rating. So parents cannot be reminded often enough of how important it is to be aware of the Ambitious child's feelings and needs. He should be encouraged to take pride in all of his achievements, large and small; and normally he does, just as he takes pride in the achievements of peers and siblings.

The age of ten or eleven is critical for the Ambitious child. The middle grades of school offer so many competitive opportunities— spelling bees, a wider range of sports activities, school newspapers, band, and so on. Consider this situation: the child comes home from school crying because she didn't win the spelling bee; she was second out of forty-eight children. The Ambitious mother can either make the situation worse by blaming the child for not having worked hard

45

enough, or she can cancel the child's poor rating of herself by pointing out that she beat forty-six other children and by praising her for having done her best.

THE AMBITIOUS ADOLESCENT

Puberty brings identification with the desirable traits and behavior of the parent generation and with culturally sanctioned strivings. At this time the Ambitious adolescent also develops a heightened fear of losing or of being rated poorly. He may even pare down his participation in activities in which he feels he has only a fair chance of winning. Competition for grades and other forms of scholastic achievement intensifies, and the Ambitious teenager becomes more aware of other students who are well equipped for academic excellence. The ante goes up, so the Ambitious adolescent who is not too sure of himself may back away from the brighter set. Once more, the tendency to displace is evident. He may seek out non-achievers with whom he can be "the best among the least," and this may be the crowd that other youngsters label "the burn-outs," "the freakers," or "the hoods." Or, if he is equipped to compete in athletics, he may displace in this direction quite productively, as may the young woman who competes and wins a role as cheerleader or majorette. The healthy Ambitious adolescent will keep trying until a favorable area of activity is found. One Ambitious Personality remembers not finding the academic side of high school too favorable for his earning good grades. Still, he took the tougher courses feeling that it was better to identify with excellence; excellence was status, and status always rates favorably. Also, he excelled in football, and always managed to date the more desirable young women—the girls whose popularity gave them a built-in high rating. Another Ambitious Personality remembers having been a cheerleader throughout her junior high years, but when she tried for cheerleader in high school she didn't make it. She felt so bad that she couldn't tell her family. That was in the fall. What she didn't tell anyone was that she had an insurance policy: she knew there would be spring tryouts for majorette, and when spring came, she won the position. So for the enterprising Ambitious teenager, adolescence can be either an enriching experience of competing and achieving, with a healthy ratio of good ratings to a few less favorable ones; or it can

46

be a crushing experience in futility, negative ratings, and defeat.

Growing up, the Ambitious adolescent finds the family to be the safest environment in which to test his wishes and strivings. At least it should be. If he finds that his wishes and efforts are acceptable and receives good ratings even when given correction and offered other options, the experience will be highly productive in his development. But if overstimulated to strive harder, or if overinhibited, the experience can be stultifying. The teenage girl, for example, who experiments in a seductive style of dress still needs personal approval— even as the dress style is discouraged—lest a sense of guilt or personal failure be induced. The young man who volunteers to be a team manager after he fails to make the team is displaying a healthy use of displacement, but if his father tells him, "That's a flunky's job," he is denied a flexible alternative; he has nothing left but a low rating. The more the individual is able to direct his interests toward a positive, attainable goal, the healthier the experience. He needs support and encouragement so that his ambitions are focused and not indiscriminate, so that his perspective is realistic and his goals are possible. He needs to learn that his competitive spirit and his strivings are normal and productive. But he also needs to know that good ratings are desirable and possible, not just for the scoring of achievements but for his own worth as a person. He should be encouraged to savor each success as it comes—his own and that of others.

COLLEGE AND COURTSHIP

As the Ambitious Personality grows, matures, and expands into life outside the home, he better defines his goals and works more vigorously and productively toward achieving them. There is still a tendency to accept challenges too readily, although his natural caution is helping him to be more selective and to proceed more thoughtfully. He diligently pursues those areas that interest him; he is willing to work long and hard to achieve his goals, and might find himself sufficiently successful, academically, socially, or athletically, to be considered something of a "big man" on campus. This, of course, would be an excellent rating, though something of a surprise to him. Compliments are always somewhat surprising since he assumes that everyone is striving and competing as hard as he is.

47

The Ambitious student will challenge the professor on a test grade she feels is not an adequate rating for all her hard work. The Ambitious football player won't understand why the coach didn't comment on his spectacular play in last week's game, yet gave him hell yesterday when he failed to score against a very tough team. The rating system seems all out of kilter and very confusing. The young Ambitious student experiences some anguish when, in college, he runs into a much higher level of competition than he has hitherto experienced. The high school football player finds himself unable to compete with larger, more skilled athletes; the straight-A high school scholar has to forego weekend outings just to maintain a B average; the prom queen discovers her sorority sisters were all prom queens or cheerleaders or the most frequently dated high school seniors. The competition gets tougher, the ratings more difficult to come by. At this stage, the Ambitious Personality benefits from a thoughtful process of re-evaluating his abilities and goals, but once he reaches that area in which his energies can be most productively and pleasingly invested, the achievements are most satisfying. The Ambitious Personality senses that he can be more discriminate in his strivings, and less desirous of an external ranking.

Not surprisingly, the Ambitious Personality approaches dating with much the same sense of competition and rating he does everything else. The Ambitious Personality is attracted to a person who has an established rating—favorable, of course—who is attractive either physically or intellectually, who is rated in the winning category but is not a competitor. The Ambitious Personality responds to someone who shows an interest in him and his goals, someone who is open and receptive. It is not at all unusual for an Ambitious Personality to pick out someone who is highly popular and heavily dated —still working the rating system, he is making choices based on predetermined favorable ratings. Whether for male or female, the system works the same way, and both are prone to leaping into love. *He* tends to promote a whirlwind style of courtship, and *she* puts emphasis on appearing seductive and on other dramatic elements of sexual interaction. Each may be said to be selling the sizzle; both need to be cautious as they approach permanent relationships. One danger is the tendency to trap themselves in relationships out of guilt feelings for having been so assertive or aggressive sexually. Another tendency is to seek out marriage partners who seem to need them, or who appear passive or naïve, persons who readily give support and security.

There is a productive tendency among healthy Ambitious Personalities to be very cautious in courtship. They know their competitive impulses going in, and they sometimes break off their engagements—not once but sometimes several times—as a way of testing relationships. They always want to be sure. But once married, the testing ends; the Ambitious Personality doesn't look back. He took out his insurance policy before his commitment.

FAMILY LIFE

The Ambitious Personality sometimes finds it difficult to gear down from all the vigorous striving, competing, and achieving of the outside world. Sometimes the temptation is to allow work and career to dominate home life, but the healthy Ambitious Personality learns to leave the job at the office or factory. Home is a haven away from the aggressive activities at work; family is an environment that gives good ratings for being tender and patient, friendly and fun. The appeal is very real and satisfying. Not that the Ambitious Personality ever discards his essential characteristics; rather, he uses them productively in creating a good family life and good relationhips within the family. As he recognizes the same personality style in his children, he is able to offer insights, counsel, and encouragement that foster growth, confidence, and healthy directions. He is able to assist his Ambitious children in healthy displacement, in overcoming indiscriminate urges to compete, in reducing rivalries. He can work off some of his energy by playing pick-up ball with his children or he might take an interest in coaching Little League or in working with youth groups such as scouting. And if he indulges in an occasional round of golf, who would deny him?

The Ambitious mother has most of the same options, especially if she also has a job outside the home. In fact, she might be a bit frustrated if she does not; she possesses the same desire to achieve and to compete, to merit good ratings. She can, of course, realize these benefits in home life, but she may feel she would like to resume work outside the home once the children enter school. She sometimes finds it difficult and frustrating at home with infants—tots do not give their mothers A's and B's for changing diapers—yet she may not mind her husband telling her she works too hard in the home; she counts that a favorable rating. When she accepts the role of homemaker and mother, she is likely to fill her time with multiple projects inside and outside the home: painting and papering the walls, redecorating, working in the garden, canning vegetables perhaps, fixing the plumbing; playing golf, collecting for charitable organizations, driving handicapped children to school, working with slow learners—whatever fulfills her sense of purpose while earning her good ratings.

The Ambitious mother *can* find herself using the rating game to her disadvantage. Take, for example, the case of a mother who spent the night in the hospital with her youngster prior to his tonsillectomy. She complained about sleeping on a lounge chair and having to do the work of a nurse, even though she was assured that this was rather usual and very beneficial to her child. Her complaint, delivered in the presence of the child, was unfortunate. She was there because she wanted to be there; she cared. But, in complaining, she was trying to elicit a favorable rating from the staff, her child, and herself: she wanted so much to be told that she was a good mother, but the effort backfired.

Take another example: the young Ambitious wife who was so excited when her father invited her husband to join his manufacturing firm. She coaxed and exhorted her husband without realizing that *her* sense of the challenge made the offer so attractive. When it was pointed out that perhaps she would have liked her father to have made *her* the offer, she backed off, thus permitting her husband to make his own decision. Similarly, an Ambitious wife might rate her husband for his ability to produce income and material things. The Ambitious Personality does not seem to value income and what money can buy for their own sake but, rather, as concrete ratings. Success has to be indicated; otherwise, how can it be scored? Thus the upward mobility of the Ambitious family—and thus one reason why an Ambitious wife might want to work. But she also might transfer her own ambition onto her husband, and she might then become the power behind a driven man. If it were not for the lingering sex-role assignments of our society, the reverse relationship would be more evident. The Ambitious male *does* push his wife in other ways—to maintain a status appearance at parties and at the club, to be knowledgeable and engaging, to be a superb cook when entertaining clients, and so on.

A parent who is Ambitious might project his strivings onto the children, attempting to live out his own frustrated ambitions vicariously. The sports-minded father might pressure his son—sometimes vigorously—to become a baseball player. This can be especially counterproductive if the child is of another personality style: here is a father shouting instructions on how to field a ball, while the child is admiring the flight of a bird across the sky. The same thing can happen with the frustrated mother who might urge her daughter to pursue the career she felt marriage had denied her. It happens. The unfulfilled Ambitious parent, however unconsciously, is in danger of putting the iron fist of his frustrations into the velvet glove of his child's life. Beware!

The phenomenon that I call *silent striving* can happen anywhere, but the home is a marvelous cover for this covert style of competition. You see it in the Ambitious woman, for example, who exercises alone before the television set to maintain her figure, which certainly is good enough to draw notice—and good ratings. It may be in the expensive and well-concealed hair transplant of the young engineer. Or it could be in the student who strives so greatly in college that she quits—perhaps gets married—simply to end the constant tension of trying and competing. Or it could be in the person who so values becoming a really good tennis player that he quits the club rather than face all that exhausting striving. Then, too, it might be in the chairman of the board, nearing retirement age, who comes back from vacation with his face lifted and his hair tinted. (And, of course, he insisted that his wife too share in the cosmetic procedures.) Or it might be in their thirty-year-old bachelor son who works over a punching bag at night alone in his bedroom. And, as one young Ambitious woman who is both careerist and wife once told me: "I can think of a few occasions when I was making love with my husband but thinking of work."

THE WORKING WORLD

When you review the essential characteristics of the Ambitious Personality, it is clear that the working world is his natural environment. There he can give full expression to his repertoire of setting goals, welcoming competition, proceeding purposefully and diligently in a rather dispassionate, well-thought-of fashion. As one Ambitious engineer commented: "Work is relaxing. There's nothing that I'd rather do than work. It's fun!" He sometimes exerts so much energy at work that there is little left for play. That reserve might be spent on a round of golf, or an evening of bowling, or a pick-up game of basketball, but his major goals, usually centered on work or career, provide the real excitement. Not realizing those goals, as one Ambitious young woman remarked, "can be devastating."

The Ambitious Personality might be found in almost any field of enterprise—anything that permits him to set goals, to be purposeful, to be rated well—if only by himself—and to keep moving upward toward the top in his field. He or she is not likely to be found in a solitary position where there is no opportunity to grow and advance. An Ambitious forest ranger will find a way to compete and compare with another forest ranger, even at a distance of twenty miles. An Ambitious physician in private practice will be active enough in the local medical society to be able to compare notes, progress in stature among his peers, and evoke favorable ratings. But more often you will find the Ambitious Personality working within a well-peopled field where there is open-ended organization offering vigorous competition and opportunity for advancement and promotion—the best sort of ratings. He enjoys sales, nursing, politics, administration, journalism, the military, contracting, factory work, owning his own small business, or any field that permits him measurable achievement.

The Ambitious supervisor is a surprisingly nice boss. With all the vigorous competition of which the Ambitious Personality is capable, he never competes in a downward direction; that would draw a poor rating from himself. Moreover, he wouldn't consider it competing at all; it would be taking advantage of those who aren't in a favorable position to compete. In his relationship with those under his supervision, the Ambitious Personality wants to be rated "Mr. Nice Guy" —a most favorable rating. Thus he might be permissive or indulgent, letting his people stray at times, but when he realizes things are getting out of hand, that quotas are off or quality is down or sales are falling, he can be quick to recover, even if he has to exert strong discipline. But he will get the effort going again, will revert to being "Mr. Nice Guy," and when the organization is moving along smoothly, when those tangible signs of success are attained—recognition awards, bonuses, whatever—he invites all his people to share the winner's circle. He always gives credit where it is due. That, too, is part of being "Mr. Nice Guy." In the Ambitious Personality's book, nice guys don't finish last; they finish first.

When the Ambitious Personality focuses on an occupational area, he becomes fully involved. He will work long hours, he will do his homework, he will appraise the environment, measure the competition, then set his goals—always upward, to the top if possible. If he can devise some insurance—some advantage, some special effort, some specialty that gives him an edge over the other person—he will. And he would expect that other person to do the same. He is always looking for that ace in the hole. It's part of the game. But he would prefer to bet on a sure thing; that's part of his caution.

The Ambitious Personality sometimes is diverted from his upward mobility by easy wins—small victories that earn quick and positive ratings. But when he re-evaluates the situation, he realizes that these easy wins are not genuine progress and he will then regroup and return to his plan. Sometimes he locks in on a rigid schedule or a planned day of demanding activities, and when his schedule or plan doesn't come full circle, he finds himself going home in the evening with a full briefcase or a nagging headache. Again, he needs to back off, to re-evaluate, to loosen up his plans and to refocus, so that the goal, not the day's effort, is primary.

Another danger to the Ambitious Personality is to alter his primary goal when a like but lesser challenge is offered. When his work is recognized and he is offered some other opportunity, he may respond quickly without fully appraising its worth—he is responding too quickly to what he perceives as a very good rating. Again, careful evaluation is helpful. Then, too, the Ambitious Personality who has worked a year or two in a position or on a job may quit because his plan for promotion is running behind schedule. He might have appraised the situation correctly; but, again, he might have benefitted by revising his schedule. Caution, in any case, is indicated. Should he discover after a year or two on the job that he may never reach the top or achieve his goal, he might also quit. But he should first ask himself whether his evaluation is accurate, or whether it is simply a matter of having been overwhelmed by competition, especially new candidates coming on the job.

RETIREMENT

The Ambitious Personality might find retirement difficult, especially if he is heavily invested in his job, profession, or career. But development of other interests is another instance of how the Ambitious Personality can use displacement to his advantage. He might get involved in senior citizens' groups, play cards, pursue outdoor activities or hobbies, particularly those that involve hand skills. Remember the point made in describing the Ambitious infant? He is very capable of entertaining himself. The Ambitious retiree will find a way to be busy and purposeful; he will locate some form of activity that is a source of good ratings. But you will not find him playing solitaire—there is no competition—and you are not likely to find him reading novels or other literature simply for pleasure. He may continue to read history or biographies or self-help books—reading material that describes how individuals have achieved or risen to the top in their fields. You will not find an Ambitious Personality sitting in a rocking chair, taking the sun and dreaming away the day. He will, as much as possible, still pursue some goal, some activity, some means of achieving and feeling purposeful. He always has an ace in the hole.

ALTERNATIVES AND OPTIONS

All Ambitious Personalities seem to have like strengths and like vulnerabilities, although the weight and emphasis will vary from individual to individual. One Ambitious Personality may display a higher degree of caution than another; one may compete more openly and keenly, while another might be more covert and diligent; one may aim straight for the top while another sets upward goals in step-by-step stages. One Ambitious Personality might be mistaken for an Accomplishing Personality because she finds that a dazzling performance draws favorable ratings. Another might prefer the quiet and deliberate sobriety favored in the executive dining room. One Ambitious careerist can leave the job at the office, but another works evenings at home.

Reactions also vary according to health and maturity or lack of them. Ambitious Personalities can be threatened by success or by failure. A sudden promotion resulting from a competitive effort might create some guilt feelings or some fear of having to strive for a high rating at a new level. Negative feelings might also come with the realization, after years of striving and succeeding, that there is less ability to compete with the younger talent coming up. Fear of hurting and alienating others in competitive situations can promote feelings of guilt, spoiling the "Mr. Nice Guy" image. That same guilt feeling can be experienced by an Ambitious spouse or parent who is turning the home into a pressure cooker. Should a close associate in a competitive situation die, the Ambitious Personality might well experience strong feelings of guilt.

While the healthy and self-assured Ambitious Personality normally handles his vulnerabilities well, he still benefits from an awareness of the alternative responses open to him. For the less sure and troubled Ambitious Personality, an awareness of alternatives and options opens opportunities to set realistic goals, to avoid indiscriminate challenges and easy wins, to reduce the level of hostility in competition, and to recognize genuine success and good ratings.

If you are an Ambitious Personality, here are some points for you to consider:

• Ambition is perfectly acceptable and desirable. Recognize genuine effort and applied talent. Permit yourself the joy that is one of the fruits of victory.

• Move away from guilt feelings that you sometimes associate with competing and achieving.

• Set limits on your goals so that they can be achieved and so that you can avoid losing.

• Judge the acceptability of your efforts without having to be rated all the time.

• Balance those seldom-received low ratings with your more frequent high ratings. It's the ongoing average that counts.

• Some things in life are worth doing even if they don't carry ratings: for instance, being tender, loving, and caring, and promoting the well-being of others.

• It's all right to make mistakes. We learn from our mistakes, so don't be afraid to stub your toe.

• You don't like to daydream, but it might be helpful to your handling of success to fantasize occasionally the good feelings that come with success. Get used to the feeling of success.

• Let your conduct and behavior be self-representing. You don't have to be embarrassed by your excitement over projects and efforts. It's not necessary to be constantly told that you are appreciated. Enjoy your excitement without fear that you are being "loud and obnoxious." And you can be liked without having to feel that you must do more and more all of the time.

• Be a team player: share the effort and the excitement with your co-workers. Recognize the value of the contributions of others. Share the winner's circle.

• Don't try to buy success or good ratings. Don't pick up the tab for the victory celebration. You don't have to pay for success. And don't pay "conscience money" for having competed successfully.

• That "tired" feeling is associated with indiscriminate competitiveness and always having to be first or best. And the guilt you associate with your competitiveness and your fear of hurting others are debilitating and unnecessary.

• It's okay to go after a goal. You needn't feel stress for wanting to achieve.

• Yes, you sometimes do have a tendency to be overambitious and to move too fast. Rather than leap ahead, pause to savor your most recent success or achievement.

• Beware of easy wins and hyped-up ratings, the kind that come with giving lavish parties, buying drinks for the house, wearing a provocative or seductive dress, seducing an easy conquest, wheeling around in your new car. But if you find yourself doing any of these, please, don't apologize.

• Try communicating without anger. Rather than finding fault with associates, look for their positive contributions; join in the effort. And don't give out instant low ratings.

• Don't always operate out of a game plan. Don't stack the deck. Don't always have an ace in the hole. Let some things just happen.

• Don't always vacation in the same place, and don't return constantly to safe areas of competition. Be open. Take reasonable risks.

• Be willing to say to yourself, and really mean it: "You can't win 'em all." You can't—and you don't have to. Many people rate you as a fine person simply because you *are*, win or lose.

• You don't always have to be "Mr. Nice Guy." That is too guilt-oriented; it is a way sometimes of apologizing for your achievements.

• Be less prone to foster guilt in others as a communications technique and as a way of competing.

• Permit yourself to win without trying to explain it away, or without apologizing for having won.

56

• Avoid using clinical jargon or scientific terminology in communicating. It's defensive.

• Be more open to sharing your feelings with others, and permit them to offer you their insights. Become more involved with *people,* rather than always chasing challenges or being locked in on a goal.

• Look for areas of interest and involvement that do not demand a rating.

• Know that when you are rating others low, you are feeling poorly about yourself.

• Quit looking for invisible vultures. Not everyone around you is competing with you, and even when you are in a competitive situation, not everyone is hostile or overly aggressive. It's only your own feeling of aggressiveness. Nobody is out to get you.

• Learn to relate without having to rate, especially to those significant people in your life—your wife or husband, your children, others who are close to you and important to you. Realize too that they aren't rating you, except, perhaps, as a lovable person.

• You don't always have to be right and everyone else wrong.

• Winning is wonderful, but not at any price. Beware of trampling on others. If your goals are prudent and realistic, measured in terms of your real talents and your true opportunities, you can win cleanly and in the open.

• And last, but most important: Stop now and then to smell the roses.

III

All I demand is perfection.
CHARLES REVSON

The Influencing
Personality

THE INFLUENCING PERSONALITY isn't interested in building a better mousetrap. He wants to build the perfect mousetrap, the ultimate mousetrap. He is ever perfecting his engineering skills or his yield per acre, his sales approach or his handball game, his batting average or his wine cellar—whatever the goal—in his relentless pursuit of perfection. His daydreams are blueprints of his constant quest for the best, lavishly detailed and larger than life.

The Influencing Personality is an organized and well-informed person who displays confidence, dedication, and self-reliance. She is the neighbor you see leaving the house every Saturday morning exactly at nine-thirty for the hairdresser, her household in order. He is your auto mechanic whose garage floor is spotless; when he tells you to pick up your car at five, he has it ready at five with the invoice tabulated and itemized. The cost may be high but the engine is humming like new, or even better than new—and there is never a grease smudge on the steering wheel.

The Influencing Personality approaches every task in life in the very same way: thoroughly, systematically, and efficiently. He is fully committed to the task. He moves toward his objective with drive and determination. He expects the maximum effort from himself and from everyone else—nothing less will do. Whatever he starts, he finishes, come hell or high water. He is keenly observant of everything going on around him, and he can spot any flaw in technique or product. He is lavishly—some say slavishly—attentive to detail. If your Influencing mechanic relines your brakes then hears the tiniest squeaks, off come all four wheels, and he reworks the whole job.

AN URGE FOR THE ULTIMATE

Whether at work, home, or play, the Influencing Personality is a perfectionist. He is possessed by an undying *urge for the ultimate*—the ultimate sales record, the ultimate rock garden, the ultimate chess game. So whatever he does must be done perfectly. And to attain perfection *he* must be perfect—the perfect salesman, the perfect rock gardener, the perfect chess player. More, the perfect result demands perfect control over the process. So the Influencing Personality is ever and always pursuing control of himself, the environment, and what he is doing. Thus he insists on being expertly knowledgeable about all phases of the enterprise he is undertaking—his equipment must be the best, and the environment so structured that it is conducive to his realizing perfection. If he is mixing you a martini, don't bother to read the label on the gin bottle. You can believe it is the best money can buy. The vermouth, also the best, is added in perfect proportion to the gin. You could test with a thermometer, but your host can tell you the degree to which he has chilled your drink. So cheers! You're drinking the perfect martini.

This urge for the ultimate and passion for perfection show in everything the Influencing Personality attempts—or he wouldn't attempt it. If he hasn't the opportunity for perfection and control, chances are that he would avoid involvement. She would leave the windows bare rather than buy inexpensive drapes, although she might plunge into debt to have them custom-made and properly hung. He would not take up tennis unless he could buy the best racket, take lessons from a professional, and dress like Arthur Ashe. It just has to be that way. First-class fare was invented for the Influencing Personality.

His conversational style follows the pattern of his other activities. The Influencing Personality isn't much for small talk, and he tends to limit his conversation to those areas in which he feels competent. Even in seemingly casual conversation, he is in control. Whether speaking of building bridges or fishing for trout, he is a talking technical manual, covering the full scope of the enterprise and the most minute details. But buried in the talk is a hidden agenda: he is taking charge; he is influencing the direction and disposition of the situation. However subtle or indirect, however charming and gracious, he is delivering the message: "Let's do it my way." And if you miss the point or choose to challenge it, he will repeat the message less subtly, even bluntly. He is not bashful, and he doesn't give up easily. If your attention lapses, he may very well clear his throat or tap your shoulder, and then repeat everything he has said from the beginning. So relax. And listen. You will find, more often than not, that the Influencing Personality is knowledgeable and informative, whether the topic is raising money or pouring concrete or barbecuing the perfect hamburger. When he tells you he knows a better way, believe him. If you want the name of a good barber or a brand of fine cigars, ask the Influencing Personality. He knows only the best. And if you inquire about the price, he may look at you unbelievingly: "You only get what you pay for."

CALCULATED CONTROL

Nothing about the Influencing Personality is casual. Even in dress, the quest is for the best. She shops the best stores and the best labels. She wants style and fashion, but today's style and an elegant label aren't enough. She must examine the fabric, inspect seams and stitching, and study every detail meticulously. He will call for the head tailor to fit him. The price tag may warrant a glance, but it isn't that important. What is important is *perfection,* even in appearance, and the Influencing Personality, male or female, is willing to pay the price.

Looking good applies to all situations. Even the casual is calculated. The Influencing Personality will costume for the occasion. He will wear an old pair of wash pants when gardening, but he will insist that they be washed between wearings. Again, he is meticulous. A volleyball game calls for sweatshirt and jeans, but hers will be the "right" sweatshirt and jeans; however studiedly unironed and faded, the tag tells you they are the best brand. Whether at work or at play, the Influencing Personality has a designated uniform of the day. And he expects others to conform to his dress code. An executive should dress like an executive, not like a bookie. A machinist should look like a machinist, not like a tourist in Miami. If others do not adhere to his notion of the right and proper, the Influencing Personality will let them know. He wants everyone to look sharp, be sharp. He abhors the shoddy and sloppy, not only in dress and appearance but in all aspects of life. Shoddiness and sloppiness are imperfections.

No matter what he is doing, the Influencing Personality is pursuing **perfection** and control. Eating out, he expects to be seated immediately **and** to be served well. If he orders three-minute eggs for breakfast, don't try to serve him a three-minute-and-ten-second egg or a two-minute-and-fifty-second egg—he knows the difference! And he might take an added three minutes to lecture you on that difference. If he orders a two-inch New York steak for dinner, measure it before you bring it from the kitchen. If he requests it medium rare, well-seared on both sides, only that will do. Anything else will be sent back to the kitchen with a sizzling comment. If he is really displeased, he may walk out, but only after he has fully registered his grievance. When the fare is excellent and the service attentive, he may say nothing. But he will tip generously. And he will come back. He tends to return to familiar places where he can expect high quality and good service, whatever the price.

THE GRAND CONVERSATIONALIST

Social occasions offer the Influencing Personality scope to display charm and grace. He or she is socially poised, open, and affable. Everyone is aware of his presence—another instance of control. As always, he is articulate and persuasive. Quite often he is a truly gifted storyteller. He can weave a web of words that is sure and smooth. Still, however glib and delightful, the Influencing Personality, unlike the Accomplishing Personality, is never simply entertaining. He is attempting to impose verbal control over the occasion. Thus he tends at times to monopolize the conversation, and when someone else is speaking, he may lose interest and let his mind wander away. He is less interested in what others have to say than in what *he* has to say. And he does say it all so well, with so much charm and grace that you usually want to listen. Not that you always have a choice!

The Influencing Personality is a hostess who knows so well how to organize a dinner or a party and how to keep it lively. Guests are selected so that they complement each other; the bar is stocked, and the meal is prepared to perfection. Everything is just right. The Influencing Personality is the social spark who keeps things exciting. She would never wear the lampshade at a party; that would look idiotic—imperfect—but she might on impulse persuade someone else to wear it. She is always aware, keeping small cliques from forming, seeing that no one feels out of it, keeping every glass filled and the hors d'oeuvres circulating. It is always a grand party, and your hostess is always the perfect hostess. Strange . . . at your last party she wasn't so sparkling. The reason is the same: her quest for perfection prompted her to note that your canapés were a bit soggy, that the ice was always running out, that the roast was overdone, and that you sat her next to a dull partner who wanted to do all the talking. The Influencing Personality is indeed a grand hostess. But she can be the imperfect guest.

TIME AND SCHEDULES

The Influencing Personality's passion for control demands not only dominance over the situation but command of time. His schedule is dear to him; never disrupt it. If he has a dental appointment at nine and the dentist is late, the dentist may be reminded—or the Influencing Personality may look for a more punctual dentist. If he is a jogger, you can set your watch by him. He will pass your window every day at the same time. If he schedules a working conference for two in the afternoon, he will be there at two, in place, notes before him—and he will expect everyone else to be punctual and prepared. If he moderates the meeting, he will address the topic immediately. He is all business. When the meeting ends, he closes his notes and leaves the room for other pressing matters.

Even in family affairs, the Influencing Personality insists on maintaining his schedule. If he normally shaves at seven, the bathroom had better be available. If he expects breakfast at seven-thirty he will be seated, napkin in lap. And, please, *three*-minute eggs! If he has an appointment at three-thirty to have his car serviced, and his daughter should call to be picked up from dancing class at three, she may find herself walking home on very tired feet. His schedule is sacred. If October 15 is the date he breaks out his winter wardrobe, he will be smartly dressed in a winter-weight suit that very day, even if the temperature soars into the eighties. Only the weatherman is imperfect.

HOBBIES AND HEALTH

Hobbies are genuinely relaxing for the Influencing Personality, but they are never a matter of idleness or killing time. You rarely find an Influencing Personality lying in the shade or in front of the TV set with a can of beer in hand. Leisure has to be productive. Doing nothing is an imperfection; there is nothing to control. So relaxation has to be constructive and productive. Recreation is tantamount to creation. The Influencing hobbyist is doing something: fishing, camping, backpacking, model-building, collecting coins, restoring old cars, gardening, sports. Hobbies are pursued with all the Influencing Personality's quest for perfection. If he builds model planes of World War II vintage, he will research available technical data, the history and use of each plane, the leading pilot who flew that plane, his unit, and its insignia, and how many bombing missions or kills were credited to him. As much as possible, all the information will be reflected in the detail of each model, constructed and painted precisely, rendered to scale. The Influencing rock gardener will be as thoroughly knowledgeable and invested, and his design of space will be a studied arrangement of beauty and splendor, texture and color, peace and tranquility, planned down to the last pebble. Nothing is left to chance, and money is never skimped. Since perfection is the goal, the Influencing rock gardener may have his eye on the vacant lot next door for future expansion. The ultimate is elusive, but it always beckons.

Since the Influencing Personality cares so much about his appearance, perfection, and control, he may take an intense interest in keeping healthy and fit. Illness—his own and anyone else's—disturbs him; sickness is a reminder that no one is perfect. If he missed a day due to the flu, he would rather tell associates that he went to the races. If he is feeling fortyish and thick in the waist, he may plunge into a strict diet and a routine of exercise and jogging. And once he begins, he will not be satisfied until he has reached his goal of losing ten pounds and two inches off his waist. You can bet that he will reach his goal. The Influencing woman with a weight problem is no different, but when she reaches the size she wants to be, she may go out and purchase a completely new wardrobe. She will feel that she deserves a reward—and nothing less than the best.

VULNERABILITIES AND CRISES

What we have seen of the Influencing Personality's urge for the ultimate and quest for control indicates the great strengths and opportunities for success and self-fulfillment for this personality style. Here is a person who is dynamic, well-informed, well-organized, endlessly patient, conscious of quality, willing to work long and hard to reach his goal. He is meticulous, attentive to details, tenacious, capable of coaxing the best effort from himself and everyone around him. He or she is always looking ahead and planning for the future, always building toward a well-defined goal. The Influencing Personality's enthusiasm and confidence are persuasive and contagious. He can articulate his objectives with consummate skill.

But these very same strengths when expressed negatively become weaknesses. The Influencing Personality's demand for control can lead to rigidity, inflexibility, manipulation. When things aren't going according to his schedule or blueprint, he can be irritable and abrasive. His tendency to impose verbal control can result in long lectures, tiring monologues, and abusive tirades. The danger is that those around him will back off from the Influencing Personality, yielding him too much control. That doesn't help him; he hears too little feedback. Interaction dies, or the chemistry sours. The already frustrated Influencing Personality slips into isolation. His rigid scheduling prohibits new ideas entering the mix or his taking advantage of unexpected opportunities or chance encounters. His exacting attention to detail can submerge him in trivia and minutiae. He loses sight of priorities, and since one detail is as important as another, everything has the same priority—or no priority. He becomes the prisoner of his own control of time and situations.

The Influencing Personality finds it difficult to accept other opinions and criticism—the message he hears is that he isn't perfect. He pulls away into long moments of logical analysis; and when it comes to logic, he is the complete logician, another Aristotle. But again, he isn't hearing the sort of feedback that would benefit him. Once more he drifts into isolation—at a time when constructive comments might help him to get back on track. Yet he can be his own worst critic—he is always the first to detect a flaw, however slight, and he often misses the worth of his work. If something isn't one hundred percent right, it is all wrong. Take it apart. Do it again. And if he is supervising the work of others, he can be just as tough. He is often critical and judgmental of others, even when he isn't involved or hasn't been asked. He is strongly opinionated, apparently feeling that he always has to have perfect knowledge and the perfect answer.

A constant problem for the Influencing Personality is his expectation that any event must be "perfect" to have significance and meaning. The ski trip has to be monumental, the vacation grand and glorious, the evening out stupendous, a movie spectacular. His ultimate urge causes him to miss the everyday pleasures and the many small joys in life.

The Influencing Personality never has a small problem. His is always the ultimate problem that provokes a colossal crisis. If the Influencing Personality were to discover a spot on his tie during a job interview, he would see it as a screaming statement of his imperfection. His worth would wilt. He might walk away with no further effort to secure the position—he doesn't deserve it; he isn't perfect. It is no different when he can't solve a problem or complete a task. He is miserable and hell to live with. Whatever goes wrong is a catastrophic reminder that he has failed—and failure is the ultimate imperfection. His worth drops to zero. He can become brooding, sullen, depressed. Anything can ignite his anger, and his anger too tends toward the ultimate. He can explode into a monumental rage, he can weep a torrent of tears, and he is known to lash out physically. Those around him, friends or not, might do well to grant him a wide neutral zone. His bark is ferocious, but his bite is worse. He would rather fight than flee. What he is doing is struggling mightily to restore control over the situation. He will maneuver, push, pull, strain, and shout, and if he fails to recapture control, if he is defeated, that is indeed the ultimate failure, perfect worthlessness. If you have contributed in any way to his failure, beware. The Influencing Personality has a perfect memory for grudges.

GROWING UP INFLUENCING

The Influencing child usually begins to show recognizable characteristics by age two. He is the child who may resist parental attempts to toilet-train him. His behavior pattern is a rather emphatic "no." Yet when his parents let up, he may respond by wanting to use the toilet—he seems to be expressing his desire to initiate his own control over bowel functions. This is the child who wants order in the familiar things around him. He is the tot in the high chair who insists that a wet washcloth be placed on his tray, that his bowl and spoon always be located in the same position every meal. Or he may be more stubborn than other children in resisting eating what he doesn't like; he may even throw the bowl of oatmeal. A tearful tantrum might follow. His clothes, his playthings, his bedding, and his nap schedule may all evoke some struggle. And since one of the parents is also an Influencing Personality, there may be frequent clashes between that parent and the Influencing child. But the parent, with insight into the shared personality style, can pursue alternatives that can diminish the struggle greatly. Wherever possible, the child should be permitted some leeway in handling those things that he considers his and to find his own napping routine. He does have a sense of order that is an advantage to parents, and when he is allowed some latitude in arranging his own world, he is a most agreeable child.

The Influencing child is normally aware and interested in his environment, and as he develops, will attempt to organize himself further within that environment. He will sometimes show frustration when his painstaking efforts do not succeed. He has a tendency to try to do everything too well, and whenever he feels that his autonomy is threatened, he will resist vigorously. Even at an early age, his measure of his self-worth is his ability to influence the situation through his control. The typical Influencing pattern of struggle for control and perfection shows increasingly throughout childhood as he meets new and more testing challenges. His greatest need, perhaps, is to be encouraged to share in group activities, and to relate to siblings and other children in a free-flowing, give-and-take manner.

Entry into school is usually uneventful, and the Influencing child is readily accepted by peers and teachers. In the primary grades, he may at times resist the teacher, but not in an overt way. All goes well for the Influencing child until about the fourth grade when his manner of contesting the teacher becomes more open and defiant. What the Influencing child is doing is attempting to establish his control over what he wants to learn and how he wants to learn it. This attitude, sometimes expressed in disruption but more often as simple resistance or restlessness, may give the teacher the impression that the child is not adequate as a student. A bright Influencing child is sometimes labeled "dumb" because of his resistance to standard classroom procedures. One teacher informed the parent of a stubborn Influencing child that she was recommending the child be held back a year. But the mother, herself an Influencing Personality, was able to offer the teacher insight; she had been through the same problem as a child. The result of the parent-teacher discussion was that the child was permitted to participate more freely, pursuing learning in his own structured and organized way, after which the child began to do very well.

Another school problem for the Influencing child is his fear of making mistakes. Trying so hard to be perfect, he becomes bogged down in checking and rechecking his work, fussing and fretting over small details and neatness, so that he can miss the large flow of the learning opportunity. He hesitates to give spontaneous answers in classroom discussions, even when he knows the answers. Here, again, insight into the problem produces the solution: the child needs to be encouraged to participate more freely without feeling that he has to be perfect—the way he can learn more effectively is to learn through his mistakes.

Why these problems surface in the fourth grade—and again around the eighth grade—is not clear. But it is helpful to parents and teachers of Influencing children to recognize that these children can have problems relating to control and perfection during these years.

Some phobic concerns and scrupulosity may emerge in the Influencing adolescent, but the teen years normally present a clearer picture of his concern for order, neatness, and maintaining an attractive appearance; his pursuit of his own values and interests; and his continuing quest for control and perfection. As he begins to date, his interest in the opposite sex centers on physical attractiveness and the same good personal appearance that he values in himself. The Influencing teenager will try to find a job after school a bit more diligently than other teenagers. He wants money to buy the clothes that assure him an above-average wardrobe. He wants to be able to take his dates to the right places. He will want to buy a car as soon as he can to give him greater control over his own activities outside the home. However old the car, he will maintain it in good running order, and he will keep it looking good. He is less prone during adolescence to run with the crowd—unless he dominates or is recognized as the leader. He will shun those situations where he feels he cannot do well or cannot control the direction of what is happening.

College is a welcome opportunity to the mature Influencing Personality. Here he can focus his energies and organizing skills on his special area of interest, improve his disciplined approach to problems, and benefit from his tenacious perseverance. But the Influencing Personality who is not flexible in his passion for perfection can demand too much of himself. A university campus and abundant academic offerings are simply beyond the scope of his control mechanisms. He has to learn to bend, to limit his sights, to challenge his talents; otherwise, his purusit of academic excellence—expressed as a goal of straight A's—can be exhausting and frustrating. A better goal would be to do his best and to accept the results. It is interesting to note that the Influencing student, in pursuing his high goals, isn't competing for grades. He really doesn't care that much how well others are doing, and he isn't interested in the challenge. The Influencing student is simply locked into his passion for perfection.

THE WORKING WORLD

The adult Influencing Personality is usually a productive person in whatever occupation he chooses. But he especially enjoys those areas that permit him to function at a high level of structure, organization, quality, and control. He does particularly well in the sciences, engineering, electronics, tool-and-die making, accounting, banking, construction, carpentry, and, in medicine, surgery. He also excels as a pilot, policeman, investigative agent, or umpire. And, of course, he does exceptionally well in the military where order and structure are prized. He enjoys going by the book. And it had to be an Influencing Personality who invented the white-glove inspection! He enjoys command and power, the impersonal style of the military, the predictable routine. The Influencing Personality will function well in any group enterprise where there is a clear line of responsibility, especially when he has the opportunity to exert leadership. He is quite comfortable doing detailed work, systematic analysis, and planning—anything that permits the Influencing Personality a logical, structured approach. Logic permits consistency and control.

The Influencing woman will enter the marketplace with the same energy and purpose as her male counterpart. She will pursue her goals with the same quest for excellence and control. If she encounters sexual discrimination in the working world, she won't hesitate to fight for her rights—remember, the Influencing Personality would rather fight than flee—but she might feel slightly greater pressure to excel and to demonstrate her competence in a male-dominated situation. Male or female, the Influencing Personality is not driven so much by ambition and competition—as the Ambitious Personality would be—as by the need to be productive, efficient, and qualitative and to maintain control of his own enterprise. His goal is not necessarily to be corporation president: he wants to rise as high as he can commensurate with his ability to maintain quality of product and control of his working environment. The pursuit of excellence is his prime concern, and it endures throughout his working career. The Influencing Personality never slackens in his quest for perfection and regulation of his work. He becomes only more of a perfectionist, sometimes too rigidly so. He tends to take few chances that would lessen his control or reduce his efficiency and competence.

Attitudes toward retirement vary according to situation. The self-employed Influencing Personality might work as long as good health permits. He enjoys the continuing opportunity to be productive and in command of his own enterprise. If the enterprise involves a large organization, he might be hesitant to step aside to permit younger talent to assume control of *his* operation. When the Influencing Personality is an employee, his employer would not be particularly pleased to see him retire; he is a valued producer. But when retirement comes, it poses few problems of adjustment. The Influencing Personality usually pursues alternative interests that permit him to sustain his sense of worth, quality, and control. During his retirement years, he would tend to keep in touch with former working associates, as he would family and close friends.

The Influencing woman who chooses home and family is no less interested in maintaining control over her environment and performing efficiently and well. She too will be driven by the urge for the ultimate, and she tends to be an immaculate housekeeper. What interests her particularly are outlets for planning and organization. If she is interested in cooking, she is a superb cook. If she has a flair for design and arrangement, her home is a showplace. If she makes her own clothes, they will be studies in elegance, style, and quality. Sometimes, however, she may sabotage her relationships with spouse and children by being too insistent on order, tidiness, and schedules. She may frequently chide the children for having dirty shoes, her husband for being late for dinner. She finds the telephone a nuisance; it interrupts her household schedule, and how do you control a telephone? She resents salesmen who come to the door and friends who drop in to chat and stay too long. She can make a terrible fuss over how the children fold the towels and linens. If the toothpaste cap isn't replaced properly, she can give a ten-minute demonstration lecture during dinner on how to recap tubes properly. One Influencing wife repeatedly asked her husband to quit leaving his coat and sweater draped on his chair in the living room. He ignored her. "Finally," she reports, "I took them both out to the garbage can." On another occasion, when she had spanked her daughter—"well-deserved, mind you"—her husband questioned the use of physical punishment. Only then did she feel any qualms—and not for having spanked the child. She felt that her husband was saying that she wasn't the perfect mother.

COURTSHIP AND MARRIAGE

The Influencing Personality is drawn to the person who is physically attractive, neat in appearance and dress, and attentive. His courtship rite is rather deliberate: he wants to make a strong showing and a very good impression—extensions, again, of his desire to be

perfect and to maintain control. He will take her places that reflect his tendency to extravagance and quality. He will plan evenings
out with studied precision.

Quite often the Influencing woman will tend to maneuver her
dates into following her direction in their activities. She isn't a bit
hesitant about suggesting dinner at the best restaurants or good
seats at the theater. She will coax him into trying skiing, if that is
what she likes, even if he is not particularly interested. If he pleads
poverty some evening, then she will invite him up to her apartment
for some of her gourmet cooking. She will tend to control the relationship, or at least try.

The Influencing Personality may choose a partner in marriage
whom he can dominate—or at least one who will permit him at least
enough scope to pursue his quest for control and perfection in all
essential matters. The Influencing woman may choose a man "who
needs me" so that she dominates. The male, similarly, may choose
the childlike submissive woman. But this need to structure and
control the relationship sometimes creates tension and conflict. Not
surprising would be a marriage where the partners maintain independent careers and separate interests, a style of peaceful co-existence
that would keep the marriage intact.

The Influencing woman might be content early in marriage to
be a homemaker and mother, but given the opportunity, she might
enjoy blending a career outside the home with her role as homemaker—but only if it did not diminish her self-image as the perfect
wife and mother.

The Influencing partner likes to maintain tight schedules, long-
range planning of family life, and control of the budget. He is
tempted to instruct everyone on how to do the various housekeeping
tasks. The Influencing husband would not hesitate to show his wife
how to make a bed with hospital corners, or how to iron his shirts,
or even how to vacuum the carpet.

The Influencing parent and spouse has a difficult time avoiding
the myopic way of seeing things only from his own perspective and
interests. He is prone to go his own way, and expects others to accept his determination of how things ought to be. One example is
an Influencing wife and mother who viewed her husband's company
Christmas party as a chore and a bore. It was outside of her sphere of
interests—and control. But something happened one Christmas party

to change all that: "I didn't want to go. It was all so boring until suddenly I began to see it from my little girl's point of view. Then I had a ball." This remarkable insight was productive for both mother and child.

One Influencing father demonstrated how his desire to dominate family life came close to disaster. He purchased a sailboat that required a crew, so he recruited his wife and three sons. The family spent Sunday after Sunday at the lake sailing—and doing little else but sailing. The father wouldn't permit swimming or sunning on the shore, or even barbecuing hamburgers—peanut butter and jelly sandwiches aboard the boat would have to do. The family was drilled and drilled to become the perfect crew under his insistent command. One Sunday in July, wife and sons mutinied. The boat was sold, and sailing hasn't been mentioned since. The incident reveals another characteristic of the Influencing Personality: he admires spunk and candor in others.

When the Influencing parent becomes involved in the lives of his children, he is tempted always to exert a forceful influence. If the Influencing mother values high grades, she may insist that her children bring home high marks; she may schedule study periods at home that are meant to guarantee the excellence she expects. Both her demand for good grades and her schedule are, of course, convenient controlling techniques. But if one or more of her children is also an Influencing Personality, then there can be friction and conflict, even sabotage. The Influencing child, remember, wants to control his own learning direction. The Influencing mother who desires that her daughter take ballet may be asking her child the impossible. And her Influencing daughter may cause the disruption of a dozen other children who really want to learn the art. The same Influencing mother may be so insistent on having her children help in keeping the house clean and tidy that they begin to feel like indentured servants. Beware of the coming rebellion.

The Influencing Personality can be the father who is heard to say on so many occasions: "Children should be seen and not heard." He is likely to set rigid hours on television viewing and bedtime hours, dating, and after-school activities. If his wife is not quite the housekeeper he expects, or not prompt enough with meals, or not always neat and attractive in her appearance, you might find him pounding the table and giving directions on how to clean the kitchen or how to shine his shoes. If sports are a keen interest, you might find him at every one of his son's games second-guessing umpires and coaches. Or he might be one of the umpires or coaches—if he is a coach, winning every game isn't necessarily his goal: it is how well everyone plays the game, meaning *his* game. The Influencing father might urge his son to attend *his* university, pursue *his* major, and join *his* fraternity.

ALTERNATIVES AND OPTIONS

The Influencing Personality's great productivity, his pursuit of quality and excellence, his great efficiency, his leadership ability, his diligence and determination offer much to his personal life and to the life of his community. But his singular point of view and his drive for control and perfection can be limiting and debilitating when carried to excess. Insight into the dynamics of his personality style and the possible extremes of his urge for the ultimate can help him to avoid rigidity and narrowness, and the fear of failure and imperfection. Those persons close to him, whether family, friends, or working associates, can also benefit by being aware and by contributing to his awareness of his style of behavior.

The key to understanding the Influencing Personality is recognizing his identification of worth with his urge for the ultimate, his passion for perfection, his need to control his environment. The best way to prevent his tendency to excess is to help him become involved by relating openly to others in a free-flowing way—and without attempting to exert control over the relationship.

Preoccupation with solving problems is often a barrier to closer relationships. This may create an artificial sense of involvement. But the involvement is with things, not people.

The Influencing Personality needs to understand that making mistakes is an acceptable part of learning and improving. Failure doesn't mean he isn't perfect.

The Influencing Personality needs to know that in the journey through life he doesn't always have to be the driver to enjoy the ride.

If you are an influencing personality, consider the following:

• Relate, don't manipulate.
• Consider the high price you pay for your struggle for control—

your resultant anger, crisis, panic, tantrums. Realize that you are capable of feelings other than anger. Don't deny, minimize, or suppress feelings of tenderness and closeness—they are very productive and healthy emotions.

• You don't have to be so opinionated. People don't expect you to be the perfect font of knowledge; they enjoy you for who you are, not for what you know. Consider that others may have helpful ideas and feelings.

• Beware of your bullying tendency. It is another technique for controlling the situation, but it destroys good relationships with your children, your spouse, your co-workers.

• Intellectualize less. That is a flight from feelings. Logic and analysis are open-ended processes that can be manipulated by whatever the logician puts into them. More, they put you out of touch; their excessive use is a substitute for feelings. You need to feel more, think less.

• Quit clinging to grudges. Holding on to anger is another way of avoiding feelings.

• Listen more and talk less.

• Stop trying to change people. Try working with them, enjoying their opinions.

• Order is less important than interaction. Organizing people is manipulative when it doesn't produce genuine interaction and open communications.

• Look for the small pleasures in life. Quit expecting life to provide an endless series of grand and glorious experiences. Enjoy the company of friends for the sake of friendship.

• Don't let your concern for neatness and appearance become a fetish for perfection. People, again, judge your worth by your total person and not by the clothes that you wear.

• Beware of imposing your friends and your interests on your spouse. Try to take more of an interest in his or her friends, his or her activities.

• Let the spontaneous into your life. Open your schedule to unexpected moments of surprise and innovation. Good things, good feelings have a way of popping up unexpectedly.

• Learn to quit short of a flawless production, whether it is work or play or conversation. Again, openness to innovation happens when you aren't so concerned with every infinitesimal detail and procedural step.

74

• Don't isolate yourself so often in your pet project or your work. You are avoiding people and feelings.

• Be less extravagant. Money can't buy perfection.

• Let yourself laugh. It's very human, and it is no loss of control—and it is the perfect antidote to anger.

• No one is perfect. No one *has* to be perfect to be of great value and worth to others or to himself.

• Freedom demands flexibility. Rigidity is a self-imposed form of slavery.

• What people like about you, what attracts them to you, is *you,* not what you can do or what you can buy. Discard some of the baggage and clutter of things and projects so that people can relate to the real you.

• Tenderness is a more perfect human expression than anger, love is closer to the ultimate human feeling than control, the quality of life is measured more by feelings than by purchasing power. Love, human contact, giving *and* receiving, bring out the best in all of us. And you want the best.

IV

*After you've done your
best, the hell with it.*
ANONYMOUS

The Accomplishing
Personality

"ALL THE WORLD'S A STAGE," wrote the poet. And every
Accomplishing Personality is stage-struck. Male or female, child or
adult, he or she wants the opportunity to perform well—brilliantly
if possible—to impress others; to earn their approval, affection, and
applause; to take a bow. Whether at work or at play, among friends
or family or co-workers, he is alive with purpose and energy, driving
hard and striving to excel. Whatever he is doing, he is doing his best.
Nothing less will do. If his is not quite a stellar performance, it isn't
that he hasn't tried. More likely he has tried too hard. And if at
first he doesn't succeed, he is willing to try, try again. And again.

The Accomplishing Personality looks on life with a robust appetite for doing all the things that appeal to him. He is the sort of
high-energy person who might put in an eighty-hour work week,
then dash off to the golf course to play eighteen holes before appearing fresh and glowing at the Saturday-night party where he can be
expected to dazzle till dawn. She is the housewife who leaves the
dinner dishes in the sink while she sits up half the night writing
what she hopes is the great American novel. He is the high school

trumpeter in the pep band who blows all those lip-bruising screech notes until the applause dies out or his lips give out, whichever comes first. She is the spunky ten-year-old who jumps off the garage roof with a home-made parachute to impress the other neighborhood youngsters. And if she breaks a leg, that great white cast is sure to dazzle them.

Exaggerated? Not to the Accomplishing Personality. A bit of exaggeration is part of his style. It shows in the way he works, in the way he plays, in what he expects to accomplish, in the way he talks, in the way he expects others to respond to the flair and flamboyance of his performance. His expectations of himself, like his expectations of others, run high, and they can only go higher. Onward and upward. The sky's the limit. Or is it? Consider this version of a dream rather common to Accomplishing Personalities: "I'm flying over the city, and the people below are waving at me. I had one heck of a time getting off the ground. But I kept flapping and flapping my arms, and I made it! It took a lot of doing, but I kept flapping and flapping, rising and turning, soaring and dipping. Everyone below me was really amazed."

THE DAZZLING URGE

What is so evident in the style of the Accomplishing Personality is his willingness to work hard and to play hard, to make the maximum effort, to commit all available energy and imagination to the task or purpose at hand. More, he does it all with such charm and good cheer, such exuberance and enthusiasm, such verve and vitality, that onlookers usually are impressed. And this is exactly the reaction that the Accomplishing Personality hopes for. He dearly wants others to recognize and approve of his performance. This is what we call the Accomplishing Personality's *urge to dazzle.* He wants always to astonish, amaze, impress. And, more often than not, it happens that way.

The Accomplishing's techniques and tools are many. There is charm: a cheerful manner, an easy smile, small courtesies and compliments that make a fine first impression. There is a sense of purpose: an energetic enthusiasm, commitment, and plenty of hard work that invite substantial approval. There are communication skills: an artful eloquence, glibness, an openness to conversation that persuade, delight, and prompt others to think well of his or her viewpoint. And there is optimism: an expectation that good things will happen, a hopeful tone, an encouraging outlook that is contagious.

Put them all together and you can begin to understand the underlying essence of this personality style: the great importance that the Accomplishing Personality places on performance, productivity, obtaining approval, and making others happy. Now the themes of the Accomplishing dream cited above become clear: to make a great effort, to perform grandly, to amaze, and to please all onlookers. Ever onward and upward. Applause, applause.

SIDETRACKING

Not every Accomplishing Personality, however, performs all that well, or at least not all of the time. There is an impulsive streak to his style. He tends to react spontaneously to whatever is going on around him, and he sometimes is distracted from his purpose. He is easily sidetracked.

Suppose that I am an Accomplishing Personality and my purpose at hand is to write this chapter, but in the middle of the chapter my neighbor phones and tells me he has just purchased a new riding mower. Would I like to give it a turn around the lawn? Why not? Ten minutes won't hurt. So I take a few turns around the neighbor's lawn. Fascinating! Another two laps. Fun! It's hot, so the neighbor brings out the beer. Why not? He turns on the ball game, and we sit, sip, root for our team. The six-pack empties. I run out for another. Our team wins. One more beer to celebrate the win. Oops! Ten minutes have lapsed into four hours. Now it's dinnertime. And after dinner I always nap. Oh, well, there's always tomorrow.

That is sidetracking. And it is ever a temptation for the Accomplishing Personality. When it is time to do the dishes, the teenager complains, "But, Mom, I've got homework by the ton." And what was going on when Mom announced the dishes had to be done? Television. That's called two-track sidetracking. Here's another prime example: Mary goes off to the store for ice cream, but she runs into Martha on the way out of the market, and the ice cream is melted before Mary has caught up on all the neighborhood news. For Mary, even the path from the kitchen to the trash barrel is booby-trapped with invitations for the Accomplishing Personality to side-track: neighbors to the right of her; neighbors to the left of her; the kids' Frisbee game; rabbits in the lettuce patch; the dog wanting petting, and Mary wanting his tail-wagging approval. Suddenly: "What am I doing in the backyard? And why am I holding this sack of trash?"

Wheel-spinning is another hazard for the Accomplishing Personality. Again, suppose I am an Accomplishing Personality writing this chapter. I am eager—and anxious—to do it well, to please my editor, and to impress you readers. But I am a little too eager and much too anxious. I write a paragraph. Not good enough. I rip out the sheet. In goes another sheet of paper, and up goes the tension. I sweat and I strain, and a new paragraph slowly takes form. Not quite right. A new sheet, another false start. The neck muscles tighten. My mind goes numb. An hour later, still nothing on paper. I am sitting and staring at a blank piece of paper. This is wheel-spinning at its anguishing worst.

The Accomplishing Personality wants so much to excel, to do his very best, to warrant approval and recognition. His motor is running hard, all revved up and roaring, but sometimes all it does is spin wheels. The Accomplishing Personality would be more productive if he would pause to give himself one small pat on the back for trying. Better still, he should tell himself that doing his best is enough. Giving 110 or 125 percent is simply too much. After 100 percent, the additional energy expended produces a negative ratio of return. His best is enough.

JOLLY JEKYLL AND HORRIBLE HYDE

The Accomplishing Personality is often described as charming and witty by friends, hard-working and competent by colleagues, productive and promising by superiors, but a slavedriving tyrant by subordinates. All of them might just be right. However, this Jekyll-and-Hyde image is not the result of duplicity or a double standard. Rather, it is explained by the Accomplishing Personality's hard-driving pursuit of excellence in performance, his craving for recognition and approval, and his tendency to define roles for others. He is intent on being a doer of deeds, and he assumes that everyone has the same high purpose and the same willingness to devote the same energy and long hours to the task.

This is role-defining. When others aren't as intensely committed, or when they approach the task with quiet reflection and deliberation, the Accomplishing Personality either feels frustrated or wonders why they aren't going about it the way he would. If a subordinate did not perform up to his expectations, he might be intensely critical, perhaps taking over the task himself. He sometimes tends to feel that others are less committed and less capable, but frequently he doesn't really give them a chance to get the task done. And it is of little consolation to the chastised subordinate to know that the Accomplishing Personality never asks more of others than he asks of himself. He is prone to ask too much of both.

But woe to the Accomplishing Personality when he himself is criticized. When he is told that he hasn't done well, or that he hasn't produced sufficiently, he is shattered. He bruises easily, and when he is wounded he is a bleeder. He can become depressed when he is told that he performed poorly. Suppose even that he did the job well but the customer complains that the price is too high: the Accomplishing Personality will take the complaint personally. His wife tells him at a party that he is talking too much. He is crushed. The Accomplishing mother buys her daughter a new swimsuit as a surprise. Her daughter doesn't like the color. Mother is wounded. The husband brings home roses, but the wife asks how their budget can afford such an extravagance. The pain is terrible. He is the big winner at the Friday night poker game, yet he wants to be told what a great game he played: he wants all the money *and* applause. His poker-playing buddies snarl. He is pierced. He would exchange all his winnings for their approval.

VULNERABILITIES

The great vulnerability in the life of the Accomplishing Personality is his exaggerated expectation of himself and others. He finds it difficult to accept limitations. He tends to overwork and to overplay, to overestimate his abilities and to underestimate problems. He tries to do too many things at one time; he diffuses his energy and his purpose. He tries to exceed his capabilities. And he wants always to dazzle those around him with his energy and talents, his productivity, his intelligence, his friendliness, and his wit. He is driving ever onward and upward, higher and higher, with abandon. He expects the moon and the stars from himself. And, in his role-defining, he expects just as much from family, friends, co-workers, and teammates. He wants everyone to match him stride for stride. He views any human limitation as nonsense; anyone can do better if he is willing to try hard enough.

The Accomplishing Personality is everywhere at once, trying to be all things to all people, sometimes with great inconsistency. At once he wants to be the hard-driving supervisor and one of the boys, to be witty and to be taken seriously, to have the first word and the last, to be parent and pal, to be the exacting spouse and the super-sexed lover. And when he is mesmerized by his own exaggerated sense of being able to accomplish so many things, he begins to believe that his strength is indeed the strength of ten. Who needs a phone booth to change into Superman?

The Accomplishing Personality, as noted above, is easily bruised by criticism. But even more perilous is a well-rounded compliment for a job well done. In his heart, the less mature Accomplishing Personality yearns for this sort of approval. But he simply cannot enjoy the compliment when it comes. He cannot say, "Thank you," and take a bow. He interprets compliments as statements of still higher expectations. He decodes the praise to mean that next time he will have to put forth that much more of an effort, perform that much better to please his source of approval. The more lavish the compliment, the greater the expectation. If it is praise on the grand scale, the overwhelmed Accomplishing Personality can become paralyzed. How can he possibly outdo that kind of a performance?

When the Accomplishing Personality's motor is purring and he is performing at a high level—perhaps above his cruising speed—others become accustomed to his momentum. When he can no longer sustain the pace, they may become a little critical. Once more, this is the high price the Accomplishing Personality pays for projecting exaggerated expectations and for overperforming. His response, having realized that he has overperformed, may be to withdraw. Emotionally, if not physically, he disappears. He can't sustain the effort, and he can't do better. So he exits. And should he fear that the source of approval will continue to withhold praise, he will continue his state of withdrawal. A better response would be for him to remain at the task but at a greatly reduced but steady pace.

But slacking off, just relaxing, is difficult for the wound-up Accomplishing Personality. He feels that when he ceases to produce or perform, he ceases to exist: he is nothing, no one. So even at a party, he is usually driving hard. He has to dazzle. He has to maintain a steady flow of glib and witty chatter and seemingly casual remarks. Wherever two or more cluster, there is an audience. The show must go on. He needs those "Ohs" and "Ahs," those approving nods, those smiles, that laughter. True, he can be enjoying the party and relishing the applause, but he is wound up and working hard. He needs to come down before he moves up to the level where his dazzling produces more heat than light.

The Accomplishing Personality is a very social person, and he does benefit from the approval of others. When he is healthy, he can accept the spotlight, perform, and then walk off the stage to the sound of applause; can take his bow and then relinquish center stage to others; can resist the urge to return for encore after encore. Not so the less sure and more tightly wound-up Accomplishing Personality. Urged on by approval and applause, he begins to behave like a Roman candle: one blazing burst after another, fired off in all directions, until suddenly he is reduced to a burnt-out ember. Too much.

The Accomplishing hostess, for example, who has a problem limiting her expectations is giving a dinner for six. She prepares enough food for twelve. Every drink served is a double-double. Wave after wave of hors d'oeuvres, hot and cold, are served. Her idea of a steak is a two-inch porterhouse that overlaps the plate. The wine flows in Biblical abundance. Three kinds of crepes, all aflame. Hers is always a four-star dinner, a three-ring circus, and a two-Alka-Seltzer evening. And yet she worries if it was dazzling enough.

Gifts, given or received, can provoke a crisis for the uncertain Accomplishing Personality. A gift given invites approval. A gift received is like a compliment. So any gift comes wrapped in the problem of expectations. The Accomplishing wife goes out to purchase her husband a birthday present. Simple? If she is on the healthy side, yes. But if she is anxious, no. She can spend the day shopping here, shopping there, looking at leather goods, clothing, liquor, records, whatever, without being able to make up her mind. After spending all day and all of her energy, she comes home exhausted with nothing, because she was afraid she wouldn't pick the right gift that would please her man and merit his loving approval. Or, she comes home with a gold-plated, rhinestone-encrusted putter. He is so stunned that all he can say is, "I'm stunned." She reads it as stunning approval, and now she has a whole year to anguish over what she can buy him for his next birthday that will top the putter.

Receiving gifts can be equally disconcerting, loaded with hidden messages of expectation. The Accomplishing wife is overwhelmed when her husband has the kitchen remodeled. She could have read the message as a pat on the back for being such a great wife. But she perceives the message as his expectation that she work even harder to be a fine wife and a good cook. She dreads entering that sparkling new kitchen. What does he want? Gourmet breakfasts?

GROWING UP ACCOMPLISHING

Parents usually describe the Accomplishing infant as a very pleasant child. He is a good eater, bubbly and affectionate, a child who shows little temper and few tears, a child who rather early returns his parents' smiles. And he soon begins to display an emerging pattern of energy, affability, and desire for approval. He learns quickly to do those things that elicit his parents' favorable reaction.

As he learns to walk and to probe the larger environment, the Accomplishing child is curious about everything within his horizon. He enjoys the excitement of doing new things, making new discoveries, developing new friends. He explodes in a flurry of activity, proud of building his first mud dam in the rain; she delighted by her first fingerpainting. You can usually find the Accomplishing child out of doors, climbing trees, playing ball, flipping a Frisbee, sledding down the most treacherous hill in the area—doing those things especially that draw spectators and cheers of approval. He prizes athletic events that emphasize energy, endurance, and teamwork. He is outgoing and not particularly prone to worry. When he comes home with an assortment of cuts and bruises, each bump and bruise, each cut and scrape, is just one more opportunity for a large dose of tender, loving care. The Accomplishing child heals quickly.

The Accomplishing child is full of affection for people and for all of life. He isn't particularly interested in competing with friends or siblings. He would rather enjoy their friendship and have their approval. He can be very helpful to his mother, happy to run for a diaper or to warm the baby's bottle. And when Mother smiles back her appreciation, he is delighted. But when the day comes that he is expected routinely to make his bed or dry the dishes, he isn't all that thrilled. The new and the special excite him: daily chores are just that—chores. They don't provide excitement, or evoke much approval.

From the first day of school, the Accomplishing child fits in. He works hard, is responsive, and makes friends. As early as kindergarten, he discovers the rewards of a dazzling performance.

Item: "At the end of our kindergarten year, the class put on a show. I was chosen to lead the band. Afterward, a friend of my parents came up and gave me a big box of candy. I was really pleased. And when I heard them say how good I was, it felt so good that they were proud of me."

The Accomplishing child is impulsive, and there is a streak of daring in his love of excitement. He is always curious, and he tends to leap ahead with abandon. But sometimes his daring doesn't evoke the response he desires.

Item: "I was about six, I guess, and my buddy and I were playing on the schoolground slide. We jumped off the top, maybe ten or twelve feet off the ground. We ran in to tell the teacher how brave we were. She said that we weren't brave, we were dumb. I felt hurt because I thought it was a big accomplishment."

And here is a rather significant comment offered by the teacher of one Accomplishing child: "Things will always be brighter and jollier with Billy around. But, sad to say, all things that produce a great abundance of light and jolliness soon burn themselves out. Billy, you must learn to conserve and use wisely this natural ability of yours. Many times you are so busy shining and entertaining everyone that you can't see your own mistakes. Your personality will be your strength only when you learn to control it and use it instead of the other way around."

The Accomplishing child's keen desire to try everything sometimes creates frustration. The six-year-old boy wants to play Little League baseball, but he isn't eligible until he is eight. What to do? Do you simply say, "Wait until you're eight," or, "Learn to be patient"? Neither. With the Accomplishing child it is never wise or helpful to discourage his enthusiasm. Always look for a way of maintaining his interest. In this case, you might encourage him to play pick-up games with other youngsters his age in the neighborhood, or practice with him at home, or find out if there is a T-Ball league in the area (the minimum age requirement is six).

A danger to the development of the Accomplishing child is the overprotective parent who stifles his performing or his desire to explore new things. Worse is to urge him to take it easy or not to try at all. The opposite danger is to encourage him to try harder. The Accomplishing child normally performs at 100 percent of his ability. To tell him to try harder is to invite him to try too hard, to become so charged up that he begins to fall all over himself trying. The net result is a very frustrating experience not likely to be attempted again.

CHANGE AS CRISIS

Adolescence brings on the usual problems, but the Accomplishing youngster on the brink of adolescence encounters a vulnerable situation on entering junior high school. He may have moved along through the elementary years with no major problems and with much success. Now, suddenly, he changes schools. And with the change in schools comes a change in environment: new teachers, new expectations, and often largely new classmates. The new and unfamiliar mix interferes with his ability to gauge the appropriate level and style of performing and accomplishing. The Accomplishing youngster can no longer anticipate what sort of response he can expect. He may be tempted to launch into an exaggerated surge of dazzling to elicit recognition and applause. Or he may withdraw if he fears that such an effort won't promote a favorable response. There is also the danger that he might become so pesty in his performing that he risks becoming the class clown. Worse, he may turn to drugs or alcohol or some other harmful behavior. One way or the other, positively or negatively, he will find a responsive audience.

This is a time when parents need to proceed cautiously and with much patience and understanding. Remember how greatly the Accomplishing Personality desires affection and approval, especially from his peers. Remember how important it is to him to be able to perform well. This is the time for parents to spend some time reviewing with the Accomplishing child all of his expectations, interests, and feelings. This is *not* the time to make more demands of him. What he needs to know is that all he can expect of himself—all anyone, including his parents, can expect of him—is his best. And since the Accomplishing Personality normally takes an optimistic view of life, he can be expected, with a little help from his parents, to settle in to new experiences, new achievements, new friends. It will all come with time. And what is learned in this period will serve both parents and the Accomplishing child when the environment again changes in high school and then again in college. The same sort of critical moment also comes whenever the family moves, with a resultant change in schools.

Teachers in the classroom also need to be aware of what is happening inside the Accomplishing teenager. Failure to recognize the essential characteristics of the Accomplishing Personality can either stifle effort or create disruption. The students to watch for are the ones frantically waving their hands in the air after every question addressed to the class, or the voices in the back of the room firing off wisecracks that trigger outbursts of laughter. Teachers may counter negatively or harshly at their own risk. The Accomplishing teenager is easily humiliated but seldom humbled. True, he may withdraw, but he is more likely simply to double his effort at dazzling. The better response is to acknowledge his desire for recognition and to encourage more appropriate means of performing that invite positive approval.

The Accomplishing teenager enjoys the many opportunities that high school offers for excitement and accomplishing and making friends. Once he settles into the new environment, it all begins to happen. He will go out for those sports that meet his talent and energy level and that permit him to perform well, especially before an audience. He may become involved in the school newspaper, the yearbook, theatrical activities, the band, cheerleading, drum-majoring, contests—anything and everything that provide an opportunity to achieve.

The Accomplishing Personality isn't interested especially in competing; he doesn't want to hurt anyone's feelings, and he doesn't keep score. Nor is he interested in leading the parade, although peers may find his enthusiasm so appealing that they choose him as their leader. Interests outside school can be as many and as varied: scouting, camping, hobbies, sports, or just socializing. He will be eager to find a part-time job after school. She very well may be the busiest babysitter in the neighborhood, eagerly sought after for her charm and enthusiasm. His or her home might be swarming with friends at all hours of the day and night. In short, the Accomplishing teenager can become so busy in and out of school that some days he may come home exhausted, wanting nothing more than to fall across the bed and go to sleep. Let him. Napping is one very acceptable way for the Accomplishing Personality to wind down.

Throughout childhood and adolescence, the Accomplishing youngster tends to identify rather closely with the same-style parent. He admires that parent's optimistic and robust approach to life and his or her energetic ability to get things done. But here, too, there is a danger. The opposite-style parent may have a very different point of view—for example, a desire for order and regulation, a set time for chores and duties. The Accomplishing parent may wink or smile at the child when the other parent is trying to impose routine, which makes the Accomplishing child a co-conspirator, drawn into a contest between parental styles. This shouldn't be allowed to happen; parental problems ought to be contained between the parents.

Another danger is the Accomplishing parent's tendency to role-define for everyone in the family. He or she may expect too much of the Accomplishing child who already expects so much of himself. Here is how one Accomplishing Personality remembers it: "My mother was a great person. You would have liked her. She laughed a lot, and she could do almost anything. She was exciting to be around, and I always wanted her to be proud of me. But I never seemed to be able to please her. She was never satisfied, and she was always saying to me, 'You should be able to do that,' or, 'You should do better than that,' especially when I brought home my report card."

How unfortunate, really, when all that Accomplishing parent had to do was give a smile of approval or a pat on the back for an honest effort rather than keep raising expectations higher. When the Accomplishing parent can resist communicating such high expectations—role-defining—then he or she can provide the kind of encouraging environment that the Accomplishing child needs to achieve at his own level of competence. Then they would have so much to share, and without inflicting wounds. There is this too: the Accomplishing Personality, child or adult, looks for heroes and heroines. The first and most natural hero for the Accomplishing child is that parent of the same style. How crushing and how sad not to be able to please that hero. And how terribly sad when that unpleasable hero is also the parent.

COLLEGE

Entering college presents problems similar to those experienced on entering junior high and high school. The environment is so much larger, is totally populated with strangers, and offers an enticing variety of opportunities, both scholastic and social. The Accomplishing collegian finds it all exciting, but again he might be tempted to project exaggerated expectations. The ways to glitter and glow are so many, and unless the Accomplishing youth is mature and disciplined and his goals sufficiently clear, he may charge impetuously in all directions, diffusing his purpose, dissipating his energy, sidetracking.

The Accomplishing Personality, however, is somewhat pragmatic, and this may be his saving grace. As he samples the many opportunities college offers, the right social environment and the right academic pursuits may suggest themselves. On the other hand, the major area of concentration may remain a problem for some time. The Accomplishing collegian may mull over the options, try this, change majors, try that. Also, he may be inhibited by parental pressures. He would like to be a doctor, but his parents are urging him to pursue a career in engineering, and he is caught up in his urge to please them. Or maybe he has thoughts of becoming a surgeon, but he has exaggerated images of Christiaan Barnard and Michael DeBakey. The immature Accomplishing aspirant might wilt in contemplating the exalted images of such heroes. He might become so paralyzed that he quits college, or, if parental expectations are so high, he may avoid college altogether. The Accomplishing Personality contemplating college and career benefits greatly from competent counseling to help him measure his potential and his limits, his strong interests and his abilities, so that goals can be fixed and pursued realistically. Once the Accomplishing Personality sets his sights on his primary goals, his energy and his desire to accomplish move him forward productively; but until his goals are clear, he tends to charge off in all directions: and even when his goals are clear, he can easily be sidetracked if he is not healthy. The extremes of this style's tendency to exaggerate expectations are typified by two cousins, both Accomplishing personalities. The one, long the cherished child of his mother's high hopes and exalted expectations, fled in the face of two scholarships; the pressures were too great. The other cousin, shortly before entering college as a freshman, tacked this note on the family bulletin board: *I will have a 4.0 grade average all through college. Signed* . . .

DATING, COURTSHIP, AND MARRIAGE

Early dating can be something of a mixed experience for Accomplishing Personalities. They may have initial fears of not performing well or not pleasing—not dazzling. And if they don't know the other person well, there may be a temptation to prejudge the situation. In any case, the Accomplishing Personality may try hard—too hard— to make a good first impression. But, after the initial date, especially if it goes well, dating is looked upon as another opportunity to make a good showing and to receive approval and affection.

The Accomplishing Personality is so eager to please that he is willing to take his date to better restaurants, expensive shows, the better clubs. He is willing to pay the price as insurance that his date is impressed, that she have a really good time. And all those fine places add a touch of prestige and elegance, qualities that are dear to the Accomplishing Personality—even if he has to subsist the rest of the week on peanut butter sandwiches. The Accomplishing woman who is the recipient of such a lavish evening is capable of entering into the spirit of the moment with a display of dazzling appreciation —if she is healthy; otherwise, she might view it all with alarm: "Good grief . . . Now what do I have to do?" Like a gift or like a compliment, she may read an expensive evening as a heavy demand that she perform—and, of course, she might be right.

Courtship can be a marvelous interval for the Accomplishing Personality, male or female. The newness, the excitement, the approval, all make it a delightful experience. "He was very thoughtful," remembers one Accomplishing Personality, "and *very* attentive. And he liked to do what I wanted to do." And he remembers: "She was really great. She had this tremendous personality, always talking and laughing and just having fun." Here, again, the Accomplishing Personality needs to be aware of his tendency to role-define. What he looks for and seeks may not conform to the reality of the other person. He may exaggerate and amplify the good qualities of the other person while choosing to ignore for the moment the less attractive ones. And the reverse could be true; he might dwell so intently on a person's lesser qualities in his role-defining that he might miss completely her strengths.

The Accomplishing Personality of either sex often seeks a spouse who is physically and socially attractive, someone he can expect to make a good impression, who will give him positive feedback. And he or she might marry for social or financial security, or for prestige. Or he or she might choose a mate who is attracted by his or her sweet and gentle ways, who responds approvingly to what the Accomplishing Personality says or does. But, as time passes, there may be a problem when all that immediate approval wanes or is less frequent and enthusiastic. And there will be times during the marriage when the Accomplishing spouse can be too impetuous in his desire to dazzle: he may want to tell her all about the great day he had at work as she is busy frying chicken; or he may have an urge to pinch or pat as she is loading the dishwasher. Bad timing. And when she pushes his hand away, he interprets her action as disapproval and goes off to the corner bar to soothe his wounds and to seek a more receptive audience.

The Accomplishing spouse rarely has a problem with frigidity or impotency. Quite the opposite, in fact. Sexual interaction is another opportunity to perform well and to elicit approval. Multiple orgasms, male or female, are interpreted as a grand performance. Positive feedback is desired and sometimes sought: "I really don't enjoy sex unless she (he) is satisfied." Sex may be discussed enthusiastically and pleasantly, and since expectations always run high and can go higher, the Accomplishing partner may want to pursue a variety of sexual experiments. Sex may be used by the Accomplishing partner as an outlet for frustrations. Many a bad day at work is soothed in the marital bed, but sometimes it happens that the level of approval and response, the frequency and tone of the sexual act, are not up to expectation. Beware. The Accomplishing spouse may be tempted to stray: a one-night stand during a trip out of town or a clandestine affair loaded with heady romance, strong physical attraction, and a gratifying show of approval. The urge to perform and the desire for affection and approval are always there. The immature or wounded Accomplishing Personality finds it all so hard to resist, and if such an affair caused the marriage to break up, the Accomplishing spouse would view divorce as a dismal failure, an emphatic expression of his having deserved complete disapproval.

Parenthood is most gratifying for the Accomplishing Personality, especially at the birth of a child. He or she is exhilarated, caught up in this moment of awe and wonder, filled with a sense of having shared in the grandest of all performances, the mystery of creation. She will send out sparkling announcements, and you can be sure he will pass out cigars, the best on the market. And, as always, the Accomplishing Personality is proud—proud of this grand accomplishment, proud of the gorgeous, perfectly beautiful child. But, as the child grows, the danger is that parental expectations will grow perhaps a little too large. The first time her daughter puts on leotards, she imagines another Nadia Comaneci. Again, beware; be cautious of projecting expectations for the child, whether at home, in school, on the playing field, or wherever.

As we have noted repeatedly, the Accomplishing Personality is always prone to role-define, but especially in close relationships. He always believes he knows what is best for everyone around him, and he takes for granted that everyone shares the same energy and enthusiasm, the same interests and goals. But defining the way the other person can meet his expectations is especially harmful to the child and damaging to the parent-child relationship. It shows in both large and small things. The Accomplishing father always knows the right way to throw a curve, the only way to build a model airplane, the best way to drive a nail. The Accomplishing mother is the only living expert on hairstyles and hemlines, solving arithmetic problems and dating problems, baking cookies and picking boys' clothing. One Accomplishing father, so eager for his Cub Scout to have the best-looking and speediest car in the Pinewood Derby, took over the design and construction of the little racer, spending hours polishing the nail axles, lacquering the finish, adding lead weights. When the car came in second, the father felt terribly disappointed. His son had little opportunity for any feeling but frustration. It was a poor experience for both—and unnecessary. It would be much better for Accomplishing parents if they could resist role-defining and over-directing that stifle and overwhelm their children.

Earlier we noted that Accomplishing Personalities are rarely competitive. It sometimes happens, however, in a home with several Accomplishing Personalities that the stage becomes cramped with everyone trying to dazzle at once. There can be some jostling and elbowing as one vies with the other for the spotlight, and sometimes an Accomplishing child has to learn how to nudge gently past an Accomplishing parent to have a moment for dazzling. Those who have a hard time doing their number can become frustrated and jealous and sometimes resort to cattiness, snide remarks, and other heavy-handed means of retaliation—all negative forms of dazzling. But when Accomplishing Personalities take turns on stage, they find that the others serve as a very receptive audience—no one appreciates a sparkling performance more than another dazzler.

WORK AND RETIREMENT

The working world is always stage center for the healthy Accomplishing Personality. Here he can be expected to do his best, performing at a high level, producing great quantities of work. The young Accomplishing Personality enters the working world with high hopes and great enthusiasm. If his goals are realistic and focused, he can expect to move ahead with vigor and success, both objectively and subjectively. He doesn't mind starting at the bottom; he is confident enough to believe that he will rise, stage by stage, to the top. He is always the optimist. He expects to make a good showing, to achieve position and prestige, recognition and monetary reward. Others find his enthusiasm contagious and they appreciate his unthreatening way of not stepping on others in his pursuit of accomplishing.

There are, of course, dangers. There is always the temptation to sidetrack; the Accomplishing Personality is very sociable and easily distracted. There is his tendency to role-define and to expect too much of himself and others. He can be paralyzed by too much approval, too high a performance level, or too little recognition. If his efforts are met with criticism or indifference, the Accomplishing Personality is capable of creating his own kind of hell: anguish, depression, overstriving, perhaps an escape into drink or drugs or an affair. He is capable of a sullen rage and can also suffer all sorts of somatic complaints: fatigue, headaches, chronic indigestion, muscle spasms. And, like the Accomplishing schoolchild when he doesn't promote positive approval in the classroom, he may set up a negative situation of crisis and confrontation until he provokes his dismissal, the definitive statement of disapproval.

The Accomplishing woman carries all the same emotional equipment into the marketplace, whether on a full-time or part-time basis. If a working mother, she will feel that she has enough energy and productivity to work without stinting on her responsibilities at home, and she will find work not only fulfilling but a welcome change of pace. As one working mother commented: "I couldn't sit home and just clean house." She might tend to overcompensate for time away from home by spending lavishly on the family; the Accomplishing Personality has no problem spending freely. As the same Accomplishing mother noted: "I can't keep money in my pocket. If I had five dollars in my pocket, I would have to spend it on the kids, my husband, or myself. I'm always broke by payday." She will always be well-dressed and looking good—appearances are important to the Accomplishing Personality—and she will probably be found in a working role that permits her an outlet for her sociable nature. And when the weekend comes, she will want to make the most of it. Citing again our working Accomplishing mother: "We have to do something fantastic—a picnic or a day at the lake, dinner out, a movie, something. I want to have some fun." But come Sunday afternoon, you very well might find her asleep on the couch: "Napping is the greatest thing in the world for me." Despite her full work week, she is able to move through a flurry of housework, with which she expects the children and her husband to help, but she never feels caught up: "I'm brushing my teeth and I notice the bathtub needs washing. I can't wait to finish my teeth to get at the tub. When company is coming, everything has to look good. All my closets are crammed, but what you see looks good." She manages to get most of her housework done when her husband takes the children out for the day. "I can't stand to be alone. I hate it. But when I'm alone, I work really hard." Can she manage the combined roles of careerist, wife, and mother? "I'm the greatest," she grins, and her eyes sparkle— pilot lights ready to ignite another dazzling performance.

Retirement is a vulnerable moment for the Accomplishing Personality. It eliminates prime sources of gratification, measurable accomplishment, and merited approval. The healthy Accomplishing Personality would rather not retire; but, if he must, he will arrange a variety of acceptable substitutes. They will usually involve physical activity and skills—painting, handcrafts, tennis, golf—things that he can touch and feel and display for his own satisfaction and for the approval of others. Pursuing his normal curiosity, he might travel extensively. He would enjoy the opportunity to visit old and cherished friends for one more round of dazzling camaraderie. He would benefit from a part-time job or just babysitting the grandchildren. He needs to do something; he hates to be bored.

ALTERNATIVES AND OPTIONS

The Accomplishing Personality, as we have seen, is normally energetic and hard-working, purposeful and productive. He enjoys the reputation of being a person who gets things done with superior skill, a person who performs brilliantly in so many ways. And he relishes the approval, affection, and applause that his efforts produce. Socially he is charming and gracious, hearty and outgoing; his humor is robust and contagious. When he is his healthy best, he knows his goals, and he moves toward them briskly and purposefully —no detours, no charging off in many directions, no sidetracking or wheel-spinning. Straight ahead. Onward and upward. First things first. He knows his limits and the limits of others, and he accepts them. Do your best, he can say, and then forget the rest.

The less sure or less mature Accomplishing Personality is also capable of great success, but the cost can be terribly high and the efficiency low. He can diffuse his energy in too many directions, and can try too hard. He can be impetuous, sidetracking, role-defining, and something of a gadfly. He can't take criticism or a compliment—either can paralyze him or provoke a chain of non-productive overperformances or withdrawal. He can become a workaholic. His social moments can be Roman-candle performances that sizzle, then fizzle. He often fails to be aware of his own limitations and the limitations of others. He is often frustrated, wound-up, and wounded. His urge to excel can degenerate into easy dazzles and superficial cleverness.

This unsteady, erratic, and unhappy Accomplishing Personality could be much more productive and more relaxed in his approach to life if he would reduce his exaggerated expectations, accept his own limits and the limits of others, keep his eye on his goals, and stop occasionally to pat himself on the back. Here, if you are an Accomplishing Personality, are other alternatives and options:

• First, do you know your goals? Have you shared them with others to test their reasonableness? Are they attainable? Do you know the limitations of your own capabilities and of these goals?

• Slow down. You move too fast.

• Rather than race off in a dozen different directions, organize your routine. Know where you are going and the straightest route there.

• Be realistic in your expectations. You tend to try to do too much in too little time.

• Accept help. Everyone needs help sometimes. You tend to deny this; you read offers of help as statements of your deficiencies. We all have limits. We can all use constructive advice, support, opinions, help.

• Sometimes doing less is doing more. Trying to do too many things often means that nothing is finished—one thing at a time!

• Stop expecting 110 percent of yourself and others. You'll burn out, or burn them out.

• Ever notice that there are certain areas of life that you avoid? You won't test them because you fear your own inadequacy. Try testing them. It may be golf or dancing, or being more of a parent and partner. Try it; you might like it.

• Share the stage with others. It can become awfully hot and lonely under the lights.

• Try listening more. You are sometimes garrulous. You have a tendency to depend too much on your communication skills. And you sometimes build verbal fences around your emotions.

• Don't be so prone to prejudge the outcome of situations at hand. You miss a lot by prejudging the effort that hasn't been made.

• Give up role-defining. Really, it is beyond your competence to suppose that you know what others should or could be doing. Not everyone is as interested in accomplishing as much so much of the time as you are.

• Watch that wheel-spinning. You can burn out your motor and still accomplish nothing. Turn the key off for a moment. Cool down.

• Beware of short cuts and flashy performances. Sometimes they are more work than disciplined procedures—and less productive.

• Quit starting a home project that creates tension in the family when you are in over your head. Hire a plumber or a painter or a carpenter.

• Be a team player. Give a little, take a little. You love people, and they love you, but your urge to sweep up a task as a solitary performance is alienating.

• When you discover you have overcommitted your time, energy, and resources, back off. Reassess your expectations. Redefine the commitment. Be flexible.

• You are not responsible for all the failures and frailties of others, so stop picking up after the children, the office boy, the janitor.

• A good performance does not have to be super-dazzling to be creditable and to draw approval. Learn the difference between the sizzle and the steak.

• Sidetracking is the greatest distance between two points; it is the longest route to the garbage can, the next promotion, the love of your spouse, the achievements you so dearly desire. Learn to move straight ahead.

• There is a time to say nothing, a time to do nothing.

• Beware of your tendency to exaggerate, especially in terms of your expectations of your spouse, your children, your co-workers, your friends.

• Be realistic in assessing your own function, whether on the job or at home, whether working or playing. You tend to direct traffic. This too is role-defining.

• Invite critical appraisal occasionally rather than arranging always for others to give you approval. Critical insight may lend more to your productivity than the usual approval. But beware of projecting so much energy and enthusiasm that the critical appraisal is like your own expectations: exaggerated.

• Don't put off till tomorrow what you should do today. Don't do today what you should put off till tomorrow.

• Don't let your wounds fester. Be a quick healer. Don't hold the grudge or plot silent revenge.

• Learn that accepting limits realistically defines opportunity.

96

Limits help solve problems; they define freedom.

• You don't have to play God. No one but you expects you to have all the answers, to say all the right things, to know all the right moves.

• Permit yourself the opportunity to make an honest mistake. Then learn from it. Seek help if you need it—but don't back away and not try.

• Please: learn to accept compliments graciously. A compliment is not intended as a stimulus to still greater accomplishments and more dazzling performances. A compliment is only a compliment. Enjoy it. Say, "Thank you." But say nothing else. Just take a bow.

• Consider this: you are so much more than what you do. You are a person, a good, charming, and productive person. You are not a machine. What people love about you, what they so gladly approve of, is simply you, not your wit, or wisdom, or accomplishments—just sweet, lovable you.

• You don't have to please everyone. Accept your own evaluation of your performances.

• You can't buy approval. Give gifts, but don't use them to curry approval.

• Do your best, then forget the rest.

• Learn to relax. Take a nap—you deserve it!

V

It is not rebellion itself which is noble but the demand it makes upon us.
ALBERT CAMUS

The Idealistic Personality

THE IDEALISTIC PERSONALITY looks on life in two ways: the way it really is and the way he believes it ought to be. He compares the real to his ideal, and spends his lifetime trying to make the one match the goodness of the other. As much as he can, he tries to right wrongs, to champion social justice, to promote human rights and human dignity, and to leave this world a bit better than when he came into it. And in his effort to make this a better world, he conducts himself according to his own high standards that never give way to mediocrity or expediencies. Others may shrug and say, "But everybody's doing it." Everyone may, perhaps. But not the Idealistic Personality.

The Idealistic Personality looks on himself as he looks on life. There is his flesh-and-blood self complete with a full array of fears, flaws, and feelings—and there is his image, the self he would like to be to match his ideals. So whatever he is and whatever he does, he is attempting to elevate blood and bones up to the lofty level of his demanding image. Image and ideals impose a set of standards and a code of conduct that the Idealistic Personality resolutely adheres to. He pursues life and his goals with an exacting sense of what is good and true and proper in the life he leads, whether he is a police officer or a politician, a florist or a fashion designer, an undertaker or a used car salesman. Thus there is a proper way to make an arrest or to design a dress or to arrange a floral display—his way. No ifs, buts, or shortcuts. So if you happen to be shopping for a used car from an Idealistic dealer, don't be afraid to accept his word on the vehicle's condition—don't even bother to kick the tires. Honesty and integrity mean more to him than profit. His standards are high, and his word is his honor. More often than not when dealing with any Idealistic Personality, these traits are guarantee enough. "You can depend on me," he will tell you. And you can.

What all Idealistic Personalities share in common is the same desire to be individuals, to hold fast to cherished ideals, to adhere to high and sometimes fixed standards that each has set for himself and the world around him. The Idealistic Personality pursues these standards with a sense of purpose that is rarely compromised. His thoughts on any topic or activity are filled with definite standards and regulations: dos and don'ts, shoulds and shouldn'ts, prescriptions and prohibitions. The Idealistic Personality lives in a world of codes and convictions chiseled in stone. He embraces them tenaciously, and he expects others to abide by them, or at least to abide by standards of equal integrity. His is a rather exacting world of right and wrong, light and darkness. There is little middle ground, few areas of gray, and little that is relative. When his standards and ideals are challenged, he would rather fight than switch, at least on first impulse. If healthy, he would have second thoughts; he would listen to the other person's point of view, but, in a stressful moment, even the healthiest Idealistic Personality feels his backbone stiffen. His ideals and standards are so dear to him, so deeply felt, that he bristles when they are challenged. The more mature he is, the greater his openness to other standards. The less mature he is, the greater his rigidity and bullheadedness.

Every Idealistic Personality takes himself and his convictions seriously—that is part of his makeup. Yet a certain style and grace, wit and charm, soften the flinty edge of his standards. His courtesy, confidence, and commitment impress others. His spirit of high purpose is often contagious, and his dedication and dignity attract oth-

99

ers to his ideals. He is a persuasive spokesman for his beliefs, articulate and forceful in communicating his ideals. His vision, integrity, and courage of conviction often prompt others of like ideas to rally to him as a leader.

Still, there are times when the Idealistic Personality finds himself standing alone. Given his dedication, his adherence to ideals and standards, his tenacity, and his individuality, it is not surprising that the Idealistic Personality finds himself cutting against the grain of conventional wisdom and the status quo. He is a deeply moral person with a strong sense of duty. He hears his own drummer, and is ever faithful to the beat. He is often a rebel with a cause, and there are always ample causes for the Idealistic Personality's choosing. One may advocate food for the world's hungry masses while another may campaign for the legalization of marijuana. One may advocate abortion while another opposes it. Whatever his ideal—profit-sharing or profit-taking, open marriage or the closed shop, communism or the corporation—the Idealistic Personality believes his ideal is right and that everyone really *ought* to see it as clearly and correctly as he does. They *ought* to be as dedicated and committed. They *should* be willing to embrace standards, no matter how demanding. They *should* . . . They *ought* . . . The imperatives never end. There is always another standard to be pronounced because there is always another situation ahead that demands one.

THE IMAGE URGE

"When I was a child," one Idealistic Personality remembers, "I was taught certain standards: 'Always be a gentleman. Always open the door for a lady.' I feel bad when I'm not allowed to act that way. I really enjoy being the gentleman, lighting her cigarette, opening the door—I even enjoy putting on a tuxedo for a formal event."

Pretense? Male chauvinism? Never. Another Idealistic Personality might be the liberated woman who wants to light her own cigarette and open her own doors—or the man who finds blue jeans and bare feet a more suitable image. The very essence of the Idealistic Personality is the individual's complete identification with his standards. His ideals, his thoughts, and his actions merge into an integrated image of himself as an individual. And this we call the *image urge*—his paramount urge to faithfully communicate this image of himself, no matter where he is and what he does. His is not the sometimes superficial and illusory imagery fabricated by the advertising and media world. He has no use for mere appearance and for false façades. His image reflects the kind of person he believes he should be and tries to be. He wants to conform to the image of the ideal spouse, the ideal parent, the ideal neighbor, the ideal worker, and so on. "A good butcher ought to sell only quality meats, keep a clean shop, and tend to customers promptly." "A good father ought to supervise his children's homework, regulate their use of the television, and discipline them when they misbehave." "A dancer should eat properly, get plenty of sleep, exercise two hours daily, and practice four." Whatever he is doing, the Idealistic Personality goes by the book. And well he should; he wrote it.

The Idealistic Personality is born with his disposition toward image, ideals, and standards, but the shape of his image and ideals, and the content of his principles and standards, are acquired all through life. They are absorbed from parents, relatives, neighbors, teachers, pastors, coaches, and other influencing sources. Or they are formed in opposition to the images, ideals, and standards of the same array of authority figures. Some are acquired from reading history books and biographies, others from the sports pages and the society pages. But whatever their source, the images and ideals are refined and modified, altered and adjusted until they become fully the measure of the individual. That is why the Idealistic Personality finds it so difficult to bend or compromise. That would mean being untrue to himself; so, if he must, he will stand alone against the crowd. Even so, he doesn't flinch. The ideal is his real. His worst fear is that he might not be true to the image he has of himself.

Adhering to such high standards sometimes comes at a high price, not just for the Idealistic Personality, but for those close to him. The problem with such demanding standards is that others are expected to meet them too. Joe, a much admired and respected high school coach, laments his inability to relax his standards at home. As a result, his marriage broke up. His wife tried and tried to live up to all the standards set by Joe, but there were simply too many of them—and Joe admits it: "I tried to force so many of my ideas on my ex-wife. I should have been more considerate, I should have let her be an individual. Instead I tried to change her to the image that

I wanted her to be, which caused problems." Even now, Joe is struggling. The present problem is with his son—"He acts one way, and I want him to act another way. We have little conflicts"—but their relationship is improving. Joe is listening more to what his son has to say, paying more attention to the boy's wishes and desires. "I've become more aware of his feelings," he says. Joe has learned to be more open, to be more aware of what others project as their own standards—at least enough to admit the possibility that there *are* other acceptable standards. It isn't always easy, but it makes life a little more comfortable, not only for Joe, but for others around him who like him and enjoy him when they are permitted a glimpse of him without the armor of his ideals.

An Idealistic wife and mother notes similarly: "When the kids were small, I expected Jim to behave a certain way as a father, and when he didn't I would get annoyed. When the kids were older, I expected him to behave a little differently. I kept up an interest in whatever they were doing, and I thought he should be equally interested. It took me a long time to realize how difficult I was, always expecting Jim and everyone else to do things the way I thought they should be done. I thought everyone was that way. Now I try not to impose my standards. Sometimes I'm successful, sometimes not."

The temptation to impose standards goes well beyond the home. Wherever the Idealistic Personality goes, the standards go along with him. An Idealistic businesswoman tells of her irritation over telephone procedures in her office: "I'm very punctual about returning phone calls, but other people in the office aren't quite so prompt. I don't like it, but I try to say as little as possible about it, and that's difficult. It reflects on my business." The worst abuser? Her partner, who is also her brother. "Sometimes I can't help it," she admits. "I'll pick up the phone and hand it to him with a stack of phone messages and say, 'Here, get busy.'"

IMAGES BY THE DOZEN

The Idealistic Personality doesn't always have a single image of himself. Each stage in life may demand a separate set of standards that reflect the circumstance: there is an image of the ideal single person, the ideal spouse; the ideal worker, the ideal player; the ideal teacher, the ideal student; the ideal conservative, the ideal liberal. Every role has its own rules and rubrics; the burden is never light. Here again, Joe offers an appropriate comment: "I find myself trying so hard to fulfill the image. I put a lot of pressure on myself, and I sometimes get overbearing to the point of giving other people a bad time. I find more and more that it's important not to force this image or to let it be the only factor in my life. Now I can turn it off more than before."

The need to mix and match several layers of situations and standards can create its own problems. Jeff is a young motorcycle mechanic, husband, and father, and for each situation in life, he has an image. He demands of himself a very high standard as a competent mechanic, and he knows he is that. But there is also a way that a mechanic working with the motorcycle crowd ought to dress and behave, so Jeff wears the regulation jeans, heavy boots, beard, and bandanna tied around his head—and he is rugged enough and unflinching enough to conform to the code of his motorcycle friends and customers. He has experimented with drugs, but he gave that up when he became a father. A good parent, he felt, shouldn't mess with junk, so he limits himself to a beer or two when he is with his friends.

Jeff is a much gentler person at home. He is affectionate with his child, and he enjoys babysitting her while his wife works evenings. He doesn't mind helping out by doing the dishes; he believes that a good husband should help in the house. But one evening, two of his motorcycle buddies walked in while he was finishing up the kitchen, and Jeff was terribly embarrassed. He felt that his masculine image, so dear to him, was damaged. He was glad, though, that the baby didn't wake up crying; to have had to put on a bottle and feed his daughter would have irreparably shattered his image.

Until Jeff began to learn to be more flexible with his exacting standards, he had other problems. He was always at odds with his employer. Jeff didn't feel that the owner ran the shop as it ought to have been run. His standards of service were indifferent, the shop was messy, parts were never maintained at a working inventory level, and the bookkeeping was wretched. More, the owner was away from the shop more often than Jeff thought he should be. "When a man owns a business, he ought to be around to supervise," he said. Jeff was often chilly with the owner and sometimes downright hostile, but his employer tolerated the chill and the chiding from his hired mechanic simply because Jeff was so good at doing all the things he didn't care to do. And Jeff kept the repair work flowing. In time, Jeff was able to ease up on his rigid standards without losing his efficiency or quality. Even the customers noticed the difference. Jeff is now part owner of the shop and doing quite well.

VULNERABILITIES AND CRISES

The rest of us find so many fine qualities to admire about the Idealistic Personality: an engaging self-confidence, integrity, an insistence on living out his ideals and standards, perseverance, purposeful pursuit of goals, a quiet dignity. And for all these qualities we respect him—from a distance. There is a defined distance that the Idealistic Personality himself sets and regulates. Everyone notices the interval, even the Idealistic Personality—and that, for the most part, is just fine with him. He will tell you that he prizes his independence and freedom. He will tell you too that he likes to stand back a bit to observe and evaluate what is going on. This, he contends, is his objective approach to events and to people. True enough, but what the Idealistic Personality is not telling is that he wishes to maintain a subjective, emotional distance. He is stating, in effect: "Don't come too close." Although it is rarely expressed verbally, people usually get the message. Some say that the Idealistic Personality is hard to know. Others say that he is remote, reserved, guarded, aloof, chilly, or even cold and snobbish. Depending on the situation and the individual Idealistic Personality and his maturity, any one of these descriptions might fit.

Why this distancing? We mentioned the Idealistic Personality's need to stand back to appraise his environment objectively, his concern for maintaining his image and standards, and his cherished independence; but beneath them all is a fear of closeness. If an Idealistic Personality was not the first to formulate the axiom, "Familiarity breeds contempt," he certainly fears its truth. He fears that, stripped of the protective armor of his ideals, he might be weak and helpless, he might need others. What he really fears is the possibility that up close others might see how poorly he conforms to his image. This possibility is enough to send the Idealistic Personality hurrying back into the armor of his ideals, and to measure the distance between himself and others. The message is plain: Stay back.

The distancing techniques vary, and they are concealed in any number of intellectualized disguises. One Idealistic salesman recently told me: "I can't understand why I'm having so much trouble accepting the idea of success. I'm the top salesman with our company. If the sales manager needs one more sale this month, he comes to me. That's a lot of pressure. I feel that I should get a bonus along with the pressure." This salesman's problem is not with success or money. His problem is not being able to relax his image. He builds up the pressure by fearing that he might not live up to his number-one image, and he pushes back the sales manager by talking about bonuses.

A young Idealistic woman was asked by her sorority sisters to be their candidate for homecoming queen. She refused, disappointing her friends, who thought she had a very good chance. The reason she gave was that she didn't want to be thought of as "another pretty face," but her *real* reason for pushing them away was that she feared in the selection process she might not live up to the image of her sorority's candidate for the college's queen.

A young executive's Idealistic wife was invited by his new employer to visit the company and the community in which it was located. The wife refused to join her husband on the trip, even though her absence dampened the success of the visit. Her explanation: "I'm not part of the package, and I'll be damned if I'll be paraded before the corporate brass." What she really feared was that she might not conform to the exaggerated image that she held of a promising young executive's wife. After they moved, she avoided company social events for almost a year, but once she was able to appreciate that her image was grossly exaggerated, she was able to share in company social gatherings and in her husband's deserved success.

Each Idealistic Personality has his own way of stating the distancing problem. Says one: "I've never met a stranger, but I have no close friends." Another: "I love getting close to people—up to a certain point. When they get too close, I feel engulfed. I want room to maneuver." A very attractive Idealistic woman says: "I don't make friends easily. I have one or two close friends, but I don't feel I need anyone else." To this she adds another revealing statement: "If others try to impose their standards, I pull away." In other words, part of the fear of closeness is that the Idealistic Personality's own standards might be threatened or overwhelmed by the strong standards held by others. And this too may have something to do with the Idealistic Personality's fear of being helpless in a close relationship. Here is a brief sketch of a dream I often hear from Idealistic patients:

"I'm lying on my back in a busy intersection, and I'm frightened. Cars are moving all around me. I can't seem to get up. If I try to turn over, I'm afraid that I'll get hit. The intersection is near my doctor's office."

Only in his dreams is the Idealistic Personality able to allow himself the luxury of being helpless.

Every winter around the holidays, when the slopes are white and powdery, we see a few "ski-trip casualties," victims of the distancing phenomenon. What happens is this: two young people fly off to Vermont or Colorado. For several days they experience a wonderful closeness. Then, on the flight back home or soon after arriving home, they have this terrible fight. After they break up, the one who is the Idealistic Personality comes into my office to complain of his terrible loneliness. Again and again, winter after winter, I hear the same story. I always explain that what he was actually fighting was the feeling of closeness. Next year, perhaps, he can be more aware of his own dynamics. Perhaps he will be able to lessen the image. Perhaps by then he won't feel the need to fight off the warm emotions he experiences. Perhaps he will realize that tender feelings are a source of strength, not weakness. Perhaps.

How far will a troubled Idealistic Personality go in his flight from feelings? I recently saw an Idealistic patient who had returned a month earlier from Alaska. He stated that his reason for going there for a year was the high salary paid by the construction company that hired him. But was it a coincidence that just a month before he signed up for the job he had become engaged? And was it coincidence that shortly before his return the engagement broke up? He might have spared himself a cold and lonely year in a construction camp half a world away from home had he realized how frightened he felt whenever he became emotionally close.

There are ways of maintaining distance without having to stray so far from home. An Idealistic Personality may date someone much younger or much older to avoid the sort of relationship that might grow and become close. Or he might date a person he feels certain he would not marry for religious reasons. He might chance a casual affair that wouldn't involve him emotionally, but if the other person showed signs of wanting a closer relationship, he would break it off or manage to provoke rejection. The immature Idealistic Personality will continue this distancing pattern until he begins to appreciate that tender feelings are not a weakness but a strength, that closeness does not require compromise or lowering of standards, that inter-dependence can be an exciting adventure in mutuality and shared happiness. He might come to appreciate that while the view from Mount Olympus is grand and godlike, it can be terribly lonely.

The less sure Idealistic Personality is highly critical of others whose standards he deems less than his own or too lightly practiced. Yet he is oversensitive when criticized, and sometimes displays a harsh streak, nursing old injuries and settling personal scores. When challenged in his exacting standards, he battles mightily, especially when he is feeling vulnerable. When that happens, he digs in for the siege, never giving ground. He insists, he defies, he demands, he scorns. He voices lofty judgments, scolds, chides. And if himself defied, pushed, or scorned—or if others move in too close—his anger blows like an Arctic wind, bitter and biting. His sarcasm cuts. But whenever he is angry, beneath the chill there is likely to be a warm layer of feelings he is fighting to stifle. It is always easier to show the anger than the true feelings; thus the warmer the feelings, the greater the fear, the colder the anger. Friends, family, and colleagues—and the Idealistic Personality himself—might find it useful to remember that he is so much more of a person than this angry surface that he presents. Don't be overwhelmed by his cold blasts of anger—or his surges of independence, or the force of his ideas. Encourage him to permit the rest of him—his suppressed feelings and emotions, his tenderness and gentleness—to surface through the storm. In time, he may become aware that his feeling for others, his warmth and tenderness, are his greatest strengths.

GROWING UP IDEALISTIC

The Idealistic child is usually described as pleasant and cheerful; although he is not overaffectionate, he has a tendency to cling. But what may be the most typical characteristic of the Idealistic child is the intensity with which he goes about everything. Even when he is sick, he seems to get awfully sick. When he has a cold, for example, it seems to be worse and to last longer than with the other children in the family. This reaction to any illness continues into adulthood when, as we will discuss, sickness becomes a personal challenge.

Hints of the Idealistic Personality's desire for independence and his standard-setting show up early. He may learn to talk and read at a comparatively young age, but school itself can be difficult. Although one Idealistic child may adjust quite well to school, another may struggle with his teacher, even in the early grades, when he finds that his own developing standards and ideas clash with those of the teacher. He has his own emerging image of himself and how he ought to relate within the learning process. He may protest, "I want to be myself because I can't be somebody else." Or he may voice somatic complaints: "It hurts my head," or, "I have a stomach ache." These complaints surface when the child doesn't want to do what the teacher tells him to do. Very early we may be experiencing the Idealistic Personality's rebellious streak when he constantly says, "It's too hard." What he means is that it is too difficult to deal with the situation other than in terms of his image.

The same rebellious streak may show at home. A child may hold his stomach while he complains to his mother, "You made me get a knot here, and I have to get it out by myself." In this situation, the Idealistic child is trying to set standards for the parent. The response of the parent—or of the teacher during a similar confrontation in the classroom—is very important to the Idealistic child's healthy development, especially when the adult with whom he is interacting is himself an Idealistic Personality. The adult's temptation is to impose his own standards on the child without considering the child's standards. An impasse develops. A more productive approach would be to introduce to the child the idea that his standards and image of himself are quite acceptable while encouraging him to accept the idea that other people have their own standards and images that are also acceptable. Suggest that perhaps the problem—the knot in his stomach—can be worked out together. A six-year-old can understand an interpretation of the impasse in a statement like this: "You hide your hurt feelings under the chair, then you bring out angry feelings to cover them up." The real danger is to permit the impasse to continue. Parents and teachers might consider the possibility of transferring the child to another class or another school rather than permit the struggle to continue.

Not all or even most Idealistic children rebel against the standards of parents and teachers. To the contrary. Many Idealistic youngsters thrive on the standards and ideals offered by admired adults. Idealistic parents sometimes send their children to private schools for the emphasis given to discipline, and many Idealistic children respond well, accepting discipline as their own standard. But should a child attending a private school, especially military school, rebel, a quick transfer is the recommended response—and everyone ought to look on the problem and the solution as a no-fault situation.

The Idealistic child may have an image of the good student as one who makes good grades, or he may have a parent whose standards include good grades. If the good-grade standard is comfortable and reasonable, the Idealistic student will work hard academically. Otherwise, he can be expected to pursue interests that reflect *his* standards and image—which may not include grades.

Because of its high ideals and standards, scouting often interests the Idealistic young person. One Idealistic adult remembers his scoutmaster with much affection and gratitude: "Here was a genuine leader, a real friend. When he gave me a goal he didn't stand over me to tell me how it ought to be done. All he said was, 'There it is. Do it.' Then he walked away. That was my first real exercise in freedom." This is a fine example of an adult recognizing and reinforcing the strength of a personality style—in this case the Idealistic Personality's self-confidence and love for personal freedom. This example also illustrates the fact that in childhood the Idealistic Personality gets along best with those adults who allow him a reasonable amount of freedom.

The relationship between the Idealistic parent and Idealistic child at times can be difficult. Each has his own standards and image. When they run on parallel tracks, the relationship is pleasant and mutually supportive, and the child benefits greatly; but when their standards differ, the relationship can be strained and difficult, and a terrible clash always threatens. In this sort of relationship, the Idealistic child often seeks out the other style parent to talk things over and to get help with decisions. The Idealistic parent is then viewed as distant and uninvolved: "You never knew what he was thinking because he kept so much within himself." The Idealistic child may fear that this parent might turn away from him, and in some instances it happens. Often this parent tends to be a harsh disciplinarian. When the Idealistic parent is absent physically or emotionally, the young person often chooses an older person to fill the vacant role—a relative, a neighbor, or perhaps his minister, rabbi, or priest. Or it might be that understanding scoutmaster. Quite possibly it will be a grandparent who is idolized: "She took me to a lot of places, and she always praised me and bragged about me. She was the one person in my life whom I could go to and say whatever I had on my mind."

The young Idealistic Personality can be terribly disappointed in a flawed parent—the parent who can't hold a job, or the parent who has a drinking problem. Even later in life he may find it painful to remember the shame and embarrassment that parent caused the family. He may also view the parental flaw as a potential flaw in himself.

THE TEENAGE REBEL

The same trend that occurs in the development of the Idealistic Personality prior to adolescence generally continues into teenage. If the person has experienced permission to conform to his own image, if he has been supported and encouraged in his quest for ideals and standards and personal freedom, the self-assurance and confidence that are so admired in the Idealistic Personality begin to blossom. But counterpressures and conflicting standards imposed by adult authorities can produce a rebel. One Idealistic teenager, for example, came home from school to find his mother standing in the doorway with a heavy scowl on her face. She told him that she had opened a letter addressed to him, written by a girlfriend who had recently moved to another town. The mother delivered a ten-minute tirade on the "vulgar" content of the letter. She had felt compelled to tear it up. Her son was furious: "I felt I was being stomped," he said. So he ran away from home.

A mother told me of an eighth-grade rebellion that took place several years ago in a parochial school where Friday afternoon confession was still a tradition. She related how this one Friday afternoon when the teacher ordered her students to assemble in the church, they refused to leave their desks. A student acting as spokesman told her that the class had decided to stage a sit-in rather than be forced to go to confession. He explained to the teacher that confession was a matter of the individual's conscience; it couldn't be forced. The teacher realized that what the students were saying was exactly what she had taught them—in theory. The practice of a set time for confessions was discontinued, but what surprised the mother, in hearing the story from the teacher, was to learn that the student leader of the sit-in was her Idealistic son.

An Idealistic father kept up a running tirade against his son's long hair flowing down over his shoulders. "A disgrace," declared the father. His image of masculinity was a Marine-like appearance of clean-shaven, close-cropped neatness; he associated long hair with hippies and drugs. So one Saturday he ordered the boy to get his hair cut "like a man." The boy refused. His father responded with silent fury, and Idealistic father and son didn't speak for months. Neither would budge from his standards. The first sign of a thaw came when the wife was able to persuade the father that their son's love was more important than his image of his own masculinity. More, she helped him realize how much he shied from showing any outward affection toward their son. The father didn't respond immediately—the Idealistic Personality insists on making his own decisions. When he did speak to his son, the two awkwardly compared notes on their standards and images. Both were able to admit to their love and affection for each other, and both realized that their feelings for each other, so well-concealed, were more important than their standards on hair length. Father and son hugged each other for the first time since the son was six, and the cold war ended.

Self-imposed standards increase during adolescence. Joe, our coaching friend, was a star athlete in high school while maintaining a straight-A average. He was very much a leader among his fellow students: "The other guys had this image of me. You know, they had me on a pedestal. I felt that I had to live up to that image." But at the same time, Joe expected his fellow athletes to live up to his standards. He trained hard, very hard, and he thought that everyone else should: "When someone goofed off, it would really get to me. I had plenty of conflicts, even with the coach. He had his ideas, I had my ideas." Joe notes that he learned to relax his standards for others only after he gained confidence in his own abilities. He learned to appreciate that most of his fellow athletes—and the coach—were as dedicated and hard-working, but each according to his own standards.

ADULTHOOD

The time of some concern in the life of the Idealistic Personality comes with graduation from high school. He is caught up in a flurry of activities and involvements still linked to high school, but at the same time he faces a new series of options and decisions about the future. He is re-evaluating old standards and an adolescent image while contemplating new standards and the forthcoming image of adulthood. He dearly desires sufficient freedom to make his own choices, but often, just as he is so busy with past, present, and future, concerned parents and teachers apply pressures on him to consider some of their recommended standards and options. It can be dangerous. The young Idealistic Personality may feel that his freedom of choice is being stifled. So parental and other outside pressures need to be applied lightly or, better, applied before the young person has developed solid interests. Otherwise rebellion is very possible—if not now, then later.

The campus rebellions we witnessed in the turbulent 1960s may have been provoked in part by the enormous pressures exerted by our society, and especially parents, on young people to pursue higher education at every level. Society said, in effect, "If you want to get ahead in our society, you must have a college degree." Then too there was the rather bizarre choice posed by the Vietnam War: be drafted, and become involved in an unpopular and very dangerous war, or go to college. And there were the glaring discrepancies between what society and its major institutions preached and what they promoted in practice. Idealistic youth, perhaps more than other personality styles, was keenly sensitive to this warping and manipulation of ideals and standards—remember, the Idealistic Personality insists on the integrity of principle and practice. So the sixties very well may have been the decade of the Idealistic rebels, polarized by the imposition of standards not their own and confronted with mutilated standards, while they tried, sometimes desperately, to establish and express their own standards and ideals. These Idealistic rebels were not the nihilists who wanted only to tear down the institutions. Rather, their desire was to build new institutions based on their own standards because they believed that traditional values had failed them and their world.

Idealistic youth's rebellion against outside pressures and imposed standards didn't start or end with the 1960s. And it is not likely to end until pressures to conform end. The current style of rebellion is less radical, less militant, less strident. It is expressed more on a personal or small-group basis with less attention given to the media and by the media. The way to avoid a rebellious reaction among Idealistic youth is to avoid the cause: too many standards and too much pressure applied from without. While the Idealistic young person very much needs and benefits from concern, support, and presentation of available options, he also needs freedom from pressures to make his own choices.

Leaving home is the first of three major life-changing events that confront the Idealistic Personality. Leaving home, whether to enter the job market or to attend college, can be an exciting and challenging moment; it represents the opportunity to be independent and to make one's own decisions. The second major life-changing event comes when the Idealistic Personality forms a significant relationship requiring that he give up some of his independence. The third comes when he re-establishes his independence, either by going into business for himself or by changing careers through special training.

Since he cherishes his independence—and since he finds close relationships difficult—the Idealistic Personality can remain single noticeably longer than other personality styles. As the Idealistic Personality passes from adolescence into young adulthood he is often avoiding attachments, drifting through a period of searching about for values and convictions, testing his independence, and seeking after adult models who can fire his imagination and kindle ideals. This drifting is a time for image-building great and small. An Idealistic youth may justify his drifting by declaring as his standard: "It's okay to have fun until you're twenty-five; but after that it should be all business." His may be the swinging single's image. Yet another Idealistic youth may find this a time to work as a volunteer campaign worker for a politician whose views he admires. Still another may ponder a military career, while another considers a training program to work with handicapped children. Whatever, the Idealistic young person very much wants it to be a matter of his own choosing. Still, he is very busy living up to his image and standards of the single life. He can get caught up in political programs and human-rights campaigns, social organizations and charitable agencies, church groups or ski clubs, dating around or visiting the singles bars. Whatever he is doing, the Idealistic Personality does it according to his own standards and with great intensity.

Take Sarah as an example. Sarah is twenty-seven, single, but living with a young man she has known for four years. She attended three different universities but was never graduated. She is actively involved in interests ranging from scuba diving to macramé, from water-skiing to gourmet cooking. Sarah isn't a competitive person; in fact, she leans the other way: "I want to be different. I don't feel I can compete with the frilly-frilly types with all that mascara and eyeshadow and long hair. I guess I don't want what everybody else wants." Sarah would rather pack up her water skis and head for the dock with her boyfriend MacArthur—she always calls him by his family name; she considers his given name too common; MacArthur suggests more stature and dignity. But really, it is a sign of Sarah's feelings for him.

Sarah and MacArthur had what she called a beautiful relationship for over two years. They had interests they shared and interests that each pursued independently. She might have lunch with male friends, and he might lunch with other girls he knew and worked with. Fine. Life was interesting and very good for both Sarah and MacArthur—until recently when they purchased a house. Suddenly, Sarah began to take another look at the girls MacArthur was taking to lunch. She also began to feel a little less sure of herself.

Suddenly . . . What happened to Sarah is what so often happens to Idealistic Personalities. Her relationship with MacArthur involved a good deal of outward affection, but Sarah maintained a certain inward detachment—a safe emotional distance. However, when she and MacArthur bought the house together, she suddenly felt the emotional distance shrinking, and she wanted to push away. She began to fear that she might not be the strong, clever girl she saw herself as; her weaknesses might show, especially in comparison with those girls with whom MacArthur lunched.

This sudden awareness of getting close can surface at seemingly strange times. An Idealistic husband is married five years and the marriage is going along smoothly, sort of a peaceful co-existence. Then one Christmas he gives his wife a very expensive and thoughtful gift. Suddenly he has to take a business trip for a week. What happened was this: that special gift after five years of marriage signified that the Idealistic husband had really begun to feel close to his wife for the first time; so he had to back off. The same thing can happen when any relationship suddenly begins to grow closer. Can he live up to his exalted image of what the relationship requires? It can happen in an engagement, a friendship, a working relationship. Then *suddenly* . . .

COURTSHIP, MARRIAGE, AND FAMILY LIFE

We noted earlier that the Idealistic Personality often seems to marry later in life than other personality styles. He seems to have some conflict making a final decision, not only on marriage but on any relationship that supposes deep commitment. This crisis of commitment is again caused by a keen awareness of the high standards involved and the demand to conform to those standards rigorously. For the Idealistic Personality, the commitment has to be total, so the temptation always, when faced with all those grand ideals and lofty standards, is to back away. When the ideals are love and marriage, what could be more grand and lofty? Hear what one Idealistic wife has to say about love: " 'Love' is a word that we throw around carelessly. I think it should have more substance than we give to it. I look on love as something that grows; it means giving all of me." Adds another Idealistic Personality: "We fall hard when we fall."

The kind of a person that attracts the Idealistic Personality seems to vary a bit according to the sexual stereotypes of our society. Idealistic women report interest in men who are "quiet, stable, the right age, the right background, the right financial bracket." "He was quiet, nice, pleasant, and always the gentleman. He seemed like an old friend rather than a sexual being." "He presented a nice appearance, he was good-looking, and he was always the gentleman." The Idealistic male reports being impressed by the "friendly look on her face. She talked easily to me, and it was very easy for me to talk to her." "I liked her grace. She was a very likable person." "She was quiet and warm. She seemed so secure and honest." "She was bubbly, concerned, and she showed a real desire to do things for me."

Courtship can have its ups and downs. The Idealistic Personality feels an emotional attraction and then backs away. When the emotional feelings rise up again, he pushes away again. But each time the distance grows less, and the pushing becomes more a token than a shove. Still, he can be abrupt, seemingly insensitive at times to the other person's feelings. It takes patience to deal with the Idealistic Personality in love. He projects his own image strongly, and he declares his standards demandingly; as he grows closer and closer, especially in an engagement, the hemming and hawing increase. The excuses for delaying setting a date multiply: debts need to be paid, it's the wrong season, Aunt Emma can't come East till August, and so on and so on.

The post-marriage Idealistic mate can be something of a shock. Here was this funloving, very hip, good-times bachelor. Now he insists on church every Sunday, quiet evenings at home, trips to the library. What happened? Remember, the Idealistic Personality has a different set of standards and a definite image for every stage of life. A bachelor behaves according to one set of standards, a husband and a family man behaves according to another set of standards. It's that simple—or that complex.

Life around the Idealistic home is sometimes described as "almost obsessive" when it comes to doing chores. The Idealistic husband tells of spending much time reading through handyman books. If a lock on the door won't work, he lives with that lock until he has its every mechanism down pat. He can become so engrossed in fixing the toilet or mending the mower that he may wonder if all the time spent was worth it. And when he is bogged down halfway through a repair, he finds it hard to ask for help and usually doesn't. Once again, he has his standard: "I feel a man should know these things." The possibly worse situation would be if his son walked up, stood watching, then asked: "How does a faucet work, Dad?" If he couldn't tell him, his image as the family handyman would crumble. Male or female, the Idealistic Personality at home would sometimes shun those chores that he feels he can't do well or might have to ask for assistance in doing.

The Idealistic woman who has had a career and then marries might find the change of roles difficult. The image and the standards change: the woman who successfully ran her own business might find running her kitchen wearisome. And she has her sparkling new image about the proper relationship with her husband. If he indulges in a playful pat on the posterior on coming home, she might state her preference for a proper kiss. Male or female, the Idealistic partner sets standards for the other partner and for the children: "Little boys never cry." "Little girls should always sit with their legs crossed." "Parents should love their children but should never display affection in front of the children." If religion is valued, church attendance might be mandatory. If literature is valued, you can expect television viewing to be restricted in the evenings while everyone reads books. If music is prized, then a piano or organ might grace the living room, and Bach might reverberate through every room in the house. Whatever the standards and values, they will be lived out in the home life of the Idealistic Personality.

The Idealistic parent might maintain a bulletin board where the children's chores are posted along with his or her own activities outside the home: the PTA, political meetings, the bridge club, union meetings, art classes, and so on. The Idealistic partner involved in organizational work can be expected to contribute strongly to the group's activities and actions, certainly as a motivator, quite possibly in some leadership role such as chairperson.

The Idealistic parent not only tends to be overly directive with the children, he or she might have a problem accepting adolescent fashion, behavior, language, and lifestyles. Remember the father-and-son furor over hair length. Remember the mother-and-son storm of the "vulgar" letter from a girlfriend. The Idealistic parent meets each new teenage fad and fashion with a corresponding standard of his own. The dos and don'ts flow, and when his standards are ignored or challenged, the Idealistic parent might respond angrily. This parent who was so playful and affectionate when the children were small might, as they become older, be less affectionate, a bit more formal, and occasionally impersonal in issuing his standards of conduct. His older children might admire him for his constancy and integrity, his unflinching adherence to values and ideals, but they might miss the tenderness. If the Idealistic parent is healthy and flexible, they might have it both ways. But if he or she is rigid and aloof, especially in extreme conflicts—drug use or a teenage pregnancy, for example—the Idealistic parent might even order the offender out of the home. And he might declare in his anger: "I never want to hear that name in this house again." Many personal tragedies result when standards take preference over persons—at home, among relatives and friends, on the job.

The Idealistic Personality is prone to idealize and intellectualize sex. Curiosity may lead to premarital sex, so long as it doesn't involve closeness. As we noted earlier, the Idealistic Personality can have an affair with a much older or younger person since there would be less risk involved. Sexual experimentation might include pornography, or even a brief flirtation with the gamut of sex, again suggesting an avoidance of any sort of emotional relationship. The Idealistic Personality might find lust preferable to love, physical pleasure preferable to emotional joy. If the person involved with the Idealistic Personality moves toward a closer relationship, the Idealistic Personality might either distance that person or arrange to be distanced. Fear of closeness might prompt impotency or frigidity. And that can cause some fear that impotency or frigidity might continue into marriage. Usually it doesn't, again depending on the level of maturity in the individual.

Early in marriage, or in an affair, the Idealistic partner might pursue experimentation in various techniques and positions, but in time sexual activity might become rather routine and frequency might diminish. Twin beds might be found very acceptable. If husband or wife is alone on a trip, he or she might feel uncomfortable if a person of the opposite sex seems attractive, not recognizing that this uncomfortable feeling really means that the spouse left at home is missed. The lonely out-of-town Idealistic partner would not be too comfortable with the notion of phoning the spouse that is missed—unless he or she could first set forth a standard that would make the call acceptable: "A good spouse should telephone his (her) mate when away from home." An awareness of the same tender or close feelings on coming home might provoke some sort of compensating distancing maneuver—working late at the office for the next few nights, going off to the library or a movie, or going to bed early with one of those famous "headaches." The Idealistic spouse might be tempted to have an extramarital affair as another way of avoiding a deepening relationship at home. Or, for the same reason, he or she might tolerate a spouse having an affair. But the more mature and healthy Idealistic partner will be the one who has learned to relate openly and comfortably and intimately in marriage without recourse to setting standards for his relationship—he simply relates. Not the less mature Idealistic spouse—he would rather embrace an ideal than a person.

118

The Idealistic Personality's love of independence and personal freedom sometimes surfaces in marriage and family life. One Idealistic Personality admits frankly that his children are a threat to his freedom, especially during the summer months when school is out. "The children stay up much later, but I still have to go to bed at my regular time. Their staying up so late cuts into my free time." How does he handle the situation? "Self-discipline. I suffer quietly." But when he feels that the balance between the freedom his children enjoy and the amount that he and his wife have left to share tilts in favor of his children, he ships them off to grandmother's house for a week.

From the same love of freedom, the Idealistic Personality cherishes quiet moments alone. The same Idealistic father mentioned above comments: "Solitary moments are very important to me—not every day but on those especially hectic days at work. I expect to come home, make my drink, go off by myself, and look over the headlines—just fifteen minutes when I don't have to worry about the kids' braces or the family budget. The only other choice would be to go out to a bar for a drink. But that's not for me."

The Idealistic Personality cares a great deal about his conduct, the conduct of his family, the conduct of everyone around him. Standards are involved. He is even concerned about proper dress; that reflects on his image. But material things generally aren't all that important—unless they have some bearing on standards and images. Otherwise, they mean little. He wouldn't care for flashy cars: "A car should be a good, dependable means of transportation." So if a car looks good, it is only a coincidence; he bought it for the engineering and the dependability. He feels that way too about his house and his yard—in which he does not like to work, but he must, as a matter of standards, maintain it properly. Status is not important to the Idealistic Personality: "I might do something to spite the Joneses, but never to keep up with the Joneses."

THE WORKING WORLD

Never be afraid to buy a house from an Idealistic salesman. You can depend that what he tells you about the house is true. The motto of every Idealistic Personality is: "Trust me." And you can. Honesty and integrity are more precious to him than his commission. So if honesty, integrity, and reliability are essential to you in your line of work, hire an Idealistic Personality: "People trust me. They know that if I'm doing something for them, it will get done. It's really important to me."

Also important to the Idealistic Personality is punctuality. Every Idealistic Personality runs on IST—Idealistic Standard Time. If he tells you he will be at your office for a sales call at 8 a.m., he will be sitting waiting in your outer office no later than eight o'clock. And if you tell him you will be there for an 8 a.m. appointment, be there: "Time is extremely important to me. I'm always on time—usually well before time—and I don't like others to be late. It really bothers me. I have to control myself or I'll say something snide." But the great benefit with an Idealistic Personality is that you can always be sure he will be where he says he will be when he promises.

The person with the best record for fewest days absent no doubt is an Idealistic worker. He hates to be sick; it violates his standards: "A good worker doesn't get sick." I know of a case where a worker missed only one day in thirty-five years, the day he had a small ulcer removed from one eye. He was back to work, eye patch and all, the very next day. And there is the story of a man who had an operation on his throat. His doctor told him not to talk for a week. But he showed up at the shoe store where he worked the day after the operation, and he had a card that he handed to every customer: "I'm not supposed to talk."

When the Idealistic Personality does get sick, he gets very sick. He has a cold, for instance; but rather than give in and go to bed, he goes to work. He fights it. He is furious. He refuses to admit that he can get sick. Then he has a cold for a week. He is more miserable about the defeat of his image than he is over the cold. But when the Idealistic Personality is sick enough to need a doctor, he is a very good patient. He takes his medicine religiously and does exactly what the doctor tells him. He knows good standards when he hears them.

The choices of jobs or careers that might interest the Idealistic Personality vary widely, but he or she will show preference for fields that permit a certain amount of self-regulation, individuality, and pursuit of high standards. Thus he might enter the military with its superabundance of rules and regulations, its demanding standards, its fixed class structures and customs. (The military also permits casual camaraderie while allowing emotional distance.) Politics and law might appeal to the Idealistic Personality for their stress on ideals and causes and objectivity. More, one doesn't have to get too close to a jury to sway it; and in politics one can shake hundreds of hands and kiss dozens of babies and then move on. Other areas of opportunity for the Idealistic Personality are advertising and selling, which effectively utilize his great concern for integrity and image, his persuasion and confidence; coaching with its demand for conformity to exacting standards and strict adherence to rules and regulations; religion with its commitment to human and moral values and its use of ritual; publishing and journalism with their stress on objectivity, intellectual assessment, and facile communication skills; teaching; business; administration; architecture; music; mechanics; technology; science; and any field that permits him to assert his own image and standards and to be relatively free to be his own individual self. Fields less likely to attract the Idealistic Personality are medicine, nursing, counseling, and social work; these areas might require interaction at too close a personal level.

Whatever his field, the Idealistic worker impresses those around him with his sense of high purpose, dedication, and confidence. His objectivity, methodical approach, and drive mark him as a productive person whose potential is limited only by his tendency to abstain from close-knit, shared enterprise—though the healthy Idealistic person can work in close relationships without being threatened—and his tendency to impose his own standards. His self-assured manner might at times annoy co-workers who might consider him a bit too aloof or even arrogant. Then too he might feel—and show—contempt for a fellow worker who doesn't behave or look like a fully committed member of the organization. "Class"—that indefinable image of dignity and spirit—is so important in everything relating to the life and enterprise of the Idealistic Personality. He feels that a shoddy job or shoddy appearance reflects poorly on everyone. His frosty glance might say so. "It's a reflection not only on him but on me," is the way one Idealistic salesman expressed his feelings about an offending associate.

Another thing that bothers the Idealistic worker is the fixed nine-to-five routine. He finds rigid work schedules oppressive, restrictions that limit his freedom. More, he finds fixed procedures boring: "It's like living in hell." The Idealistic Personality believes that he is more productive and efficient when he can work as long and as hard as he wishes. And it's true—he is very responsible, very trustworthy.

His high standards and exacting sense of time pose other hazards for the Idealistic careerist. One engineer confides that his career must progress according to his standards, or he leaves. "If I don't make the kind of money or develop the kind of products that I feel I must, then I'll be leaving in five years." He means it; he is on his third five-year plan, and he is still bothered by living up to his image of a successful engineer. Another hazard that he might share with other Idealistic Personalities is his hesitance to make a genuine commitment. As in personal relationships, an Idealistic worker can go along in a position for six months or so without really being involved, or without being fully aware of the standards expected or the devotion required. Suddenly he realizes just how much of himself must be committed, and he quits. He might tell others that the working conditions were poor, the company's standards were shoddy, and so on, but his real problem is facing up to the full standards required for commitment. Another ploy sometimes heard from an Idealistic careerist is this statement, often repeated as the demands for commitment intensify: "Always hold back a little of yourself." That means about 80 percent is available, but never the full commitment. The trouble is, holding back 20 percent means he is cheating himself that much. There might be additional risk in full commitment, but only 20 percent more risk. It's usually worth it.

Retirement is not a problem normally for the Idealistic Personality. "I'm looking forward to it," says a rather young Idealistic careerist. "I've always thought that it was kind of ridiculous to work all your life. Early retirement makes a lot more sense."

ALTERNATIVES AND OPTIONS

The healthy Idealistic Personality is a rather definite, enthusiastic, and forceful person who prizes his own integrity and ideals while respecting the ideals and integrity of the other person. He holds to convictions with great fidelity, always adhering to values and standards, even when others choose expediency and lesser values. He can be a glimpse of grandeur in a ho-hum world of apathy and indifference. His independent style often elicits the admiration of others while his conduct and confidence prompt them to follow his lead. He insists on maintaining an impeccable image, one that communicates trust and loyalty.

Whether healthy or a little less than comfortable with himself and his exalted standards, the Idealistic Personality is something of a natural resource in his community and an asset in his profession, a source of pride and admiration to his family. He might further enhance his image and be a little more accessible if he would learn to relax a bit more, to share a bit more, to be more flexible, to relate to others without setting standards for the relationship. Then he might have his life of high purpose while enjoying warmth and closeness. With fewer mountains to climb, he might enjoy the view from the heights already attained with much greater satisfaction simply because others can then share his moments of glory.

How? If you are an Idealistic Personality, look at these points:

• Consider that warmth and closeness are not weaknesses but great inner strengths. They don't need the rigid armor of ideals for protection.

• Love and being loved enrich a person's image. Far from rendering a person helpless, love shared is an endless source of energy.

• When you learn to accept the help of others, you are better able to offer them your help and the benefit of your vision and ideals.

• Independence sometimes comes at an exorbitant price: loneliness. No one is self-sufficient or ought to be.

• So often your standards are brittle. You may fear closeness because brittle objects tend to shatter on contact.

• Practice saying "I need" rather than "I should," "I want" rather than "I ought," and "We are" rather than "I am."

• You have a delightful sense of humor, but sometimes you use it to nudge others back a bit. That's manipulation and not genuine joy.

• The most noble of images are cast in metal and placed on pedestals for everyone to admire. But they are so remote that they are accessible only to pigeons.

• How does this sound as a description: "He was enormously appealing but somewhat inaccessible." If the description fits a little too tightly, trade it for something more comfortable.

• You love a compliment; that means you are meeting standards well enough for others to notice and comment. But you seldom give compliments. Is it that you are so rigid in your standards for others that they can't possibly live up to them?

• It is perfectly fine and admirable for you to be a lady or a gentleman. But be a warm lady, a kind gentleman. Pneumatic devices can open doors, but they can't smile.

• Others could admire you more if they could come a little closer. You don't look real from a distance.

• Be careful of being a snob.

• Your tendency to be critical is equivalent to building a twenty-foot moat all the way around you. It keeps everyone at a safe distance.

• It is easy for you to say, "You can depend on me." But is it so easy for you to depend on others?

• When you begin to notice that your wife is looking a little heavier, or that her feet are too big, beware. That probably means you're getting closer. But if you get close enough there is no possible way for you to notice her feet. And while you're that close try to guess her weight. That's close enough to whisper, "I love you."

• With all your integrity, confidence, enthusiasm, and decisiveness, it is truly unbelievable that you could be helpless or weak—at any distance. Everyone seems to share this attitude but you.

• Question: Is the love of your children worth your exalted standards of dress, behavior, and hair length?

• Question: Is your finest and most noble ideal finer and more noble than the love of your spouse?

• Is your cold anger preferable to the warmth of friendship? Know that when you are your coldest, something warm is being stifled inside you.

• You tend to treat people as stereotypes. They are people—feeling people.

• Whenever you get the feeling you want to run, turn around; someone you love is straight ahead. Don't flee from your feelings.

• Again and ever: realize the great strength of tenderness, the power of warm love, the joy of sharing.

• Be open to relating without imposing structures on the relationship.

• Making a commitment is less risky than walking away.

• Come close enough to feel how much family and friends love you.

• If you insist on putting distance between yourself and others, then don't complain about being lonely.

• Speaking of complaining . . . you sometimes complain when really you would like to ask for help. You say you are honest. Why not honestly ask for what you need? Or the person you need?

• Listen more. Pronounce less.

• A relaxed smile is much more comfortable than a stiff upper lip—not only for you but for everyone around you.

• You can't take an ideal to lunch. Ideals don't get hungry. And ideals can't share your joys and your sorrows—people can.

• Being haughty is naughty.

• Always anguishing the follies and frailties and flaws of human nature is defeating. Don't be disappointed. Get involved—but without your exalted image and your demanding standards. Your commitment might make a difference.

• You cherish your freedom of choice. Fine. But do you sometimes limit the choices of others by forcing your standards on them? When you deny them their freedom of choice, you forfeit your own.

• "Compromise" doesn't have to be a dirty word. Compromise is the art of the possible in a world of conflicting standards. When you hold your convictions so rigidly and so exaltedly and so inflexibly, they become unattainable. When that happens, you are the one who has compromised them.

• Feelings are always real. Images can be dishonest. You prize honesty, so don't let the image cheat you.

VI

The Patient Personality

WHAT THE APOSTLE PAUL wrote of love in his first letter to the Christians of Corinth comes remarkably close to describing the strengths of the Patient Personality:

"Love is patient; love is kind. Love is not jealous, it does not put on airs, it is not snobbish. Love is never rude, it is not self-seeking; it is not prone to anger; neither does it brood over injuries. Love does not rejoice in what is wrong but rejoices with the truth. There is no limit to love's forbearance, to its trust, its hope, its power to endure" (1 Corinthians 13:4–7).

The Patient Personality is indeed patient and kind and even humble. He is rarely snobbish or rude. He values trust and truth; he is ever hopeful. His forbearance, tolerance, and endurance are remarkable. He is known to be a bit jealous and to brood—no one is perfect—but he softens this with silence. What is so noticeable about the Patient Personality is his great generosity. He is always giving to or doing something for others in a quiet, unpretentious way. The Patient father will willingly rake the baseball diamond after his son's Little League game. The unmarried Patient aunt might help finance a niece's college education. The Patient neighbor would be willing to babysit your children while you keep a doctor's appointment. The last doctor in town to make house calls very well might be a Patient

126

Personality. No doubt there is a disproportionate number of Patient Personalities among the ranks of Scout leaders, Sunday-school teachers, Big Brothers, and Candy Stripers. Wherever and whenever help is needed, you are likely to find Patient Personalities on the scene. But one point needs to be made: the Patient Personality really isn't that prone to volunteer. Rather, others sense that the Patient Personality is available and willing to give assistance when asked. The Patient Personality, sometimes to his regret, is as aware of his availability. Still, he responds; he finds it difficult to say no.

Not only is the Patient Personality generous and giving of self, but he goes about it in a calm and unruffled way. He is both responsive and responsible, genial, understanding of others, and straightforward in manner. He does what he must do with simplicity and common sense. He may mutter about all the endless demands, but only to himself. One father we know could always be depended on to provide transportation for his daughter's gymnastics team. He never said no. One sunny Saturday afternoon, he noted the other parents waving their greetings from doorways and shaded lawn chairs, and he thought to himself: "They sit at home on their duffs while I take their kids everywhere." In his own gentle style, he negotiated with other parents to form a car pool. The other parents really didn't mind; they were only surprised that he hadn't asked earlier. And he was glad that he asked, especially on those Saturdays when he could wave to them from his own shaded spot on his front lawn.

THE GIVING URGE

What prompts the Patient Personality to give and give all through life? The essential element of his style is his desire for security, particularly his emotional security. The Patient Personality fears that unless he gives in any relationship, the other person(s) might desert or abandon him. Thus his *urge to give*. To protect his security and to avoid getting hurt, the Patient Personality will respond to anyone in his environment who seeks his assistance.

But the give-and-take usual to relationships is lopsided when the Patient Personality is involved. He readily responds to the needs and wishes of others, but he is reluctant to make his own needs and desires known. This is the vulnerability the Patient Personality fears:

"If I say no to others, I'll hurt their feelings. But if I ask for something, it might burden them and they might say no. That would hurt me." So the Patient Personality is saying, in effect: "It is safer to give than to express needs." And so, quite literally, he is generous to a fault. Since this is a great big world of endless needs and desires, the Patient Personality finds himself giving endlessly. Sometimes he finds it overwhelming. He is tempted some days to stay home with the blinds down and the phone off the hook, fearing even to open the morning's mail lest it too bring demands for giving, giving, and more giving. After an exhausting day of meeting the demands of clients and customers and responding to the needs of family and friends and even strangers, the worn and weary Patient Personality sometimes feels as limp and trod upon as a doormat.

But how can anyone give constantly and never deal with his own needs? He can't. The Patient Personality has his own special coping mechanism for surviving the deluge of demands. We call it the *will-struggle*. One Patient Personality nicely defined it as "a sweet way of saying no." It is also a silent way of saying, "Not now." The will-struggle is essentially a delaying tactic. Ask and the Patient Personality will give; but *when* he responds is a matter of his own choosing. He may feel compelled to give, but the choice of time is his. "Honey, will you iron a shirt for me?" will give you an ironed shirt—perhaps now, perhaps later, perhaps Tuesday. You never know. But don't nag. That will guarantee Tuesday, and not necessarily next Tuesday. This is the will-struggle of the Patient Personality, his way of dealing with the seemingly endless stream of requests and demands that he feels obligated to meet. He very much wants to make you happy, but in his own time. He won't say no; you might not like him if he did, and he doesn't want to risk abandonment. So silently and even sweetly he or she is saying, "I'll do whatever you ask of me. But I'll do it when I'm ready." So be careful when making a request of the Patient Personality, particularly on a harried day. Always be sure the request you put before him is a real need, one that is clear, sincere, and immediate.

This silent will-struggle may appear to others as plain stubbornness. It is, but to the Patient Personality it is a necessary defense. Consciously or not, he is protecting himself from having to give too much too often while not risking abandonment, which he fears so much, and the pain that might be inflicted by a hardedged "no." All of these elements are well-displayed in the case of Mrs. P. When she married, she put her rather substantial savings into a joint bank account with her husband. Several years later, she inherited a large sum of money from her father's estate, but this time she put the money into a personal account. Her husband didn't understand, and he became somewhat annoyed when Mrs. P. didn't explain. She felt that she couldn't—or wouldn't—even though she felt guilty about her silence. What she couldn't tell her husband was that she felt that she had given enough. Moreover, she wanted the money in her own name for security, but, typical of the Patient Personality, she found it difficult to admit that she had needs, even a need for security. So she stubbornly maintained her silence and her will-struggle, never even hinting at her feelings. All she could say to Mr. P. was, "I've made up my mind and that's it." Had Mrs. P. been able to share her feelings with Mr. P., he might have been able to support her in this need for security. Instead, she did what she dislikes most; she hurt her husband.

SECURITY FOR OTHERS

What the Patient Personality wants for himself—security—he wants for others, for whomever he feels responsible. For the Patient parent, that means security for home and family. For the Patient businessman, it means conservative business practices, sufficient cash reserves, a decent profit margin, fair wages and adequate benefits for his employees. For the Patient workingman, it means a job with a well-established company that is stable and has an early retirement plan, insurance programs, job security, seniority rights, and few demands to work overtime. Whatever he does, the Patient Personality tries to minimize risk and any threat to his security. He isn't a gambler, he tends toward thrift—unless the urge to give intrudes, as it so often does. Still, he tries earnestly to maintain a budget; he buys smartly; and, if possible, he stashes a little something away in savings. Last year's wardrobe will do another season; everyone else's needs come first. The car may be driven until the wheels wear off. The home will be maintained as a comfortable yet unpretentious place to live. The Patient parent will tend to worry when the children are away from home. The Patient mother will sleep ever so lightly until she has heard all of her teenagers come home; and should her husband stop for a beer with the boys, she will want a telephone call—her indirect way of hinting that she would prefer him home with her. In any case, home for the Patient Personality is where the heart is. Home must always be a safe haven, a place of peace and security.

There are times when the need for security and the need to give clash. The solution depends on the individual Patient Personality and his maturity. If mature, some sort of compromise can be worked out—the Patient Personality has a knack for practical solutions, although he may take his time making them—but the less mature individual sometimes finds the urge to give overpowering, even when his personal security is threatened. Sam, for example, is divorced and he pays ample child support, but his two children occasionally call to tell him of special needs, like a new pair of skates for hockey or a new dress for the high school dance. Sam skims from his car payment to buy the skates and the dress; he plans to give up bowling for the next month to compensate. But the boys on the bowling team need Sam's 186 average. Once more Sam can't say no, so he bowls. But the following week on bowling night, one of the boys has to pick Sam up. His car has been repossessed.

Along with his need for security, the Patient Personality is protective. He wants to safeguard his own from any form of evil and harm. We know of a story about an immigrant couple that makes the point. The husband, adapting to the American scene, invited a group of co-workers to his house for a poker game. He got into an argument over a hand, and the dispute worsened due to his language problem and the effects of a few drinks. Tempers flared; fists flew. The husband, a small man, was losing badly when his Patient wife, hearing his shouts, rushed from the kitchen with a rolling pin. This usually quiet and gentle woman pounded and pummeled her husband's hefty opponent until he ran from the house. Beware of the Patient Personality protecting his—or her—own.

With this story in mind, it may seem incongruous to note that the Patient Personality abhors violence, but it's true. The case cited is simply an instance in which security took precedence over abhorrence of violence—the immigrant woman's prime concern was to protect her husband from harm. The Patient Personality dislikes violence in any form, physical or emotional. He is not your cops-and-crooks television viewer or your war-movie buff; he dislikes bullies and demagogues, tyrants and tormentors; he wants no part of bigotry and prejudice. On the contrary, he supports the rights of others and the remedying of injustices, but always in a nonviolent fashion. He is ever and always the peacemaker. He doesn't even care to argue, and he hates to be hassled—either provocation will prompt a will-struggle. He doesn't like to confront anger in others, and he tries very hard to keep his own anger in check. He will avoid saying anything that might hurt the other person. He would rather suffer abuse than inflict pain. The Patient Personality at times is capable of tolerating a great deal of abuse; he sometimes plays the martyr. He seems to be willing to pursue peace at any price. Almost . . . Remember the ire of the immigrant wife. The Patient Personality is able to stifle his anger for a long, long time. But when it erupts, it is awesome. So beware. Never underestimate the Patient Personality.

VULNERABILITIES AND CRISES

The Patient Personality normally handles stress very well. But when the frustration of demand after demand piles up, when he begins to wonder when it will all end, when he has given and given and given, he is prone to slip away to a quiet spot to weep silent tears. This is part of the tendency to be martyrish—even when the burden seems too great, even in tears, the Patient Personality is reluctant to state his problem or his feelings. After the catharsis of tears, he is likely to return to the task of meeting others' needs, saying to himself, "I can take it. I've got broad shoulders." It would be much healthier if the burdened Patient Personality would allow others, especially those close to him, to know his feelings, wishes, and needs—and much less confusing and frustrating for everyone. Also, he would discover that sharing is a more productive way of relating. Interdependence would permit him to relax and to relate without always feeling that he has to be doing for or giving to others. Then, too, he would enhance their happiness by letting them meet some of his needs.

Any discussion of the Patient Personality always comes back to his tendency to give. All this generosity is not always healthy. It can be obsessive and even destructive. When the less mature Patient Personality becomes too preoccupied with concern for whether people like him or not, and with his fear of abandonment, he can glut himself on his own generosity. He becomes what we call the *selfish giver*. The pace and range of his giving and doing for others becomes exhilarating. He gets high on giving—he gives and gives and goes higher and higher. He is like a broken gumball machine that keeps spitting out bright balls of bubblegum without having to insert a coin.

The selfish giver is the doting father who spoils his children by giving them more than they can handle maturely, the mother who never insists that her children make their beds or fix their own lunches or pick up after themselves. She is the young college student who spends all her savings for a car, supposedly for transportation to and from the campus; but really she wants it for her less financially able boyfriend so that he can have transportation. What the selfish giver doesn't realize is that he paralyzes others with his bounty; or he makes them feel inadequate. One way or the other, his gluttonous giving is stunting, debilitating, and confusing. This is the mother who raises her daughter's two illegitimate children, the uncle who supports his nephew's drug habit. She is the young woman who permits her roommate and boyfriend her bedroom while she sleeps on the couch. This is selfish giving far beyond anyone's good. Everyone suffers; no one benefits.

The insecure Patient Personality is jealous, fearing abandonment all too easily. Mrs. J. sees Mr. J. noticing an attractive younger woman. She is tormented by jealousy; she interprets her husband's roving glances as a statement that she hasn't done enough or given enough in their marriage. She fears he might leave her, so Mrs. J. gives more and more to Mr. J., indulging him in every way. Suppose Mr. J. is doing more than just looking. Suppose he has an affair. Does Mrs. J. rage at him? Does she deny him her bed, board, and body? Does she confront the other woman? None of these. Being a Patient Personality, Mrs. J. is terribly loyal, even now; so tolerant, in fact, that she appears to others as a bit naïve and gullible. She plays the Pollyanna. Mrs. J. may tolerate the affair a long, long time while she tries desperately to find out what more she can give or do for Mr. J., making their home as pleasant as possible, shrugging as she says to herself, "You can make the best of a bad situation, if you're willing to try hard enough. He's only hurting himself, not me." With that she might withdraw into herself, letting her anger build as she denies her need for him. The jealousy, the affair, the anger might all have been prevented had Mrs. J. only shared her real feelings with Mr. J. Oh yes, she *thought* that her loyalty and tolerance expressed her feelings, but Mr. J. had read her silence and her tolerance as indifference. Open communication of her love for him and her need for him might have convinced Mr. J.

The insecure Patient parent is also capable of jealousy. Suppose our Mrs. J., having given up on Mr. J., now focuses all of her giving on her bachelor son. She cooks his favorite meals, tidies his room, buys all his clothes, lends him money, and makes her car available to him. Her reward is having the opportunity to do so much for her son—and he is grateful, occasionally taking his mother out for dinner. But the time comes when the son finds a girl who is willing to cook his favorite meals, care for his clothes, tidy his room, and go places with him on mother's money and in mother's car. And so they marry. Mother J. always hoped that this day would come, but when it did, she felt a little deserted and a little jealous. Yet she couldn't express her feelings to her son. She withdrew behind her self-contained ways and her silence. Had her son known her feelings instead of her silence, Mrs. J. might enjoy more than an occasional dinner shared with her son and her daughter-in-law.

Happiness, even for the healthy Patient Personality, is never having to ask. The Patient Personality projects onto the environment his own giving ways. Doesn't everyone give when they know there is a need to be met? He feels that he shouldn't have to ask for help or to seek a favor. Besides, as noted earlier, he fears that his needs might be a burden or his wishes might overwhelm you, and you might abandon him. So he never openly shares his needs, desires, or wishes. He simply won't ask; the risk is too great. Rather than ask for two hours off to keep a dental appointment, the unsure Patient worker might not show up at the shop at all that day. He might later state that he was ill, or that one of his children was ill. Everyone accepts illness as a reality; so for the Patient Personality, that is more acceptable than having a need. He can relate somatically. The young executive might end up in the hospital with a bleeding ulcer rather than tell his boss that he would prefer to remain in his present position instead of accepting the planned promotion with accompanying transfer to Toledo.

For all his reluctance to state his needs, the Patient Personality really would like others to know; but he won't ask, and that leads to frustrations. What he hopes is that others can read his mind, antici-pate his needs and desires, but when they don't, that irritates him too. A Patient wife might silently pout all evening rather than ask her husband to take her to a movie she wants to see. She doesn't mention it, yet she remains annoyed with him for not knowing. A Patient Personality might walk a mile on a broken toe rather than ask for a ride to the doctor's office. His wife surprises the Patient Personality with three handsome new sport shirts that he has wanted but hasn't mentioned; she observed him admiring them one day shopping. His reaction? Protest. He doesn't like her knowing that he has such desires, needs, or wants. He can't permit her the good feeling of having given to him. This is a variation of the selfish giver, and his attitude is less than healthy. Neither is the attitude of the Patient wife who complains at noon Sunday that she hasn't had time to have breakfast. This is a double-barreled complaint. She is at once subtly complaining about all the giving she has had to do all morn-ing for the family and voicing her frustration that her husband didn't take her out for breakfast. She could have asked, but she didn't.

There are times when the Patient Personality may resort to stealth to promote something he wants, although not too likely for himself. The Patient Personality is persuasive in a gentle and patient way. He never likes to make waves; he plays a waiting game; his strategy is low-keyed; he bides his time; he avoids risk. A Patient working wife wants snow tires for her car as a safety and security measure, but she doesn't want to ask her husband to purchase them for her. She is not at all unhappy the day she comes home on a slippery winter day with a dimple in the front bumper. She can tell her husband how she slid on the ice and came close to a serious accident. That same evening she is delighted when he goes out to purchase snow tires and she didn't have to ask. If she were healthier, she would have asked long before the first snow.

This same Patient woman for years kept up a small conspiracy with her children to protect her husband from the many household problems that she thought might annoy him—and would advertise some need for his help. The rallying cry—or whisper—was: "Don't tell Dad, he'll get mad." Dad did get mad the day that he discovered the conspiracy, and he was a bit short in his comments. That was a mistake. If "hell hath no wrath like a woman scorned," that scorned woman is a Patient Personality. His wife's intention was to protect him from problems, and he wasn't a bit grateful. "What more does that man want? What more can I give?": she rehearsed her grievances while fighting back her anger. He wisely slipped away when he felt the heat rising.

GROWING UP PATIENT

In infancy, the Patient Personality is a rather quiet, undemanding, pleasant child. "He's such a good baby. He's never any trouble," is the way you usually hear the Patient infant described. He is the child that cries little and can remain content in his crib or playpen for long periods of time. The pattern of quiet contentment continues through childhood; so does his tendency to be pleasant. The Patient child is apparently untroubled by many of the situations that other children often find frightening, such as the dark, a windstorm, or a thunderstorm. If he is scared, he doesn't complain—perhaps an early forecast of not being willing to communicate his needs. Even illnesses and accidents are handled well, especially when the Patient child is assured the security of a caring parent. Thus he would react comparatively calmly to a tonsillectomy if his mother were to spend the night with him in the hospital before the operation. Whatever apprehension he feels in the doctor's office awaiting shots or stitches is handled with quiet resignation. He tries very hard not to make a fuss, even when a hint of concern shows in his eyes.

The danger in the serenity of the Patient child is the possibility that he can easily be taken for granted. He is not the foot-stomping, yelling child who manages to have his way. He is the quiet one on the sidelines when the other children are bumping and nudging to be first for ice cream. As he grows older, he is the child who willingly babysits the younger children. He rarely says no to parental requests; even at an early age; he won't risk abandonment. As one of the younger children, he is prone to take all the teasing and joshing that goes on in a family. He is even reluctant to state preferences when asked. He is prone to noncommittal answers, even to direct questions: "Do you like apple pie?" "Sort of." "Would you like to go to a ball game?" "Maybe." One Patient father who understands the problem tells of a family practice of taking the birthday child out for dinner to a place of his choice. His Patient daughter when asked always responds: "I don't care really. It doesn't matter, whatever you want to do." The father always has to explain that this is something nice for everyone, that she needn't worry about making a choice of some place that is too expensive. If it is, he will tell her. After some coaxing, the daughter finally names a modest restaurant. The Patient Personality never wants to seem to be asking for anything or to have desires, even when asked. To others, it appears to be an attitude of indecisiveness. It isn't. Still, it can be vexing. One needs to be patient with the Patient Personality. The more secure he feels, the more likely he is to express his needs and desires. Never fear; they will never be excessive.

The first day of school may distress the Patient child. His security is momentarily threatened by the new and unfamiliar environment. He feels vulnerable when mother leaves him at the classroom door; he may sob and wail and cling to her. As one Patient Personality remembers, "I thought my mother had left me forever." The fear may persist for several weeks. During this time the child needs a tremendous amount of understanding and assurance from parents and teacher. Once the Patient child adjusts—and he does—school becomes a comfortable and secure environment, and he does well. The Patient child responds calmly and with few complaints to the discipline and routine of schooling. He is rarely demanding, but he will remember fondly those moments when he is given special attention or when his needs are anticipated, as against those times he had to ask. He may be the child who has an "accident" rather than have to ask to go to the bathroom.

The Patient student is rarely if ever a disciplinary problem, but should the teacher have a bad day and be short with the class, the Patient child may be uncomfortable. Should the teacher snap at him, he may feel that the teacher doesn't like him, and this would trouble him, threatening his security. He may suppose that he hasn't responded well and that is why the teacher isn't happy. He'll work harder, give more of himself. His patience and his reluctance to make demands of others can be a problem in the classroom. When he doesn't understand instructions or explanations, he won't ask the teacher to repeat or to explain further. He simply endures. His teacher may sense his frustration, but no one really may be aware of the problem until his report card comes home with poor grades. Now his parents are frustrated. Even with a poor report card, the

Patient child may be hesitant to tell of his problems and his need for help in his studies. He may continue to struggle; he may accept parental exhortations quietly, even accusations that he hasn't studied hard enough, rather than admit that he needs help. The problem can be compounded by the Patient Personality's own very deliberate, unhurried pace. He can't be rushed. Sometimes this will-struggle over learning is identified as the problem of a slow learner or lack of ability when really it is the personality style's pattern of not stating his needs and problems and of resisting what he feels is pressure to do more.

This will-struggle can create problems for the Patient Personality throughout his education unless parents and teachers recognize the struggle for what it is and then deal appropriately with it. What began as one child's failure to communicate need for help in reading in the early grades became a massive struggle with her concerned parents that lasted well into high school. During that time, her parents provided special tutoring, eye examinations, summer school, and reading clinics. Nothing helped. The parents were perplexed—perhaps the child was indeed dull. The child, on the other hand, tried to tell her parents not to worry even while she felt their concern as a heavy demand to give more of herself as a student when she was already doing her best. Stalemate. The struggle went on until one evening in great frustration the Patient teenager told her parents: "Look, you can lead a horse to the library, but you can't make him read." Something clicked in the memory of the mother, herself a Patient Personality. She recalled having a terrible time with algebra but had never admitted her problem to anyone—not her parents, not her teachers. Mother and daughter began to compare problems. The daughter admitted her own reluctance to confide her need for help. The pressure began to drop. With a little remedial work, real progress was made in improving her reading skills.

Throughout childhood, the Patient Personality gets along well with siblings, peers, and playmates. He never imposes himself, but his pleasant ways make it easy for others to invite him to join in whatever is going on. Once involved, he is a contributor, always pleasant and helpful to others. He is the peacemaker who arbitrates quarrels and breaks up fights. He never thrusts himself into the spotlight, but his way of getting things done practically makes him a welcome and well-liked member of the group. But he seldom realizes just how much others enjoy his presence; even this touch of humility is attractive to others. He is always comfortable to be with. The Patient Personality enjoys the camaraderie and the excitement of sports, but he may prefer baseball, tennis, or track to the hard contact of football or hockey. He doesn't much care for the violence.

The generosity of the Patient Personality begins to show at an early age. He or she is helpful around the house. Walking home from school, the first-grader may pluck a handful of spring dandelions as a bouquet for his mother. In crafts, she fashions a lumpy ashtray for her father—one part of clay to ten parts love. Both gifts are small gifts of self, presented with eyes sparkling in anticipation of the parents' joy. The danger is that parents in this hectic, fast-paced world of ours may fail to perceive these gifts, however humble, for what they are: genuine symbols of self. Not only is a moment of joyful sharing missed, but the child may feel that he hasn't given enough, that he must give more or do more.

ADOLESCENCE

Adolescence for the Patient Personality is much what it is for all teenagers: a time of searching after relative freedom and independence, of re-examining values, of testing new environments—a mixed moment of trial and error and, if all goes well, of learning and maturing. The Patient Personality does it gracefully, although he has his moments of frustration. He may display his tendency to will-struggle with his parents as he seeks to assert himself more, still with the typical reluctance to declare his needs, wishes, and desires. He may, for example, struggle with parental pressure to attend church regularly. But parents needn't be too worried, and they should avoid responses that feed into the will-struggle. This young person is well-disposed to all matters religious and moral. He prizes truth and loyalty and personal integrity. So if given enough room for reflection at his own pace, he usually will make decisions quite acceptable to his parents. But they must permit him his own deliberate pace—he won't be hurried, and he wants to make decisions that are fully his own, not someone else's. When he makes his decision, it is firm and resolute—unless he is forced into conflict over fear of abandonment or possibly hurting someone such as a parent. Then he might waver or will-struggle. So a light hand is recommended. And parents might look for those occasions that permit them to reinforce his decisions.

The Patient teenager's worst hazard in adolescence is his desire to be liked. He tends to let others walk all over him; he is afraid of being deserted if he states his needs or feelings. Unsure of his limits, his level of confidence fluctuates, and he may give too quickly and too abundantly, committing his services beyond his capacity to deliver. He finds it difficult to state an emphatic no, and he can be sullen and even depressed when his eager generosity is refused or is not appreciated. He very much needs to experience appreciation. This is the child in the family who will complain least while giving greatly; he is the one who doesn't fuss when he has to wear the hand-me-downs of an older brother or sister. Should he have a part-time job during high school, he will want to buy many of his own clothes —perhaps because he doesn't want to make his needs and desires known—but here again there is little cause for worry. He is sufficiently frugal, so he isn't likely to spend excessively, at least not on himself. He is more likely to spend money on others.

The Patient teenager is usually liked and enjoys a wide range of friends, but he tends to fix on one or two close friends, male or female. "Emotionally, we tend to put all our eggs in one basket," is the way one Patient parent explains it. Here again there is some concern for the Patient Personality's tendency to give too readily and sometimes too greatly, especially if that special friend is less well off financially, less gifted, or less capable. He may even choose a friend who is handicapped in some way, and then give abundantly of himself to meet that person's needs. His friendships resemble his decisions; they are made slowly and deliberately with firm commitment; so when the Patient teenager overcommits himself, he may be deeply disappointed if that friend doesn't appreciate his giving or should move away. There is the danger, too, that the other person may find his boundless generosity stifling and push away from it. The Patient Personality always has difficulty when people leave him for whatever reason. He may not say much, but he very well may go off alone to shed silent tears. This is the desertion he always fears. When it happens, the family might take note and try to give him support, and with support security. But say little—remember, he doesn't like his needs or his feelings known.

Since the Patient Personality is warm and friendly and responsive, he or she usually enjoys a good social life. Dating tends to follow one of two patterns: (1) as in the friendship situation described above, he may date those persons whose needs he can meet; or (2) he may be attracted to the kind of person who spends freely, who is attentive, who anticipates the other person's needs, who is outgoing —the kind of person who goes places and does the things that the Patient Personality would like but never request. Thus he or she is often attracted to the dazzling style of the Accomplishing Personality, the take-charge ways of the Influencing Personality, and the winning manner of the Ambitious Personality. These outgoing personalities are the Patient Personality's entrée into the social scene without having to assert himself or to reveal his needs. He enjoys the glitter and the glow and the good times, and the Patient Personality has no trouble in taking it all in. He just loves it—so long as he doesn't have to ask.

The Patient Personality will wait patiently for the person whom he considers "nice, kind, pleasant, and mannerly"—and with enough sparkle. And he or she would have to be rather dependable, someone he could count on doing whatever he would say he do. The Patient Personality would then explore the possibility of forming a relationship in a rather forthright way. But he can't be rushed; the Patient Personality has his own pace and has to make decisions for himself. But then, as one Patient Personality described it, something wonderful happens: "All of a sudden, that person meant something to me. He became part of my world, part of my life."

Marriage can be most rewarding for the Patient Personality. Or it can be difficult. He or she can adapt to a mansion or to a hovel so long as emotional security is part of the environment. He is willing to work very hard to develop the relationship and to meet the needs of his spouse. As we saw in the case of the immigrant wife, the Patient Personality is fiercely loyal. The danger is that the Patient partner might overwhelm his spouse with selfish giving, never allowing his spouse the joy of giving to the Patient Personality. Or he might maintain a reserve that suggests a lack of involvement or indifference—this again is his reluctance to communicate his needs, wishes, and strivings, and a hint of the will-struggle. He sometimes doesn't give his partner feedback; he can make it difficult for his partner to make him happy.

The less mature Patient Personality can be attracted to someone who has a crippling need such as alcohol, drugs, or neurosis. The Patient partner can be too patient, too understanding, enduring verbal, emotional, and even physical abuse or privation. Sometimes a Patient spouse confides, "Maybe I walk on eggs around my wife too much of the time." He doesn't recognize the problem as a problem. Rather, he believes that if he gives enough and loves enough, everything will come out all right. But if something is wrong, the Patient Personality tends to blame himself: "I didn't give enough." The Patient spouse, remember, can remain in a troubled or hopeless marriage for a long, long time, and he may even contribute to the turmoil by being too patient or by being the selfish giver. He is willing to be of service and to give in a bad situation simply because he enjoys giving. He may recognize that he will go to any lengths to gratify his partner, even while realizing that he can frustrate that person by allowing too few opportunities to reciprocate—the partner is effectively stifled in his own desire to give.

The Patient Personality's feelings are hurt when all his massive efforts fail to please or are ignored. What the Patient Personality perceives as abandonment—any rejection, real or imagined—prompts him to clam up. He will not state his hurt. Instead, he withdraws, and when this happens, the possibility of abandonment becomes very real. Still, the Patient Personality can't express his emotional needs. Instead, he may try to give more and more when all he has to say is, "Golly, I need you." Sometimes something in the emotional circuitry switches to another channel. Even in an extreme situation, the Patient spouse can assume an attitude of unreal optimism: "Everything will work out somehow, if only I try hard enough." Or, "I let things bother me more than they should."

The Patient Personality is prone to be a self-contained or self-sufficient person, even in marriage. It may sound strange and incongruous, but one Patient Personality once told me, "My belief is that I'm the only one who can make me happy. I've always worked very hard to be self-contained and not to need anyone too much. My security is in myself. You've got to be able to meet life on your own." This, again, is a product of his essential need for security. The security that comes through marriage and the love of the other person reinforces and enhances this quality of self-sufficiency—it produces that serenity which is so much a part of the charm of the Patient Personality. But it also produces that sense of reserve, that hint of the loner about the Patient Personality. In fact, he does like moments alone, he prizes intervals of solitude, he protects his privacy. Spouse and family will grant him that, recognizing that the busy, giving Patient Personality needs a break from so much doing and giving for others. It can be a problem, however, when the Patient Personality is also reluctant to share his needs, when he is practicing his grand silence, when he supposes, as he does, that everyone else is giving and protecting privacy and not sharing feelings. It all comes together as one large package of frustration for the other persons in the life of the Patient Personality. Once again, the danger is that others can misread the solitude and silence. It would be beneficial for the Patient Personality to remember that the root meaning of the word "mystery" is "a secret shared."

The Patient husband might find himself feeling the pressure of a threatened layoff or another child on the way or unpaid bills piling up, but he says nothing to his wife, feeling: "If I let people help me, I'll be vulnerable." So he sits there saying nothing, giving the impression that he is uninvolved, or that he is just plain stubborn, or that nothing really bothers him. He also might give others the feeling that they are inadequate to his needs or that he doesn't care for their affection. He does care, and he would like their help. But he can't ask.

The Patient Personality's sense of service, patience, and common sense are great assets in times of stress. The Patient mother can spend long hours with a sick child in the hospital, yet organize the household in such a way that a routine of life keeps going. The Patient husband might be very willing to take his aging mother-in-law into his home. The Patient wife will care for the children of a sick neighbor, take a foster child into her home, whatever is needed. The Patient husband might find himself acting as a Big Brother for a succession of fatherless boys. The Patient wife and mother, God bless her, will work long hours through the night helping her children with their homework, writing out checks to pay the bills, helping her husband check over his expense account, pressing band uniforms, washing baseball uniforms, typing out a child's report long after he has gone to bed so that he can hand it in on time. She might serve herself and her family better if she would insist that others might do a bit more for themselves. But when she finally sags into a quiet corner after everyone else is asleep, who would deny her that solitude and that small glass of wine? The small moment of solitude is a cherished pause. And it does refresh.

The Patient wife, always home-and-family-oriented, might not be as prone as women of other personality styles to work outside the home. She will if it will increase her sense of security or extend her ability to give to her family. Or she might want to take a job as a way of fleeing the many demands she faces at home. This last impulse to work is most likely to surface either when school vacation begins and the children, especially teenagers, begin to place more demands on her, or at the time of the year when the bills are piling up. But when her husband's income is adequate and things are going well, the Patient mother is quite content to remain at home doing what she can for her family.

Sex is normally satisfying to the Patient Personality. Here again the Patient spouse is quite tolerant, ready to respond to the needs expressed by his or her partner. Still, he or she has trouble communicating his own needs and preferences, even in bed. Yet at times he may use sex as a way of vicariously expressing needs and desires that he finds hard to communicate openly. There is a danger that the self-contained manner and the silence of the Patient partner may be misread as coldness, but frigidity or impotence is rarely if ever a problem for the Patient Personality. Sex is approached with much pleasant anticipation, if silently, and the Patient partner, while not assertive, is loving, affectionate, open and responsive to the initiative of his spouse.

THE PATIENT PERSONALITY AT WORK

The Patient Personality seeks employment or a career that permits him to make good use of his service orientation: social work, nursing, medicine, law, counseling, teaching, administration, secretarial work, customer relations, guiding travel tours, industrial relations, and so on. Any responsible work that involves people is attractive, especially when appreciation is one of the compensations. Comments of gratitude or visible signs of having helped go a long way toward making the day for the Patient Personality. He can return home feeling that he has contributed to the well-being of his fellow humans.

The Patient worker thrives on a job where supervision is casual and the routine predictable. He doesn't like the unexpected; he prefers the working situation where he can plan and organize and produce at his own pace. Since he is so responsible, he does his work well and is highly productive. But when supervision is rigid and demanding and the schedule hurried, you can expect the Patient worker to resort to his silent will-struggle as his way of expressing his discontent. Otherwise he is a well-disciplined, responsible worker who is industrious in pursuit of his career goal. He works well with others—his desire to please others and to conciliate are tremendous working assets. While he might not actively seek a leadership role— he doesn't like to compete; he wouldn't want to hurt someone else —he very well might be boosted for that role by his co-workers or by an aware superior. But when he holds a supervisory position, his patience and tolerance of the faults of others might be viewed from above as a weakness. Indeed, he can be overly patient.

His worst fault may be his dislike for placing demands on others. Since he feels so responsible he expects that others simply ought to know what is expected of them; and if they do not perform as expected, he might try to help them by doing the job himself. The Patient Personality, in fact, is sometimes so busy making others look good that his apparent work performance suffers by comparison. But he will say nothing—unless, perhaps, his seniority or security is threatened. All in all, the Patient Personality is well-liked and respected on the job, the kind of worker or supervisor who is prized for his talents, purpose, and productivity, who builds team spirit while keeping things moving toward the goal.

His home orientation and his focus on family life may prompt the Patient careerist to decline a promotion that would involve relocation or would require him to spend more time at the office or to take work home. One high-salaried project engineer, for example, found his work increasingly conducive to spending more and more time on the job. He was given the more interesting and challenging projects. The best people were assigned to his group. Whatever was needed to complete a project was made available. But late one night this Patient engineer realized how much of the time he was away from home and how much he missed his family; he began to feel guilty that he was so seldom available as father and husband. Within a month, he located a new position with a much lower salary and with far less prestige. But he was able to spend evenings and weekends with his family, and he felt more alive and much more involved in those things that mattered most to him. Once again, ever and always, home is where the heart is.

In a business world that values the aggressive styles of the Ambitious, Accomplishing, and Influencing Personalities, the great worth and the low-keyed contributions of the Patient Personality are undervalued. This is a person who has a great capacity for reducing issues to their essences. He insists on dealing with facts in a straightforward, thorough, and deliberate manner, resisting impulsive actions and pressure tactics. He keeps the goal always in mind. His unassuming style invites others to share in the enterprise. He is able to promote conciliation and consensus through patient persuasion. And he is able to reduce risk by proceeding cautiously and patiently, always advocating "letting the dust settle." The Patient Personality takes his time making a decision, thinking through the alternatives, and working through problems in a gradual, yet direct fashion. When he makes a decision, it is firm and resolute, and he pursues it forcefully. He does all this without bluster or pretense and without bruising egos. All in all, the Patient Personality is a highly productive person. He knows how to achieve, he enjoys success, and he is quite willing to share his successes.

Retirement is rarely a problem for the Patient Personality. He usually enjoys travel and a variety of recreational activities such as gardening, golf, or tennis, or just walking in the cool of the evening. The Patient Personality maintains contact with family and friends, always remembers birthdays and anniversaries, always makes himself available when there is sickness or a problem where he can lend a hand.

ALTERNATIVES AND OPTIONS

Family, friends, and working associates all note that the Patient Personality is modest and moderate in all things, loyal, genial, and gentle. He prizes honesty and integrity, truth and moral values. He wants others to like him, and he strives never to hurt anyone or to get hurt. He is something of a loner, tending to be a bit reserved and self-contained, and he also tends to define the ground rules of his relationships. He is usually viewed as a strong person, although in a quiet, unaggressive way. He pursues life with great simplicity, disdaining pretension and vanity. He is noticeably plainspoken and direct, yet never threatening, given to ending statements with comments such as, "Don't you agree?" or, "Isn't that right?"

The Patient Personality sometimes appears to others as rather indecisive. But, in fact, he pursues decisions with unruffled deliberation, choosing to follow fact and his own instincts. As others observe, "He knows his own mind." Still, he is capable of compromise, except in moral values. Whether at work or in social circumstances, the Patient Personality is a gifted listener, always attentive, responsive, and understanding. He can also be an artful talker, though he tends to guide the conversation away from his privacy and any declaration of his needs, wishes, or desires. So sometimes he is evasive, but always in a kind and gentle way. He is also prone to protect the status quo as another tactic for defending his privacy and security. This sometimes gives the impression that he is shy or conservative; while he maintains a wide circle of friends, only a few really know him intimately.

Family is always the center of the Patient Personality's world. Here, if anywhere, he can form close and enriching relationships, relax, find interests and activities that deflect the worries and stresses of the outside world. If he is open and flexible, home is the secure emotional environment that permits closeness and interdependence, the place where he can admit needs, wants, and desires. Still, wherever you find the mature Patient Personality, he is contributing significantly yet in a quiet and unassuming way to everyone around him.

Given his tendency to give too readily and too widely, the less mature Patient Personality can find the stress excessive, and then he has the urge to withdraw or to engage in a will-struggle that is silent yet tenacious. Or, at other times, he can be the selfish giver who often paralyzes the recipients of his largesse, often making them feel inadequate. And he can stifle the efforts of others to meet his needs or to make him happy, frustrating others by evasive responses such as, "Whatever you say," or, "Whatever you want to do." When troubled, his greatest fear is that others will desert or abandon him. Giving is his way of paying dues for membership in the human family—he fears that if he fails to pay his dues in the currency of service and giving, he will be expelled from the company of other people. So he pays and then overpays. He tries very hard to hide his own needs and wishes, fearing that he will burden others who might then hurt him by abandoning him. He finds it hard ever to admit his needs or to say no to the demands of others.

There are options and alternatives for the overburdened Patient Personality to consider, insights to ponder and pursue, choices to be made so that what may seem like vulnerable moments may in fact be great opportunities for happiness.

If you are a Patient Personality, consider these points:

• No one can read your mind. Share your needs and desires. Don't hesitate. Communicate. Let others be as giving to you as you are to them. Reality is sharing—giving *and* receiving. Healthy human relationships suppose mutuality and reciprocity.

• It is selfish, not generous, to deny others the opportunity to be generous.

• Oysters need shells. People don't. Your needs and feelings and desires aren't so demanding that others will shun you or abandon you. So unless you're an oyster, avoid stewing.

• Your quest for security is potentially a great building block; used wisely, it can be a solid part of the structure of your happiness. Otherwise it can become a stumbling block or a roadblock.

• Your home is your castle, but don't consider it under siege every time someone approaches who might make a demand of you. Keep an open-door policy. Let people and ideas flow in and out and all around your life, even your home life, without supposing that you will have to give more. Security is as much a matter of attitude as it is of locks and keys.

• Expect to be disappointed and you will be disappointed. This is a self-fulfilling prophecy. Here again, be open-minded and optimistic, but not to the extreme of playing Pollyanna.

• "Peace at any price" comes at a terrible price: no peace at all, only an illusion. Reality has to be faced, decisions have to be made, risks have to be taken. Security and peace have to be earned. Happiness has a price: dealing realistically with problems on a day-to-day basis. Don't play the waiting game. Problems won't simply fade away. This is another illusion that worsens problems.

• Beware of paralyzing others with your selfish giving. People feel helpless and inadequate when they are never permitted to do things for themselves. Or they may begin to overexpect of you, not realizing that you too are human. Or your abundant giving can so overwhelm others that they may do what you fear the most: shun you. Glutted generosity is terribly discomforting.

• You are afraid at times of not getting enough. This is one reason you never admit your needs.

• Stop being so subtle and devious about your desires. Understatements are like whispers in a windstorm—no one can hear them. Speak up. Be direct.

• You have a right to moments of solitude, but don't let these moments stretch into isolation. Your tendency to keep a distance between you and others is another of your protective devices against the threat of having to do more.

• You have a right to remain silent—unless your silence is making others unhappy. And it does. So much silence can be misread as sullen anger, displeasure, boredom, coldness. Occasional expressions of your true feelings can prevent your silence from being misread. Others will feel better knowing your real feelings, and so will you.

• Beware of the will-struggle, that stubborn streak in you that runs silently and deeply through your threatened moments. Such a struggle! You fear that everyone is demanding too much of you, but the real pressure is only from you. So stop struggling. Go fishing or golfing or bicycling. Better still, open up. Let someone do something for you. Ask, and don't fear a no. Those close to you are just waiting for any chance to give to you.

• For every time that you find yourself giving and giving, try to make a small request of the other person.

• You operate well from the stance of "letting the dust settle." But too often you are still waiting long after the dust has settled. This is like holding your breath—nothing good happens. After the dust settles, settle your problems. Then comes genuine peace and security. Keep in mind this comment by Edmund Burke: "The only thing necessary for the triumph of evil is for a good man to do nothing."

• The person who clings to a security blanket clings to a fragile and flimsy fragment. The greatest hazard to happiness is to risk nothing. Only the person who can risk life and love and joy is a secure person—that is, a free and alive person.

• Practice saying no. Otherwise you might become known as Patsy Patient, the person who is unable to distinguish the appropriate from the inappropriate request. If you learn to say no, your fear of always having to say yes will diminish significantly.

• Avoid answering offers and invitations with ambiguous remarks like "Maybe" and "It's okay."

• Don't play the martyr. Martyrs are venerable, but they aren't easy to get close to or have fun with or to make love to.

• Your silent tears won't wash away your pent-up feelings of being so heavily burdened. Sharing your feelings is a better way of dealing with frustration.

• Time, you can take it. But should you? Your shoulders wouldn't have to be so broad if you would speak up. It takes less muscle to speak up than to carry the world on your shoulders.

• Don't rehearse your grievances. Speak your mind when the situation that irritates you is present.

• Try to remember this slogan while you are busy doing for others and giving to others: "I can have my piece of the cake." But don't settle for dessert by missing the whole meal that goes with it.

• It isn't too realistic to be always self-contained. Everybody needs somebody sometime, even most of the time.

• Quit supposing that the rest of humanity is made in your image and likeness. It isn't fair, really, to suppose that everyone should be as security-conscious, as self-contained, and as generous as you are. Nor is it really fair to suppose that others can read your mind.

• Try to see yourself as others see you: a strong but gentle person —strong enough in your remarkable talents to be attractive and valued, gentle enough in manner to be admired and respected and desired as a good friend. What you are as a person is much more appreciated than simply your impulse to give.

• If you keep your eye on your goals, and if you organize and plan your approach to your goals, you will find that you feel less burdened than when you approach every task in a haphazard fashion.

• You are a very important person in the life of your family and friends, but your belief that "no one can take my place" only adds to that burdensome feeling that you have to do everything for everyone. This is a selfish illusion.

• Don't always be so humble. You underestimate your worth as a person and your value as a friend.

• Doing less won't make you less a person. It will give you more time to be relaxed, refreshed, and just the pleasant person people like so much.

• Sometimes being so understanding is self-indulgent, a mushy way of dealing with others—and sometimes a crippling way of handling relationships.

• Ever notice that you are a different person out for an evening, away from the demands of home and family? If you haven't, your spouse and friends have. You are delightful and radiant, not that serious and burdened workhorse always busy doing and giving. Go out more often. You deserve it. And having you relaxed and having fun is something others deserve.

• To those whom you need, say, "I need you." They would very much like to hear it. To those whom you love, say, "I love you." Love thrives on communication. To those who give to you, say, "Thank you." That would be generous.

VII

*Independence, creativity,
and self-reliance are
all facilitated when
self-criticism and self-
evaluation are basic and
evaluation by others is of
secondary importance.*

CARL ROGERS

The Anticipating
Personality

SHOULD YOU WONDER about that fine, old chair stored in
your grandmother's attic, consult an Anticipating antique dealer. If
he says it is an authentic Morris chair, you can believe him; the
Anticipating Personality appreciates authenticity; he himself is genuine. If you are shopping for quality clothing but feel you know
nothing of cloth, cut, or style, you can rely on the Anticipating
clothier—he is concerned about quality; he knows quality. If you
are considering setting up a retirement fund, you would do well to
seek the advice of an Anticipating investment counselor. The Anticipating Personality is fully attuned to the future, and would anticipate your needs with great care and planning. But if what you need
at the moment is a touch of warmth and good feeling, then invite
an Anticipating friend over for coffee and conversation—the Anticipating Personality has a knack for generating warmth and good
feelings.

In a world that sometimes caters to synthetics and substitutes, to instant fads and electronic fakery, the Anticipating Personality is the real thing. He wants to be genuine and authentic in everything he does; he cares about the quality of life and about the quality of his contribution to life. And who he is is important to him; he sees himself as a rather creative, capable, self-reliant person who pursues his objectives in life with conviction. At the same time, he holds those close to him in high regard; each is a very important person, and he always seems to know when and how to encourage, to compliment, to praise, to applaud. And he does it all so convincingly. His presence is refreshing and reassuring. He radiates charm and generates optimism, making the future look believably bright. The Anticipating Personality, you might say, is life's own cheerleader.

The Anticipating Personality is convinced that he or she is a very adequate person who will succeed in whatever tasks he accepts. If she is writing an advertising campaign for a new soap, she is convinced she will do a terrific job of making the product known to everyone who bathes. She believes that the key to the success of this soap is her advertising effort.

The Anticipating Personality's faith that his role is pivotal reflects his concept of self as important. The very essence of this style centers on the question: "How important am I?" And there is only one acceptable answer: "I am important, and what I am doing is important." And when the Anticipating Personality says so, you can believe it. He insists on being genuine, and he possesses the tools to assure that what is happening will reflect the quality the Anticipating Personality expects: a probing, searching, experimenting involvement giving order to all the elements in the task; the ability to anticipate the results and all the steps necessary to the task to produce good results. Thus the Anticipating Personality has reason for feeling confident about his own importance. It has nothing to do with a puffed-up ego; rather, it has a great deal to do with a sense of contributing significantly to one's own life and to all of life around him.

THE WORRYING URGE

If the essential element of the Anticipating Personality is how important he sees himself, how important he feels, and if he is so concerned to inject that quality into whatever he does, then there is the danger that he can carry his planning, arranging, and anticipating too far. He becomes caught up in the *worrying urge*. He is so concerned that everything go right he begins to anticipate everything that might go wrong. He goes too far, and he ends up worrying. Then he hesitates. He faces the task before him, and he wonders: "How well will I do?" If he is reasonably healthy, with good feelings about himself, he can realistically measure his talents and competence against the scope of the task—he can anticipate the appropriate outcome. If he and the project at hand are reasonably matched, he can be expected to plan and organize efficiently, then move into the task, confident of doing a quality job. But if the Anticipating Personality is less mature, less sure of himself and his competence—however appropriate his talents are to the task—he might back away. He very well might anticipate every conceivable problem, every possible pitfall, every snag, every danger—even a few that aren't too possible. He feels less than adequate to the task. He supposes that his personal resources are inferior, that he will do poorly, that he will botch the job. So he might put off the task, wait for another opportunity—there is always tomorrow.

Take, for example, our advertising copywriter who is an Anticipating Personality. She is aware of her writing talents, and she realizes how important an advertising campaign is to the success of a new product. She has fully digested all the laboratory reports on the new soap, so she is confident that this is a better bath soap than exists on the market. But she is somewhat hesitant about the scent. If they like it in Louisville, will they like it in Los Angeles? She has studied the market research, and she wonders if the copy she is considering for the East will go over well in the South. How effective is the name, the design of the wrapper, the model's image for the soap, the tentative slogan? Will it all mesh into one singular impression of a quality bath soap? She wonders. She worries. If she is that healthy, self-reliant Anticipating Personality who knows how well she can write, how her copy always reflects her own ability to charm and persuade, how fully adequate she is to the task, then she can move ahead, confident, as always, that she can put all the pieces together. If the campaign goes well and the new soap is a success, she will be able to assess her own contribution and give herself credit. Even if it doesn't turn out to be an overwhelming success, she will be able to acknowledge that she did her best and still give herself credit.

On the other hand, if our Anticipating advertising writer is less confident going into the campaign—this product and this campaign are something new—she may worry too much about Louisville and Los Angeles, too much about the scent and the wrapper and how she will handle the slogan. She might roam around the agency seeking reassurance from colleagues. Or she might decide to hold up writing copy until she has a look at proofs of new photographs being shot at the studio. Meanwhile, she might quarrel with the designer of the soap wrapper, snipping and sniping, trying to cut him down to her own feeling of inferiority. That contagious confidence and radiant charm have dimmed to gloomy gray. Fretful and unsure, hope soured, she may even begin to worry how the results of the coming campaign might affect her future with the agency. "Maybe I should quit before they fire me." Doomsday looms large, even before she has written the first word of copy.

VULNERABILITIES AND CRISES

What could happen to convert a perfectly confident and capable, personable and optimistic young woman into feelings of gloom, doom, and inadequacy? Change. Something new. The Anticipating Personality thrives on the familiar, the usual. If he is surrounded by a familiar environment while pursuing a familiar task, the outcome is relatively certain. Every step along the way, like the outcome, can be anticipated. But a new situation, change, or anything else that might pose a threat can prompt feelings of unsureness. It not only impairs his perception of the task, it impairs the Anticipating Personality's perception of himself. He might consider himself inferior to the task; worse, he might consider himself inferior to others approaching the same task. He gets very down on himself, and strange things happen. This warm and charming person can become anxious, irritable, and negative. Self-assurance teeters and sometimes topples. Confidence may collapse. His certitude about his own importance and adequacy might dwindle into a faltering sense of inadequacy and inferiority. Why, he wonders, isn't he as confident and capable as the next person? The words "dumb" and "stupid" creep into his vocabulary—in reference to himself, in reference to everyone else involved: "If I make a mistake, I ask myself, 'How could I do such a stupid thing?' And when someone else makes a mistake, I don't mind telling him about it." This blunt style of criticizing seems very negative, but beneath the harsh words and cutting tone is the deep-felt desire to move his own performance and that of others up to a higher level.

When things aren't going well, the upset Anticipating Personality may just as easily take the tack opposite to sniping. He might praise and even flatter others as an expression of his lowly feelings. When he says, "Hey, you're really doing a great job," to a colleague moving ahead with a job, he may be saying that in contrast to the way he feels about his own performance. What he feels is, "I'm doing a lousy job." Whether praising or cutting his colleague, he is grading himself as inferior, and he really supposes that everyone else thinks he is inferior. His expectations of himself are so exaggerated in terms of quality that he begins to back off, slow down, hesitate. He fears testing his skills and competence; he anticipates failure. He would rather hold off than produce something of poor quality, and, as every Anticipating Personality who has had a bad day knows, it is difficult to feel genuine or important when you sense nothing but forthcoming failure. Better to do nothing than to botch the job. And just that feeling is the mother of every cop-out, a tactic all too familiar to the anxious Anticipating Personality.

ONE STEP AT A TIME

For all the fretting and fussing, the uneasy Anticipating Personality is remarkably like his self-assured counterpart when he is coaxed into action through one form of reassurance or another. Even better for him is self-motivation; if he can talk to himself in a positive, confidence-building way to get moving, he has learned a technique that is helpful in any uncertain moment. But either way—through the assurance of others or self-assurance—he benefits. Once he takes the first step, he can do the job. Once he stops worrying and starts working, he becomes productive. He discovers that he really isn't inferior or insignificant. He can succeed at the task, performing smoothly and well, and it doesn't matter whether the task at hand is writing advertising copy or a sales report, changing a diaper or changing middle management—he can do it with conviction, confidence, and sureness of purpose. And the quality shows.

But, alas, praise the less steady Anticipating Personality for the job well done and you risk another kind of problem. Compliment him and he well might shrink back into a worrying state. He wonders, "Did you really mean that, or are you putting me on?" Remember, he sometimes compliments others as a way of putting himself down, so he isn't sure that you aren't doing the same thing. He suspects you are flattering, faking praise.

The Anticipating Personality seems to function under the norms of Newton's first law of motion. An Anticipating Personality at rest tends to remain at rest—that is, he doesn't seem sure enough of what lies ahead to get started; but an Anticipating Personality in motion tends to remain in motion—that is, he continues to function with sureness and efficiency. He works smoothly and well. Good things happen. Quality is stamped on process and product. He radiates confidence and warmth. He is great to have around. But don't change the task or the circumstance—even the healthy and confident Anticipating Personality, we noted earlier, can be threatened by change. If he is healthy enough, he recognizes his vulnerability, accepts the moment, and works through it. If not so healthy, he may revert to his unsure pattern of worrying and fretting, butterflies bouncing around his stomach. He may begin to slough, slide, and evade. Cop-outs loom in every direction.

This pattern of threat in the face of newness or change is evident whether at work or at play, at home or at school, in childhood or in adulthood. Entry into school can provoke a crisis. So can graduation from high school or college. So can entry into the job market or moving to a new neighborhood. A promotion can pose a problem. The line supervisor, informed that he has been made department head, might insist on a memo verifying his promotion, or he might ask immediately how large a raise he can expect; he wants proof; he wants to know that the promotion is genuine. But more, he is beginning to anticipate; he is beginning to worry how well he will do.

A transfer from one plant to another or from one city to another would prompt some worry, whether the Anticipating Personality is healthy or not. The children leaving home can strip an Anticipating parent of his or her sense of importance, the authenticating role as provider and protector of his children. A new home might present

156

the usually confident Anticipating homemaker with so many new tests of her adequacy: carpeting, drapes, and furnishings; color co-ordination and room arrangements. In these and all like situations, the great temptation for the less confident Anticipating Personality is to unload the responsibility onto someone else or simply to escape, to flee, to cop out.

SHADES OF GRAY

Emotional health, maturity, or how well an individual reacts under stress is not divided sharply into black and white areas. The healthy Anticipating Personality can question praise, can slip in confidence, can momentarily falter when faced with a difficult task or a new experience. And the less healthy Anticipating Personality, as noted, can perform well under familiar circumstances. The areas of gray vary from individual to individual. One facet of this style that generally comes through is the prevalent charm and social grace. You will normally find the Anticipating Personality open, easily met, and disarming. He is attentive, affable, sympathetic, understanding. His compliments are gracious, so warm and expressive and full of feeling that you feel a glow spreading over you. His manner is so engaging that you want to believe you deserve every word of praise. He will unerringly find your good points and garnish them with compliments. Moreover, in these same circumstances he is a good listener. For example, you are chatting at a party with a charming, attractive Anticipating woman, and she is attentive to every word you speak. She responds with a large smile and just the right comment that highlights and affirms your remarks; and then she immediately praises your insights and wisdom. You feel like a sage. While there may be just a hint of exaggeration in her generous response, you never question her sincerity. Nor does she; she tries always to be genuine, however casual the moment. But later that evening, on reflection, she may feel that she overdid it a bit, and for a moment she may be concerned lest she be guilty of fakery. But no; her enthusiasm and her genuine desire to be responsive and open were real enough—and she is not unaware that she has always had this personal quality that charms people.

This quality of charm and grace comes naturally and comfortably to the Anticipating Personality, especially among friends. The smaller the crowd, the dearer the friends, the greater the charm and grace. Colleagues at the office might, for example, be somewhat surprised to learn that this poised and highly professional person could belly dance at a small party for old friends: "A lot of people don't see the frolicking side. I like to ham it up with my husband and friends. We do dumb things just for fun." Alone with her husband, she might turn on the stereo and dance with him, teasing and laughing until they end up wrestling on the floor. Feeling healthy and happy, she can be as silly as she wants without worrying. Such is their relationship, so genuine and real, that she knows that whatever she does, she can anticipate her husband's full approval.

But here again there are shades of gray. The Anticipating Personality is always concerned about looking right and not looking foolish. The larger the crowd and the less familiar the faces, the greater the concern that he or she might look foolish. One very healthy Anticipating Personality commented to me that she has difficulty getting close to new people: "I can be a little standoffish. I worry that I might not do the right thing or that I might look stupid." And she admits too that if she is in a roomful of people, she may shy away from the one person she doesn't feel comfortable with: "I'm always conscious of that one person. If she is at one end of the room, I stay at the other end."

A less confident Anticipating Personality might not stay in the same room in the circumstance; he might find a convenient excuse to leave rather than chance encountering that discomforting person. And a less confident Anticipating Personality might possibly keep all social activity restricted to a very tight circle of old and good friends. Even in social situations, newness can be unsettling. The Anticipating Personality might feel a bit apprehensive when a stranger is introduced, wondering how this new presence will alter the social atmosphere, the comfortable mix of people. Given the chance, he might check out the newcomer before any personal encounter—as always, trying to anticipate: how will their meeting come off? Still, with all his resiliency, even a stranger would find the Anticipating Personality easily met and disarming. The effort is always there; the Anticipating Personality wants to be genuine and important in any situation. And he wants to be liked. That, too, is important.

158

Friends are very dear to the Anticipating Personality. He remembers birthdays and anniversaries, tries to get together whenever possible, maintains correspondence or telephones old friends who live at a distance. The Anticipating Personality wants all relationships to be authentic and true. Friendships are never casual. He tends them carefully and prizes the constancy of a relationship. Loss of a friend is painful and troubling, and the Anticipating Personality can even be possessive with friends, not wanting to share them. He can also be very generous with friends, sometimes to a fault.

For example, one Anticipating teenager, always a good student and never a moment of trouble at home or at school, was caught shoplifting one Christmas. He had no money, but he knew his best friend particularly liked this new pocket calculator, and he thought it important that his friend have it. Their friendship was special, so he took the calculator. Had he been more sure of himself and confident in the relationship, he might have avoided a very sad situation. Instead of looking good in his friend's eyes, he ended up feeling foolish and phony, just how the Anticipating Personality least likes to feel. And this young man who had always worked hard to receive the approval of others now found himself facing the disapproval of family and friends. It was a very sad and worrisome Christmas.

The Anticipating Personality is not only generous with friends; he tends to want to help *anyone* in need, especially the less fortunate. He will readily give to social agencies and community projects, whether he gives money, time, or talent. As one Anticipating Personality comments: "I'd give the shirt off my back if I knew it would help somebody. I like to see the other person happy." Another Anticipating Personality agrees: "I get a good feeling out of helping people." This might be translated to mean: "I feel more significant as a person when I am being of genuine help to others." More, the Anticipating Personality doesn't want to feel inferior, so he would do what he could to remedy that feeling in others.

One way or the other, the Anticipating Personality is a generous, contributive member of the community. But, again, there is always a chance that some vulnerability will surface, even in the exercise of strength. One Anticipating woman who had volunteered to deliver meals to elderly shut-ins had a man snap at her for banging too loudly on the door. "I felt terrible, insulted. I thought I was doing something that I could be proud of, and all I got was criticism," she said. This woman, however, was healthy enough to measure the contribution as more significant than the insult, and so she continued delivering meals to the man, needing his approval less than her own affirmative evaluation of her effort.

FEARS AND PHOBIAS

All of us have fears, large and small, rational and irrational; that's part of being human. But of all personality styles, the Anticipating Personality seems to demonstrate the greatest number of fears and phobias. Any one of us can experience fear of flying on a turbulent day, but why is it that, for example, a certain Anticipating young executive never feared flying until he was asked to attend the corporate management meeting in Boston? We might suspect that it had something to do with a totally new experience of some significance, one in which he could anticipate possibly not making much of an impression with top management. Once he identifies the coincidence of his fear of flying with this very important meeting—and assuming that the meeting went well enough—he might begin to relate his fear with the meeting, and begin to enjoy flying again. Another Anticipating Personality turns down a position with a firm where his office would be small and windowless. Claustrophobia? Yes, and fear that he might not do so well in changing jobs.

Everyone else is tempted to be sympathetic and understanding with the person demonstrating fear—we all remember childhood with its fears of the dark and things that go bump in the night—so the unhealthy fear of the worrying Anticipating Personality finds a receptive audience. Too bad. The troubled individual isn't helped; he is licensed to cop out on some very significant opportunity in his life.

An Anticipating Personality, referred to me by his family doctor after a series of appropriate tests, told me of his fear of having a heart attack and dying. He was afraid to leave home for work; he was certain he would have a heart attack behind the wheel of his car; he would never see his wife and four children again. He couldn't eat or sleep and couldn't get it off his mind that he hadn't taken out the mortgage insurance when he bought his house. After discussing the problem over several visits, we were able to date the onset of his fear to a significant moment at work. Several new safety procedures were to be introduced at the plant where he was responsible for their implementation. That same day, he first experienced the fear of having a heart attack. Once the coincidence was recognized, we could go on to discuss his anticipating that the new safety procedures would not be adequate—he had tried to convince management that they needed more careful study and testing, but he was overruled. He felt he hadn't done a good enough job of presenting his case. The underlying question threatening this man—and every Anticipating Personality in like situations—was: "How well will I function?" The phobia symbolizes the response: maybe not too well. The ultimate phobia is cataphobia, fear of failing.

A phobia is perhaps the anxious Anticipating Personality's more extreme way of copping out, but cop-outs come in a variety of sizes and shapes. The escape routes are imaginative and usually quite logical, the *apparent* solution for handling a particular conflict. However, any success that such a cop-out enjoys is deceiving. Its very success as a means of evading the problem leaves the basic problem unresolved, and it invites repetition of the phobia or other means of escaping. No one can argue with nausea or dizziness or even hand-wringing anguish when the news comes that the boss will arrive for dinner in an hour or that your income tax return is to be audited, but the evasion-prone Anticipating Personality does have other options. First, he must recognize that his worry comes from his intense anticipation that he might not be adequate to the situation. Next, he needs to back up to the present moment to utilize his sense of ordering and setting priorities that makes effective planning possible. What happens next is critical: he needs to move ahead one step at a time. The anxious Anticipating Personality sometimes tends to try to do too much too fast. But progress and genuine achievement come through a series of successive, successful steps; so to perform any task well, whether it relates to job or to family life or to a social situation, the individual must transfer his energy from the future to the present and then proceed in a deliberate, step-by-step fashion. And the last step is always so important: he needs to evaluate his own effort and achievement rather than depend on the evaluations of others. He needs to give himself credit. Worrying can be a habit. So can success. So can self-reliance.

The Anticipating Personality always needs to remember that

when he is working from an attitude of self-reliance, he is functioning from strength. The ability to evaluate his own performance and importance produces a hopeful outlook on life that embraces everyone and everything around him. It permits a somewhat intense and eager focus on the task at hand. When that happens, the Anticipating Personality displays that vibrant yet realistic optimism. He is functioning productively while maintaining a genuine regard for personal integrity—his own and that of others. He is rarely fascinated with the quick and easy solution and its brief moments of glory; his measure is long-term success that brings about something authentic, something of value and lasting quality. He is convinced his vision of his own adequacy and fruitfulness is purposeful, realistic, and attainable. He feels important—and he is.

GROWING UP ANTICIPATING

Parents of the Anticipating child describe him as a happy, cheerful child who is outgoing and affectionate. He seems to need more physical love and praise than children of other personality styles, and he might fuss when left alone. He is not selfish; he likes to share what he has. He can be very generous, devising small gifts and special treats for parents and siblings. He is neither overly aggressive nor overly independent. Still, for all his usually pleasant ways, the Anticipating child is sometimes described as either "up or very down." These mood swings that show early continue on through life; and despite his normally gentle ways, he sometimes displays a quick irritability. He also tends to be something of a worrier, almost as if asking, "Am I a good child?" He might overreact to discipline, feeling that he is receiving disapproval and then feeling poorly about himself.

The Anticipating child sometimes is hesitant about entering school, unsure of the new environment, unable to anticipate what the new experience will be like and how well he will do. But once the strangeness wears away, he does well—although he may not always be a self-starter. There are times when he benefits from some personal contact with the teacher—a nod of recognition, an approving smile—to get going. Neither parents nor teachers note any particular tendency in the Anticipating child to challenge their authority. Rather, he is usually responsive and cooperative, though sometimes noticeably shy. He doesn't, for example, like to have to stand up before the class to give an oral report.

Both parents 'and teachers describe the Anticipating child as loving and playful, as trying hard in school activities, and at home, where he might pursue such activities as cooking or sewing, building things or helping around the house. He is delighted when praised for his accomplishments. He makes friends easily, another characteristic that is evident throughout his life. He has a tendency, however, to be sensitive to teasing and to the opinions of others, and he is inclined sometimes to belittle himself, recalling later in life that "I always felt I wasn't as good as my friends." A very pretty Anticipating child may feel that all the other girls in her class are better looking than she is—or, despite her having many friends, she may feel that nobody likes her. The self image sometimes can be surprisingly poor, baffling to parents. Especially when things aren't going right, the Anticipating child is prone to minimize himself, and then he can be sullen. He may introduce a conversation with a remark such as, "I know you're not going to like this . . ." or "I know that you'll think this is dumb, but . . ." This characteristic also tends to endure even in adulthood.

Childhood memories center on the theme of the Anticipating child's own sense of desirability. When an adult—aunt, uncle, grandparent, godparent, or even a close neighbor—showed particular interest in him, he always felt very special. He tried always to be special to friends, special to parents. Gifts were perceived as verification of his desirability. So were special trips and outings alone with parents. Holidays and family celebrations are recalled warmly in later life as very special moments—not just for the gifts and the festive atmosphere but especially for the delight of dressing up, experiencing closeness and togetherness. All together, it made the child feel very special, very happy.

Another recurring theme of childhood is worry over something the Anticipating child may have done wrong—or thought he had done wrong. A remembrance of feeling "dumb" or inferior is usually associated with the memory of wrongdoing. Themes of concern over health or the well-being of someone close are remembered. One Anticipating child was playing with her aunt's glasses when she dropped them and accidentally stepped on them. She was frightened and started to cry. "All my aunt did," she remembered later, "was tell me to forget it, but I still cried. I felt so stupid." Situations such as this require some tactful handling by parents. Note that telling the worrying Anticipating child not to worry wasn't too effective; the feeling of being "stupid" was much stronger. The child needs to learn, even in a corrective situation, that he can have positive regard for himself. Some correction is indicated—"It's not a good idea to play with glasses"—but so is some attending positive direction—"Why don't you take Aunt Emily out to smell those lovely roses you and I planted and have taken such good care of?" As much as possible, so long as it is genuinely deserved, parents can help the Anticipating child mature through showing approval while avoiding reinforcing fears and negative attitudes. The child benefits especially from positive examples from a liked and trusted adult model. Encouraging the child's interests and activities, inviting him to share in household projects and even parental hobbies help teach him that he is capable while showing regard for him. More, the Anticipating Personality, child and adult, benefits greatly just by keeping busy; so if Mom is baking a pie, let the Anticipating child roll the dough; or if Dad is cutting two-by-fours for a workbench, let him help by holding the wood steady or stacking the cut lengths. That way he will feel involved; he will feel important. But if you tell him, "Go away, kid; you're in the way," you are also telling him that he isn't important—or, worse, that he is inferior, insignificant. And that would be damaging.

ADOLESCENCE

Entry into adolescence, coinciding with entry into junior high or high school, may initiate a crisis of change that can disrupt the happy routine of the Anticipating Personality. Everything is new again. "How well will I do? Am I capable enough? Will the other kids like me?" are all questions that will flow through the thoughts and feelings of the Anticipating Personality changing schools, facing new teachers, mingling with new classmates. Here he needs to remember —or to be reminded of—his accomplishments and good performances in his previous activities. But, again, once he moves into the routine, gets busy, the worrying vanishes; he does well. Nevertheless, each new opportunity or challenge will be an invitation for a new worry. "Will I make orchestra? Will I make the football team? Will I win the debate? Will I be chosen a cheerleader? Will the boys like me? Will the girls like me? Is my nose too long? Am I pretty? Will I flunk trig?" The Anticipating adolescent can work up a worry six months before tryouts for football or cheerleading or whatever. He benefits, of course, from encouraging signs of approval, but he also needs to learn to evaluate his own successes and then give himself approval. Most of all, he needs to keep busy.

During the teen years, as later in adulthood, the unsure Anticipating Personality can be concerned about his appearance. He wants so much to look good because he isn't so sure of his substance, his performance. If her date greets her at the door by saying, "You look nice," that might not be good enough; she says that all the time to her girlfriends. So her date's compliment has to be potent: "Hey! You really look terrific!" Even so, she may ask, "Really?" The Anticipating Personality tends to compliment others rather easily and sometimes lavishly. And he suspects that others might be flattering him, so he has to question just how genuine the compliment is. An hour after her date told her that she looked terrific, the Anticipating teenager might ask again, "Do you really think I look terrific, or were you just being nice?"

Close friendships become consciously important during the teen years. We mentioned earlier the Anticipating adolescent who stole a calculator as a gift for his best friend. Being important to a friend enhances the self-image, and the feedback given by friends is re-assuring; but this desire to be well liked, to have good friends and to feel important, can create pressures and mixed feelings.

One Anticipating young man remembers how badly he wanted to make the varsity football team in high school. As it happened, he not only made the team but became an outstanding quarterback. The role not only assured him popularity, but it assured him a great deal of prestige and importance on campus. He found, however, that the football crowd separated him somewhat from his other friends at school. Still, he went along with the macho style of the other athletes. "I was a good actor, and I could put it on like them when I was around them." But the other group was more his natural element, the friends he enjoyed most. Later on, looking back, he commented that he "felt like I faked it a little," that he gave up a little of his authentic feelings for himself and his other friends by putting so much emphasis on being part of the football set. While he felt he managed to avoid outright hypocrisy in maintaining two differing sets of friends, he did feel he copped out a bit by not being more committed to his truer friends.)

This same young man also noted that sibling rivalries play their part in the Anticipating Personality's need for recognition. While he was quarterback, a four-point student, and senior class president, he always felt that his mother gave more recognition to his younger brother, who seemed to merit mother's doting approval, he said, simply by being "Mom's baby." Again, the ability to evaluate one's own effort and performance effectively is very important.

The Anticipating Personality's tendency to go along with authority still pertains in adolescence. The Anticipating teenager is not your rebel; he usually avoids many of the adolescent perils such as drugs and alcohol because he doesn't want to risk losing control of himself and "looking stupid." He might be drawn to marijuana as a way of handling his worry about an upcoming test or game or dance. But if he were smoking, for example, he wouldn't really enjoy the experience because now he would be worrying about being caught —and getting caught would make him feel horribly stupid. He would feel very poorly about himself, his sense of self-importance diminished to nothing. He wouldn't want to do that.

There are dangers that should be avoided lest they disrupt or divert healthy growth. The two greatest dangers are the two possible extremes: (1) Urging the Anticipating Personality to do too much too fast, and (2) Supporting his worrying tendency. Doing too much too fast is a prelude to failure and its attending feeling of being inferior to everyone else. The Anticipating Personality does much better by utilizing his sense of planning and good preparation and proceeding one step at a time. And should he falter, it isn't to his benefit to support the lull; that only promotes worry. Better to urge him to try a little harder, to remind him of how well he has done in other areas. Should he become enveloped in worry, it doesn't benefit him either by being told to forget about it. No, he needs to get back on the track. He needs to move ahead. The worry ceases when he gets back to work.

COURTSHIP AND MARRIAGE

A person with as much warmth, openness, and social grace as the Anticipating Personality has little difficulty attracting others and

166

forming close relationships. But when the Anticipating Personality finds that one person to whom he can be very special, it is someone who is "calm and easygoing, funloving." "With her I didn't have to act or put on. I could be myself." "He accepted me as I was. And he was so much fun to be with." In effect, the Anticipating Personality is attracted to the person who will permit him to be genuinely himself.

Marriage can be either highly fruitful or somewhat frightening for the Anticipating Personality. Here is a new and profound role, frightening perhaps in its newness and unfamiliarity, its yet-to-be-tested expectations. There is a tendency to worry, anticipating possible problems through the course of marriage; yet marriage can also be a chance to assume a rich and close relationship, authentic in its opportunity for quality, mutuality, growth. The Anticipating Personality no doubt feels the whole range of concern and possibility all at once; and, as always, the worry reduces once the Anticipating Personality enters the routine of married life.

The Anticipating Personality works hard to be a genuine husband or wife. The emphasis put on his or her own adequacy and self-reliance may prompt the Anticipating partner to divide the household and chores on a "his" and "hers" basis. Noted one Anticipating wife: "The house is mine, the garage and the car are his." Each functions according to his own competency. Another Anticipating wife commented: "My husband is much better at decorating, so I want to let him use that talent in our home. But the kitchen is my province. I don't want him encroaching there. I remember one time I came into the kitchen to find him cleaning out the refrigerator, and I just let him have it. I thought he was saying that I wasn't doing the job well enough." Whenever her husband is busy, she feels she has to be busy too. Otherwise she is tempted to feel that he is more interested in the job he is doing than in her. She is prone to ask herself: "Is painting the bathroom more important to him than I am?" Thus she has learned from experience that she can feel much better about herself if she is busy baking a cake, which she does so well, than by comparing herself to the bathroom. And when that luscious smell of cake wafts through the house, she can pat herself on the back while complimenting him on his fine color coordination. No comparing, just complementing compliments.

The Anticipating Personality's concern for quality shows in all things, even while rolling a shopping cart down the aisle of a super-market. She has her favorite brands, even if they cost a few cents more: "I always buy the same brand of green beans because they have the best flavor. I don't care if I'm buying shoes or canned goods or drapes. It has to have quality. And I feel the same way about going out to dinner. If the monthly budget only permits so much for eating out, I would rather go out one night for a good meal than have two so-so meals. Otherwise, I'd prefer to stay home and cook." Her summary comment about the need for injecting quality into whatever she buys or whatever she does: "I just think there's a right way and a wrong way about everything. It should be done right. I'm a perfectionist, I guess."

A large part of being an authentic partner in marriage means putting spouse and children above everything else—sometimes too much so. The Anticipating parent can so invest his or her role identity in the children that when they leave home there is a sinking sense of loss of purpose. This parent might become terribly depressed when the last child is gone. If one of the children were to fail in college, the Anticipating parent might blame himself, feeling somehow he hadn't performed his role as a parent adequately: "I felt like I had done something—or hadn't done something. I failed somewhere along the line."

One young man remembers his Anticipating mother being so intensely involved as a mother that when he broke his arm, she turned the accident into a moment of panic—and she a nurse. "She fretted terribly, so busy asking everyone what to do that I sat there two hours before they got me to the hospital. It was a neighbor who finally took me. But once we got to the hospital, Mom was very good. She explained to me what they were going to do and why they were going to put me out. But when the break happened, she really had a hard time."

Another Anticipating young woman remembers her Anticipating mother: "I remember in high school my Spanish teacher was one of mother's best friends. And that was pressure. I was getting all A's and then I got this one B. Mother blamed herself for that B. She assumed all the inferior feelings, the sense of inadequacy. She felt that if she had done something right—what, I don't know—I would have gotten that other A. Her attitude seemed to be that she wanted to give me everything she didn't have. I felt like I was almost a mini-her going through life. She wanted me to get the grades and to be popular and that sort of thing. Funny, I wanted the same things."

The Anticipating homemaker is meticulous. "If everything in my house is looking good but there are a couple of things out of place in the back bedroom, it doesn't look good to me, and I don't deserve any praise. I hate it when people come in and say, 'Your home really looks lovely.' I'm sitting there thinking, 'No, you ought to see the back bedroom. It looks like hell.' This isn't something you learn in life; it comes built in to your way of looking at life. I don't look at what I have done. I look at what I haven't done." What she is missing is the good feeling due her for all that she has done well, but her fretful feelings about the small things that aren't done to her satisfaction steal the moment. And she really does deserve a pat on the back.

The children know too well the thorough, particular ways of the Anticipating parent: "There were four of us kids, and we all had specific jobs. Our house was always nice. You didn't just mop the kitchen floor; you got down on your hands and knees and scrubbed and scrubbed until it was done expertly. Mom always went over to the corners to see if you had scraped out the dirt. You did it again every Saturday morning. Mom would have made a great Army sergeant."

THOSE FRETFUL MOMENTS

The Anticipating spouse might find it difficult if the mate shows interest in activities away from home. The Anticipating husband, for example, might display all sorts of irritability when his wife works: the house is a mess, the meals aren't what they once were, the children look neglected. And the Anticipating wife might complain about the long hours her husband works, his fatigue, his greater interest in the job than in the children. As long as the situation remains unresolved, the greater the chances are that the irritability will develop into bitterness and full-scale nagging. The problem is that the Anticipating spouse is feeling a lessening sense of adequacy and importance with the partner's outside involvement. This sniping routine is designed to bring the other person down to his own feelings of inferiority—and when the attack reaches its full fury, everyone does indeed feel rotten. One possible way of counteracting the problem is for the Anticipating partner to pursue something like parity. When the other person is working late or engaged in some activity away from home, the Anticipating spouse might arrange to take care of a special task, to go bowling or to a movie, or to visit a good friend that he hasn't seen for a while.

Other situations that might provoke crisis in the Anticipating Personality are marital problems, including divorce, in which he would question how well he handled the responsibilities of marriage; the death of a spouse; the birth of the first child; problems in his children's lives, such as poor performance in school, unacceptable friends, or the use of drugs or alcohol; when the children leave home; job reversals or loss of employment. Any such situation prompts fretful questions of adequacy or competency, ability to cope, comparing self to others in a like situation, inferior feelings, confusion, possibly depression. I know of one Anticipating mother who experienced let-down feelings when she stopped nursing her baby. She began to feel she wasn't as needed as she had been.

A job reversal might be particularly threatening. If a younger man were to assume his responsibilities—or even part of them—the Anticipating Personality might absent himself for a time claiming illness, even if he fled instead to the golf course or the racetrack. He might exhibit jealousy, even rage, fearing that the change in his status really expressed some loss of faith in his competency or effort or value to the company. And he does not like the advent of retirement, feeling that this disrupts his sense of self-importance. A certain lingering question of his inferiority continues to roll through his thoughts.

The initial reaction in any of these situations is voiced in several styles of complaint: "I'm just not happy," "I have a habit of blowing everything," "I guess I could do better," "I don't live up to the hopes of others when I'm given responsibility"—and variations on the same theme. When this prevailing mood goes unaltered and unresolved, look for a greater show of irritability and bitterness. The worrying Anticipating Personality will begin to shun responsibility, arrange for others to perform his task and functions. Unchecked, the mood slides into depression, with anger, tears, and bitter projections of self-contempt thrust onto others.

Item: "My sixty-eight-year-old mother was visiting us, and she gave us $6,000 for a new car. I really felt miserable. Here we were, married all these years, we still didn't own a home, and we still need to accept money from my mother. So what did I do? I ripped into my husband who was out of a job. Then I began to see what I was doing. I was feeling so inferior and so put down that I had to put someone else down."

Other signs of feeling inadequate and inferior are the teasing of others, although the Anticipating Personality really hates to be teased, and prankish put-ons that are really put-downs. Or the Anticipating Personality might begin to worry about his health or the health of others. He might find himself identifying with an aunt or uncle who died at his age; then he becomes preoccupied with death. The way he feels, he might as well die, he feels that he has lost his purpose in life.

THE WORKING WORLD

The fear of new challenges, new frontiers, and new encounters might make the Anticipating Personality hesitate to enter the job market. If he is nearing graduation from college, he might be tempted to change majors in his senior year, or to go on to do graduate work, as a way of avoiding the new demands of the working world. But, as always, once he crosses the threshold of the new and unfamiliar, he becomes an energetic, resourceful, responsible performer. He is a delight to co-workers, charming while not being too aggressive in his career goals. He will pursue a job situation where he can anticipate the benefits and advantages, the opportunities for functioning well and moving along in his career. He might, of course, also project all the pitfalls and problems. But once in motion, he tends to stay in motion. He is noticed early by supervisors and management as a comer.

The Anticipating Personality works so well in so many fields that it would be difficult to suggest them all. He is a very curious person who is always gathering more knowledge in his areas of interest. He makes a fine journalist, a good investigator, an excellent public relations or advertising person. His planning skills and anticipation of problems and needs, mixed with his creative bent, make him a very good architect. His insistence on quality serve him well in any quality-control work or inspection. Because of his abiding regard for the quality and authenticity of relationships, he makes a fine counselor, whether with married couples or children; and for the same reasons, he would do well in any part of the medical professions. He might greatly enjoy acting, if not as a profession perhaps as hobby or recreation, performing well and authentically, bringing quality to a role. The least attractive working areas perhaps include any traveling position—the constant shifting of environment being uncomfortable and threatening; or trouble-shooting—he wouldn't be at his best working constantly in the unexpected and the strange. He makes an excellent supervisor in almost any field that he chooses since he has such regard for people and for relationships.

While considered so promotable, the Anticipating Personality might be tempted to shy from it—and he might decline a promotion that necessitated relocation. Transfer to another line would find him vulnerable to anticipation of problems and concern about his qualifications. He might suppose he wouldn't or couldn't do well; others might do so much better. Those insidious feelings of inferiority sneak up on him, and he is sorely tempted to cop out or to slip away from the occasion, offering every excuse imaginable. The rising young executive offered an attractive position with another firm in another city might know very well that his career is at the threshold of real success, but he is concerned about leaving his aging parents—even though his two brothers and a sister live not far from them. Then too, his children might find it hard to make the adjustment—meaning, of course, that *he* would find it hard to make the adjustment himself. And he doesn't want his wife to have to forfeit her macramé classes—even though she has expressed her support and enthusiasm for the new job. Still, on face value, he seems so genuinely concerned for his parents, his children, and his wife that you could readily believe him. Moreover, he believes himself. But, once again, his worrying urge prompts him to want to cop out, even though there is little doubt—certainly not on the part of the firm wanting to hire him—that he would be found highly competent. And he no doubt would be content, productive, confident, and would feel good about his importance to the new firm once he accepted the challenge and got to work.

If an Anticipating worker were faced with a strike at his factory, he would experience some stress, questioning his adequacy, the future of the company, the financial and social well-being of his family. At times like this, he might turn to the bottle a little too freely or simply sit around and wallow in his worry, feeling useless and inferior, pondering further reasons for viewing himself a failure. He might decide that the time off during the strike is a good time for painting the kitchen and bathroom, but when he begins to measure the walls, inspects all the cracks and peeling paint, prices the quantity of paint needed—a quality paint, of course—and consults his wife on the colors, the task mushrooms into nightmarish worry. Better to take the kids fishing to escape the fuss and worry of strikes and painting—all of which, he knows, will still be there to trouble him when he returns. But if he wanted to make it a week-long fishing trip, he might not make it at all. Worry about packing gear, getting the car ready, stocking food supplies, packing clothing and so on would so burden him that he might decide to call it off—unless he made a careful list of everything and then proceeded one step at a time. But then, there is this too: What if the fish aren't biting?

The Anticipating Personality always works well from a list and by executing items one at a time in advance of any set deadline. Notes one Anticipating Personality preparing for winter: "All my flowers are out of the ground, the bushes are mulched, the trees trimmed. Long before the cold weather hits, I have the car tuned, the antifreeze checked, and the snow tires put on. The furnace is cleaned and the filter changed. The fireplace is checked and the cordwood stacked. That way I'm ready. If something isn't right, like the furnace, I'm not caught waiting three or four days for the furnace man to come. By planning properly, I can do it all a little at a time, and I never have to rush. When I'm rushed, I always seem to bungle the job and have to do it over."

ALTERNATIVES AND OPTIONS

All things considered, the Anticipating Personality is usually a content, self-reliant, generous person who contributes significantly to the human good, even when he isn't as aware as others are of how much he contributes. In a culture that often puts more emphasis on imagery than on substance, the Anticipating Personality is greatly concerned with authenticity and integrity. If he is a plumber, he is concerned that his customers receive a full measure of skill and competency along with sound materials. No skimping. If he is a construction engineer, he will build a bridge that will survive its need. If he is an accountant, his clients and the Internal Revenue Service can be sure that both parties have their due. And if he is a photographer, he will capture the true and lasting moments of his generation. And whether plumber or engineer or photographer—whatever —those who share his work and his life will experience genuine moments of charm and grace, his deep regard for others and their well-being. To all this add a touch of mirth and merriment, hope and optimism, and you have a very healthy Anticipating Personality who functions productively, sure of himself and his capabilities, willing to share them with others. He values his friends always and gives to them generously. He is a person of convictions who lives them out with fidelity. He always wants to be genuine.

Even so, with all his marvelous traits, the Anticipating Personality doesn't always recognize how much he contributes, how much people enjoy his warmth and admire his integrity. He doesn't always give himself enough credit. He is sometimes prone to insure his substance (or lack of it) by being concerned over his appearance—like the woman who purchased new prescription glasses, but, after her daughter told her that she didn't like the style, never felt comfortable again wearing them. Anything new or different in his routine and life situation might cause him to worry, anticipating an unfavorable outcome. He may be tempted to evade the new situation or at least to temporize, and he might be too aware of the person sharing responsibility or working in a similar capacity. Also, he is prone to comparing capabilities with a tendency to grant the other person superiority, thus assigning himself the inferior ranking. His urge then is to escape the situation, to cop out—or he might lash out, attempting to downgrade the other person to his own feelings of inferiority. He nags, snipes, complains, when feeling down; he wants others to support him, to assure him, to praise and compliment him, but he has a hard time accepting praise as genuine. He tends himself to overstate compliments, feeling again that others do things so much better than he does. And while doing any or all of these things, he very well could be busy worrying and fretting, feeling the palms of his hands damp with nervous sweat.

The Anticipating Personality who recognizes himself as less sure of his capabilities can be too pessimistic, too worried to test his competence. His confidence erodes; he anticipates failure. Shrouded in gloom, he begins to tear everyone down. No one can do anything right, himself most of all. He anticipates disaster. Full of worry, he too often permits himself to be molded by others. His mood swings up, then down. He wants to be rid of all responsibility, to cop out. When these things happen, he needs to be aware that he has options that will help him move beyond worry and gloom into real productivity and regard for himself.

If you are an Anticipating Personality, consider the following points:

• Plan ahead. Make a list of things you have to do. Then do them one at a time, one step at a time. Life is a cinch by the inch, hard by the yard.

• Don't worry. Work. Worry stops when work begins.

• Keep busy. Don't stop to take that worry break. Worry is often a habit with you. Kick the habit. Replace it with the habit of patting yourself on the back when you do something well, when you make a strong effort, when you try something new.

• Be more willing to test your capabilities. Try harder. Listen for the encouragement of others who have enough regard for your talents to urge you to try harder.

• Assume more responsibility for judging your own capabilities and competence. Avoid seeking approval where the situation doesn't really warrant it.

• Avoid withdrawing from a situation that you feel might be too difficult. Don't drop out or cop out.

• Always make an effort to function at your true level of capability. If you believe you should be a B student, make every effort to work at that level. If you believe that you are capable of being a supervisor, be willing to assume more responsibility. Beware of the opposite tendency: to make excuses for not making B's or not assuming more responsibility.

• The really important effort is starting. Hear this successful Anticipating Personality: "Once I start, I'm okay. If I don't start, I feel defeated. I used to think too much before starting. Now I don't. I just go ahead and do it."

• Rather than let each element of planning overwhelm you, recognize that you plan and organize quite effectively. Write down your plans, then move ahead one item at a time. Then appreciate your effort. And keep going.

• Listen for your cop-outs. Excuses, excuses, excuses.

• Here is a test: How often have you eaten out lately? And how did you arrange to eat out so often? Listen for the subtle excuses, the persuasive hints to your spouse. Then get busy cooking dinner.

• Listen for your rather easy habit of nagging and griping about other people's faults and failings. If you listen closely, you might hear you describe yourself. You are projecting onto others your faults, your own inferior feelings. Don't put others down; pick yourself up.

• When things are gloomy, recall some other moments when you were doing well, feeling good. Let your natural optimism rise to the moment. Look for the bright side. Shine up some of your old successes. Above all, don't go looking for a bad day.

• Your fears and phobias are messages. Read beneath the surface of fear of flying, fear of crowds, fear of dying, fear of dark places. The underlying message is fear of trying.

• Whether it is a testing of your sexual adequacy or cooking ability or job competency, don't cop out with somatic complaints. Get involved. Make a commitment. Try. Then give yourself credit.

• Watch your language. Stop calling yourself "stupid" and "dumb." And don't call yourself a quitter. That is an invitation to quit when you ought to be starting. Remember: worry less, work harder.

• Failure *is* possible, and when it really happens, it does hurt. But don't let one failure paralyze you for life. The best response to a failure is to look around for other areas of capability. And give yourself credit for having tried. The failure is in not trying.

• Don't be a cliché, always putting off till tomorrow what you could do today. Again, the thing to do is get started. If you can get five minutes into the task, whether you are washing the car or designing a bridge, you have momentum going for you.

• Stop fearing being tired and exhausted. Start telling yourself you can do the job. Onward.

• Don't shop around for help when you can do the task yourself. Only one person is needed to burp a baby or mix a martini.

• Whenever you are avoiding people or work or a new oppor-

176

tunity—promotion, buying a new car, meeting your future mother-in-law—ask yourself: "Is this another cop-out?"

• Don't compare; prepare. Comparing yourself to others is self-defeating. If you need viewpoints from others or to consult, do it without putting yourself down. Make your plans, then move ahead.

• Expand your interests and involvements. Probe untried areas of interest. If you have always wanted to play the guitar, then rent one. Get started before you have time to think up excuses or reasons why you couldn't possibly play the guitar. If you have always wanted to be a writer, take pencil in hand. Begin. Try first, evaluate later.

• Try new things. Take new risks. Try change. Remember, a new problem is a new opportunity. Give yourself the well-deserved opportunity to succeed.

• Temper your tendency to compliment and flatter others. You may be nibbling away at your own self-esteem. And don't distrust the compliments of others. Be more prone to appraise yourself and your performance properly. When someone compliments you, say, "Thank you." You deserve the credit.

• The more you do, the better you feel. And the better you feel, the more you can do. It's nice when the circle comes full.

• Get more involved. Relax. Make your plans. Execute them. That way you can go more places, have more fun, make new friends, enjoy new successes, see the world. Then give yourself credit.

• Stop jumping on mistakes that your husband, friends, co-workers, children, neighbors make. Tearing them down is another statement of your sense of inferiority.

• Those butterflies bouncing around your stomach? Strange how they fly away when you're busy.

• The next time you feel like saying, "I know I can't do that," say, "I think I can." Then take the first step. Soon you will be saying, "I knew I could."

• An interesting comment from a fellow psychotherapist: "It's funny, but the only person I ever heard say a bad word about an Anticipating Personality was himself."

• You're right; you are important.

• You have all sorts of options. You can either stay home and feel fretful, or you can go out and help someone else. Helping others helps you feel significant, genuine, successful.

• Your home doesn't have to be perfect for you to be a perfectly lovely person. You can be neat without having always to keep things neat.

• Don't cling to your children. Let go. But let the love keep flowing back and forth.

• You want to be special? You are. Note the looks of love and appreciation on the faces of your spouse, your children, your friends. That lasts and lasts.

• Don't hold back. Move ahead. One step at a time. Keep the arm loose to manage that pat on the back.

• The future is now.

VIII

Truth, honor and justice
are at the basis of all
human relations.

HARRY S. TRUMAN

The Perceptive Personality

THE PERCEPTIVE PERSONALITY is quick to respond to pain and privation, not just when they afflict him, but when they happen to anyone, even to a stranger. He is the Good Samaritan who stops to comfort, to give aid, to bind wounds, to console. If he could, he would see to it that every hungry child was fed, that every disease was cured, that the poor had plenty, that every broken heart was mended, and every tear wiped away. Every stray cat would be given a home, and every dog would have his day. When his efforts to give aid are thwarted, he is frustrated, and he speaks out against the sources of privation and suffering. He demands that justice be done, that promises be kept, that injuries be redressed.

Why? Because the Perceptive Personality is compassionate. He cares. He is quick to perceive suffering, and he can put himself into the other person's pain. The good that he wants for himself, he wants for everyone. What he fears for himself, he fears for others. Thus he reacts to all forms of deprivation, rejection, abuse, and mistreatment. Thus his abiding concern for justice, truth, honesty, integrity, morality. These values promote security and well-being, and should these values be lacking or be abused, he does what he can to make

179

them a reality in his own environment—and beyond. The Perceptive Personality might notice a lost child crying in a department store and spend the next half hour locating his mother. He reads in the newspaper of a homeless family and responds by offering blankets and clothing. If the evening television news shows earthquake victims in faraway Iran, he might weep in genuine sadness over their suffering. He truly cares.

The Perceptive Personality is normally a down-to-earth person, decent and likable, outgoing and responsive, loyal and fair, a genuine friend who wears well over the years. He prizes his friends as he cherishes family and a good and happy home life; family and friends together constitute his prime sources of security. He enjoys the sound of laughter, and he finds it easy to laugh. He is pleased when he has earned the respect of intelligent people and the affection of children. He will play with every stray mutt and mongrel, and he is content to spend an hour at the window watching the squirrels gathering nuts. He loves life—all of it, human, animal, and plant; and when life around him is serene, he is content and happy. He will do all that he can to keep it that way. Thus he tries hard to be a good person, an honest person who keeps his word, a fair person who meets his obligations, a compassionate person who does what he can to remedy and relieve misery and misfortune.

THE PROTECTIVE URGE

The Perceptive Personality's worst fear is that he might be deprived of his well-being and security—friends or family, good health or good fortune might desert him. So he maintains a certain vigilance to preserve what he has, even sometimes to the point of feeling a bit possessive and selfish. While he sees himself as a giving person, he openly admits that he is prone to think of himself and his welfare first. And so, as an extra safeguard, especially when his security is threatened, he takes a self-reliant, do-it-yourself approach to life. A Perceptive woman I know had never worked during her marriage, but when her husband underwent a colostomy, her reaction was to enroll in a secretarial course and to look around for employment. Her impulse, immediately after she knew that he was out of danger, was to make sure she could take care of herself. This is the *protective urge.* While the Perceptive Personality is quick to respond compassionately to the other person's plight, inside he is saying to himself, "Dear God, this could happen to me!" Thus his second-level response is to look out for himself. He balances compassion for others with his concern to protect himself and his security.

It would be difficult to exaggerate or overstress security in all forms as the pivotal concern of the Perceptive Personality. When emotional security is absent—or when he fears that it might be withdrawn—he is subject to feelings of deprivation, rejection, or desertion. When material security is threatened, he also fears hardship, but to a lesser degree than he fears the loss of emotional security. But whatever the threat to security, the Perceptive Personality responds typically by trying to offset the feared loss by moving away toward greater independence: "I really don't need anyone. I can make it on my own." But he does need others; the more he pursues independence, the more he experiences feelings of loneliness. When threatened by loss or disappointment, it is better for him to become more involved with people than to stand off. When he becomes involved—when he reaches out to meet the needs of others—the less he experiences loneliness and the more he feels secure.

"Survive" is a word you hear the Perceptive Personality use when he feels threatened by possible loss of security. It ties in with the thrust toward independence. As one young woman remarked to me, "Oh, I'm sure I could survive. If you've got enough get up and go, and if you are independent enough, you can always find a way to survive." Another woman admits that whenever her husband shows the first sign of a cold, she mentally inventories the attic and the closets thinking that, if he really got sick, she might raise quick cash through a garage sale. A Perceptive patient once explained to me how, if he lost his job, he could always buy peanuts in bulk, package them in small bags, and sell them on street corners. His father did that during the Depression. Thus the threatened Perceptive Personality tends to practice survival techniques when he might better invest his emotional energies in counting and nurturing his blessings. Why settle for a lonely can of beans out of a survival kit when a feast is possible with family and friends?

The Perceptive Personality is not only protective of himself; he wants to extend his protection to whoever needs it. But protection always begins at home. A Perceptive wife might shovel the snow from the driveway rather than permit her overweight and over-forty husband to risk a heart attack. She might continue on to the neighbor's driveway since the woman next door is a widow; she can imagine how it would feel not to have a man around the house. Coming back into the house, half-frozen and huffing and puffing, she might feel guilty that she wasn't able to help the teenager down the street push his car out of a snowbank. Before she can get her coat off, she might head back outside to throw bread crumbs on the snow for the birds.

THE ANIMALS' FRIEND

Feeding birds in wintertime would not be an incidental gesture on the part of the Perceptive Personality. His compassion extends to all living creatures, especially those in need. A Perceptive Personality could never ignore a stray dog or cat, however scraggly. He would take it in and feed it and give it a home, offering as explanation, "They look at me with those sad eyes, and I'm lost." Or, "I don't know where he came from; he just chose to move in with us." The saying "A dog is a man's best friend" certainly smacks of the Perceptive Personality. He would view any pet or domestic animal as an affectionate creature that demands little while giving loyal companionship. Since no one is ever lonely with a pet in the house—a loved and well-fed animal will never desert you—the Perceptive Personality is inclined to gather creatures into his home like a latter-day Noah.

This concern and affection includes all animals great and small. One Perceptive young woman mentioned to me that she would love to have a baby cougar—she didn't say what she might do when it was no longer a baby! Horses are favorites always. Not all people who go to the racetrack are bettors. The Perceptive Personality would spend a day at the track just to watch the grace and beauty of this grand animal in motion. A mother told me of her Perceptive daughter choosing a particular college because she could stable her horse not far from the campus. And you could expect a Perceptive Personality driving through farm country to stop often simply to admire horses, sheep, and cattle grazing peacefully in their pastures. If by chance he should see a sickly animal alone and unattended, the

Perceptive Personality might drive up to the owner's house to ask what was being done for the poor animal. And the farmer had better have a good answer. The Perceptive Personality is a no-nonsense, plainspoken individual at all times; when he sees mistreatment, he is blunt and sharp in his criticism.

CHAMPION OF THE UNDERDOG

The Perceptive Personality is a rather open and available person who tends to like everyone—at least until he has reason not to. Yet he does not necessarily trust everyone; he is too attuned to the inequities in the world. He is so alert to every form of privation and so concerned about justice and honesty and fair play that he is quick to respond to any injustice he encounters, and thus he disdains privilege because it implies a corresponding lack of privilege. In his own conduct he avoids anything pretentious or pompous; he is noticeably straightforward, plainspoken, and candid. He identifies with the common man, and he openly speaks out against whatever is false and phony, what is corrupt, deceitful, and dishonest. He shuns the smug and haughty or whoever shows contempt for his fellowman. He abhors bigotry and prejudice and will rush to the defense of their victims. He avoids all forms of subterfuge and is wary of those who practice evasive tactics in their dealings with others. In sum, he is the champion of the underdog: the disadvantaged, the deprived, the underprivileged.

A Perceptive father heard his son—not a Perceptive Personality —mimicking another boy who stuttered, and he made his son apologize on the spot. A Perceptive woman working in a factory put her job on the line by going to management to complain of safety violations in her department. A Perceptive businessman walked out on a possibly large sales contract when the other party made an unkind comment about his partner's ethnic background. This same businessman quit his country club when he discovered that membership was restricted to white Gentiles, even though he lost golfing friends over his resignation. Still, this same man was well liked by all his employees, even down to the janitors, because he was always open and accessible, friendly and kind to everyone. He spoke to every employee he passed, greeting each by name, and when union contract negotiations came up, there was never fear of a strike or dispute; he was known to be scrupulously fair and concerned for the welfare of his workers. In return, he expected his workers to give him a fair day's work for a fair day's pay.

The Perceptive Personality is a loyal, lasting friend. He delights in visiting old friends, and he would make every effort to attend a reunion of high school classmates or buddies from his old military service unit. He might grin, however, when he notes that the once-handsome and dapper class president is now thick in the middle and thin on top, thinking, "Man, am I glad that I've still got my hair." And when he greets the girl he once thought so attractive, he is gracious and charming while thinking, "How could I have had a crush on a girl so fat?" In neither case is he being smug or unkind; he is only thinking candidly that he is glad that misfortune hasn't come his way.

There is a judge I know who is something of a local celebrity. He grew up in a poor neighborhood, spent years working his way through law school, and gained a solid reputation in his political party. Even though he is careful with his money—typical of the Perceptive Personality—he has helped finance the college education of several promising young people in his old neighborhood. This generous aid isn't generally known because he makes secrecy a condition of helping out these children of friends who haven't done as well as he has. Secrecy is his safeguard against everyone in the old neighborhood who can't appreciate the limits of his ability to help. He doesn't want to lose lifelong friends, so he protects himself with his secrecy. But the judge wasn't able to protect himself so well when the local newspaper reported that he had paid the funeral expenses of the town drunk, once the town's mayor before he was convicted of embezzling municipal funds. Few people could understand the judge giving a graveside eulogy that praised the dead man as a good and loyal friend. What they didn't know—or had forgotten—was that the judge and the dead man were once boyhood friends from the same miserable neighborhood and that the convicted embezzler had helped the judge get his start in local politics. People shook their heads, but the judge offered no explanation. As a Perceptive Personality, he took it for granted that everyone felt the same fierce loyalty to an old friend. And compassion, always.

184

VULNERABILITIES AND CRISES

The Perceptive Personality with all his compassion and concern is a boon to everyone around him. Normally easygoing, funloving, and playful, he is a likable person, comfortable to be with, a dependable friend. But the Perceptive Personality is so attuned to harm and hurt and privation that in times of trouble or stress his perceptions can become colored. He is prone to sense abuse and mistreatment where they aren't, or he tends to read more misery into a situation than really exists. He can respond by being too easily upset, or he can be overprotective, guarding himself against any threat of hurt or privation. He becomes so preoccupied with compassion that he can't go beyond his feelings to an understanding and resolve the depriving situation. He can feel like an outcast, even when everyone loves him so much, and is prone to be too quick to react, too quick to comment, bitching and blaming others for his woe. Any slight or snub or inequity sends him into a snit. His understanding of what is happening is blunted and dulled by his pessimism, his battling, his taking matters too personally. His sense of justice and fairness becomes rigid; he begins to measure what he gives against what he gets, and always he feels that he is on the short end of the measurement. "I feel like I'm used," he sighs, "but I always come back for more."

When troubled enough, the immature Perceptive Personality is extremely susceptible to any threat of loss or rejection; and rather than wait for it to happen, he lunges toward independence, feeling he doesn't want to need anyone. He slips off to a secluded spot, only to feel so lonely; or he wallows in his suffering, forcing others to share in his misery. Either way, he is singing the blues: "Nobody loves me, nobody cares. . . ." But then again, he just might laugh it all off with a "What the hell," perhaps to resurrect his complaining at a later date. Under stress, the Perceptive Personality is given to extremes.

When the Perceptive Personality's compassion goes awry, it can cause as many problems as it solves. One evening a Perceptive woman answered the door to find a very sad-looking nephew standing there. She asked him in, sat him down, offered him a piece of pie and a glass of milk, and then asked, "Something wrong?" There was. This teenager and his father had had a battle about his staying out late the night before. The young man had left the house in a huff. And now: "Auntie, can I spend the night at your house?" How could she say no? After he was asleep in the guest room, his Perceptive aunt called his parents to let them know their son was at her house; no need to worry. But alas, when she so informed her still-angry Perceptive brother, he roared, "What the hell are you doing, taking sides?" With no further comment, she slammed down the receiver. "Here I thought I was doing everyone a favor, and what do I get?" Her kindness might have been more productive had she considered the option of calling his parents *before* she consented to her nephew spending the night, thus avoiding the appearance of having taken sides in a family problem. But in her rush she didn't, and as a result, she suffered. And her family suffered. She felt so put upon and abused that for a week she couldn't put a hot meal on the table. Her family heard so much of her complaining about her brother that even her dog began to shy away from her.

The less secure Perceptive Personality can be jealous. The other person always gets the bigger piece of the pie, the big break, the window seat in the plane, the easier job on the line, the first pick of the litter. His wife always seems to dress better for her job than she does for him at home; could she be interested in another man? He spends so much time in the ball park; could there be another woman? Her brother wins a scholarship, but she has to work her way through college. Why me, Lord? Or rather: Why not me, Lord?

The Perceptive Personality has an earthy, easy sense of humor, but when feeling on the down side, he doesn't recognize how much people enjoy him; and when they laugh, he feels ridiculed. When they tease him—as he teases them—he bristles: "They're treating me like a jerk." He might not go along with the party theme of wearing a costume because he might look silly or, worse, phony, pretentious, so he doesn't go to the party, and he feels unhappy all night. Think of all those people—his friends—having all that fun without him. He sulks in his beer. The young Perceptive woman who is chosen prom queen fears she will look foolish with a crown on her head, and she is tempted to refuse the honor. But she doesn't, and she has a wonderful time.

The insecure Perceptive Personality is easily slighted and forever assuming snubs. A Perceptive husband asks his wife to meet him for dinner downtown after a late business meeting. He sets the date for seven o'clock. When she doesn't show by 7:15, he finishes his Scotch and leaves: "She's not coming." But his wife was caught in heavy traffic, and she did show—at 7:20. Too late. He is off to his favorite bar, telling the bartender how everyone lets you down, even your wife. The next morning he feels very guilty, and very hung over, as his wife explains what happened. Whoever said, "If you expect the worst, you'll never be disappointed"? A disappointed Perceptive Personality who always expected the worst and thus made it happen.

The Perceptive Personality will tell you that he wants to be independent and self-sufficient. He might say, "To get what you want, you have to pay for it." Or, "You only get what you pay for." Don't believe all these protests of going it alone or paying his own way. The Perceptive Personality is like the boy who ran away from home never to return—until suppertime. The hurt Perceptive Personality may make an effort to adopt an independent stance, but he usually stays within reach of his source of security, that person or persons whose love and affection mean so much in his life. He is trying to protect himself against hurt or rejection, but if he gets too far from his source of security, then he does indeed feel hurt and rejected. In truth, the Perceptive Personality easily feels lonely. The one evening in the year that a Perceptive mother had to eat alone—her husband was out of town and her children were at a school function—she sat nibbling at a tin of sardines, miserable in her loneliness, feeling blue and rejected. And this was the woman who was forever saying to the family, "Oh, what I'd give for one evening by myself!"

The wounded Perceptive Personality has a very difficult time forgetting unhappy experiences. Old grievances are sometimes stored away for another fray. The battle is kept going so that problems are not examined and solved or wounded feelings salved or relationships fully repaired. Hashing over grievances, old or new, is one way the Perceptive Personality protects himself. In a cruel world of deprivation and hardship, you can't be too careful. Someone who hurt you once might hurt you again, so protect yourself at all times. Thus the hurt and the memories of hurts go on and on, and in the passing of time, the blame always seems to slide in one direction: to the other person. In the protective game, it is *always* someone else's fault. Both the nourished hurt and the finding of fault only isolate the smoldering Perceptive Personality. The harmed Perceptive Personality can hardly come to an understanding of the problem or any improvement of relationships while he clings to his grievances.

One Perceptive Personality, for example, had his mother-in-law living with him. For fifteen years the two of them did battle daily, sometimes in silence, sometimes in minor sniping attacks. It all began when he first became engaged to her daughter, and the mother had said, openly and candidly, "I think my daughter can do better." He never forgot what she had said, and she never quite felt like changing her mind, so she became the resident ogre, and he kept the fire of resentment smoldering. Yet when the old woman needed a new set of teeth, it was the son-in-law who first became concerned; he called his dentist for her appointment and instructed that the bill be sent to him. It is worth noting that the Latin roots of the word "compassion"—"to suffer with"—can be understood, in this instance, in two ways.

One husband married to a Perceptive Personality described his wife as "a woman who is always picking up rocks, stuffing them into a bag, and then hitting me over the head with them." What he meant was that she tended to note every slight or snub, to store them up, and then to unload the accumulated hurt at one time. His wife hadn't realized her habit of "picking up rocks"; but when her husband described the practice, she commented, "I guess I do go along getting upset but not saying anything at the time. I don't complain. I don't nag. But then all of a sudden, *pow!* Some little thing happens, and I explode all over the place. Then I feel sort of guilty and wonder, 'What the hell is wrong with me?' " Rather than "pick up rocks," the aggravated Perceptive Personality would be more reasonable and relate better if he would speak up when he feels slighted or put down. Everybody would be much happier.

GROWING UP PERCEPTIVE

Parents usually describe the Perceptive Personality as a very loving child who is instantly and easily loved; he presents no problems with eating habits or toilet training. Yet as early as two years of age, the child may show the first signs of resistance to parental direction, perhaps sensing something negative in tone, as if he feared that correction meant the parent didn't love him or might in some way deprive him. This resistance, however, is balanced by the child's ready response to warmth and affection shown him within the family circle. This is the child who might indicate in his behavior more than children of other styles that he welcomes and appreciates the closeness offered in all relationships, inside and outside the home. He is not too shy, and anyone who pays attention to him becomes his friend; he seems naturally aware of the warm security provided by dependable adults, and his response invites them to give him more and more attention. It is not unusual for him to be the pet of parents and teachers, although he may not be consciously aware of that status. Something about him prompts postmen, metermen, and the ice cream man to stop along their routes to help him fix his skates or to lift him out of a puddle; playground instructors single him out for special attention; teachers seem to choose him for the role of Santa Claus or the littlest angel in the Christmas play. He always seems to be the center of attention when aunts, uncles, and grandparents visit; and he is the child relatives tend to nickname. Later in life the Perceptive Personality might deny that he was given all that attention, or that he liked it, but, in truth, he loved it.

The Perceptive Personality is also the child who cries over spilled milk, a crack in his cup, a broken spoke on his tricycle, a rip in his teddy bear. He feels sometimes that he is the last one served at dinner; he always gets the lumps in the oatmeal and the burnt piece of toast; and even when he is pampered by the entire family, including his brothers and sisters, he may feel that Mom and Dad like the other children better. He had a tendency to be attuned to the negative moments, and he remembers them more than the good moments. Yet this is also the child who is most responsive to a sick parent, who might bring that parent tea and toast in bed because he knows how bad it feels to be sick; he too would want someone to care for him. He is also, for the same reason, concerned for and considerate of a sick sibling. The Perceptive child is pleasant and content as long as things and events are flowing along agreeably, but when he finds himself at odds with what is going on, or when he is chided or spanked, he can be obstinate and negative; he easily feels rejected. A parent might have to spank him once for the offense and a second time for running away or for doing it again.

The Perceptive Personality shows his delight in animals early. He plays with every dog in the neighborhood, and he very well may bring them home. The protective urge begins to show very early in life.

The Perceptive child may have some problems the first day of school. His sense of security may be threatened as he enters the totally new environment, and the teacher would do well to give this child an extra moment, just sitting with him and comforting him—being compassionate toward him. It works. Given a few days and a show of concern, the Perceptive child will adapt, entering into school activities and making friends. A few problems might surface from time to time. Even when he is quite capable of doing the required work, he might balk if he perceives the teacher's manner to be indifferent or harsh; or, should the teacher comment, "I had your older brother in class, and he was really a good student," he might interpret her remark to imply he isn't that good a student. If friends should comment in any way on a Perceptive boy's having to wear glasses—even in understanding—he might suspect they are calling him a sissy. When teachers and parents are aware of this tendency of the Perceptive child to read negative meanings into positive comments, they can help him better understand what is said by always expressing their interest in a way that directly pertains to him, or by rephrasing the remark when he shows discomfort.

Teachers often find the Perceptive child helpful in aiding another child who is a slow learner or has a reading problem. He welcomes the opportunity and might even volunteer to help without having to be asked. The one caution is that the Perceptive child might become so engrossed in the other child's problem that he might let his own work suffer.

ADOLESCENCE

Adolescence for the Perceptive Personality sometimes can be turbulent. Like his peers, he wants to assert himself, to be less dependent on his parents, to rely more on his own judgments, to test previously accepted values; but he is inclined to try independence a little more forcefully. Still, he very much needs the security of home and family to fall back on when his independent efforts fail or when he finds himself feeling lonely. As long as he finds himself fully supported by reliable friendships among his peers, his testing is relatively comfortable.

The Perceptive teenager may be rebellious at times, although usually in an agreeable enough way that parents may try not to make too much of it. The Perceptive parent can be very protective yet somewhat lenient; he remembers his own teenage years as a trying time, and he wishes his child to cultivate a self-sufficient spirit. But when the Perceptive adolescent attempts too sharp a break with home or is too much in conflict with his parents, he may grab for more independence than he can handle. He might run away from home or join the military service, feeling that he can make it on his own, but, at a deeper level, he is leaving before he can be rejected, which he fears will happen. Then, as always, an excess of independence leads to loneliness—the runaway Perceptive teenager might feel terribly unhappy and lonely only a mile from home. Parents need to hold their love open to the Perceptive adolescent—and display ample signs of that love—while being prudently tolerant of surges into the wilderness of independence. Keep a light burning in the window.

Here is how one parent described her Perceptive teenager: "She was a delightful child all through elementary school, but as soon as she entered high school, she started going out with boys. I told her she couldn't date till she was a junior, but she would go over to her friend's house, and the two of them would double date. Then she told me herself what she was doing. You know what she said? 'Mom, I want to be honest with you and have everything out in the open. But, Mom, I want my independence too.' So I gave in. And guess what? After that she didn't want to go out with the boy any more. You just never know."

The Perceptive Personality, adolescent or adult, is a very honest person always, at any age. He doesn't make excuses beyond a moment of hemming and hawing. He will miss an assignment in school and then tell the teacher, "Sorry, I just didn't get it done." Never ask a Perceptive Personality to give you his honest reaction; he will. One father bought himself a new, very stylish suit and asked his son how he liked it. The son told him: "It looks a little silly on a man your age, Dad." And so it goes.

Divorce or death in the family can be very difficult for the young Perceptive Personality. When it comes to problems between parents, the Perceptive child tends to take sides, showing exaggerated protective behavior toward one parent. If there is a divorce, the Perceptive child might run away from home. That might also be the response to a death in the family. Death is viewed as final rejection, and rather than staying with other members of the family for support and security, he rushes off, feeling, "I don't need anybody. I'll get by." His grief can be long and lonely. The hurt would heal much sooner if he could understand and accept the nurturing love of his family.

In some cases, the tendency in loss is to seek a substitute source of support. One Perceptive teenager who lost her mother married soon after her death. Her attitude: "If you can't get your needs met one place, you can get it someplace else." Hard? No, hurt; but the feeling and hurt Perceptive Personality is only applying a Band-Aid to the wound. The need is to push past the pain to understanding, to see through the moment to the long-range problem and solution. Here friends and family are very important—if only the Perceptive Personality will permit them to be compassionate.

ADULTHOOD AND MARRIAGE

The turbulent teen years can be explained this way: the Perceptive personality is aware, however unconsciously, that he is approaching the time when he will be leaving home, so he practices his independence as he prepares to move away. This, again, is part of his protective mechanism at work, so that when the time comes for his graduation from high school, he has no problems facing this leave-taking. The moment is indeed a commencement for him, a new beginning, and he is fully prepared to leave for college, or for a job, or simply to launch out on his own.

What happens to the Perceptive Personality on leaving home is illustrated by Kitty, an attractive young wife, mother, and social worker. After some time in therapy, she can smile as she tells you, "I always considered myself the most independent spirit in my family. When I was ready to leave home for college, I chose a school two hundred miles from home. I said to myself, 'I can handle it. I'm never going home again. I can do it all for myself.' Out of pride, I stayed away from home on the holidays. Wow, was I lonely! And I was always so broke. But I wouldn't ask my folks for money; maybe they wouldn't give it to me. I was miserable."

After earning her master's degree, Kitty went to work in a large city several states away from home. There she met Michael whom she describes as "quiet, gentle, a bit reserved, and nice-looking. He was so friendly, but what I really liked about Mike was that he treated me with so much respect, and that's important to me." Kitty and Mike began to date regularly, and despite his attention and affection, Kitty was surprised when Mike proposed. She hadn't really been too sure how the relationship had been going. True to the pessimism of the Perceptive Personality, she didn't assign that much significance to the flowers, those surprise gifts Mike gave her, and all the special places he took her. Yes, he told her that he loved her; and, yes, she loved Mike. Mike was always so attentive to Kitty, yet she was enormously jealous whenever he spoke to another woman. Kitty later learned to read her jealousy as a sign of her fear that she might lose Mike, and she began to handle her feelings appropriately. But back then, she was sure that Mike was slipping away from her, and with him would go her security.

Their marriage began delightfully. For Kitty, everything seemed so right: a wonderful job that she found purposeful in helping others, professional associates with like concerns, an occasional evening out, a small but cozy home, long hours alone with Mike—the good life. And so it was, for a while. The two of them decided to have a child, and in due time, they did, and Kitty quit work. But then she began to feel jealous of Mike's career as she began to miss her own. "It didn't seem fair. My day was full of diapers. His day was full of people." Every evening she would probe to find out what sort of things had been happening in Mike's day, but he never felt that all the small moments were worth detailing. Kitty felt left out. Meanwhile, their home became a clutter of cloth and scraps and paper patterns and books on sewing as Kitty attempted to be a do-it-yourself seamstress. She could have sought help in her sewing from the woman down the street who was an excellent dressmaker, but that wouldn't do; that would rob Kitty of her independence. More, when she made her own drapes, she battled to put up the hardware herself rather than haggle with Mike to do the job. And when he teased about her projects—"The complete decorator, huh?"—she bristled, supposing he meant that she wasn't doing too good a job.

Kitty's one great compensation for everything she felt she was missing in life was sex. She really missed Mike when he was away at work, but rather than say so, she guided him toward the bedroom

when he came home. Sexual activity became Kitty's all-purpose substitute for expressing her needs or communicating her feelings. But
one night, feeling a bit weary and worn, Mike snapped at her, "If
you didn't want to do it all the time, you might get something done
around here." Kitty felt totally rejected, and she wept half the night.
The next morning, for the first time in their marriage, other than
when she had the baby, she didn't get up to fix Mike's breakfast.
Mike worked overtime that evening, and Kitty began to suspect there
was another woman. She fantasized an affair of her own. That was
the beginning of a long, smoldering standoff. Mike began to spend
more time at work; Kitty began to complain more; Mike upped the
hours away from home. That was how matters stood when Kitty,
terribly jealous of Mike and feeling generally deprived, sought help.

Like so many Perceptive Personalities, Kitty admires individuals
she considers strong—to her that means independent—and intelligent. Kitty's favorite is Bob, a leader in her church community who
is a man close to her father's age. "Bob is someone I would like to
be like when I am his age. I admire his intelligence. Intelligent
people seem to think more about other people. Bob is the kind of
person I can discuss things with. He's so wise, helpful, and understanding. But most of all, I like Bob's attitude toward me as a person. He respects me."

Why so much stress on intelligence? Intelligence, in the reckoning of the Perceptive Personality, means that a person is able to
work things out for himself; he doesn't have to depend too much on
others if he is intelligent enough to solve his own problems. The Perceptive Personality might typically say, "I have to make it on my own.
I have to pay my own way in life." He has to look out for himself,
be independent, even though what he really wants is for someone to
make him happy. Only he fears that no one can—or will. Thus the
interest in self-help and do-it-yourself books and courses that the Perceptive Personality is always pursuing. In his quest for independence
and self-sufficiency, he takes a pay-your-own-way attitude, not liking
to be obligated or indebted. He sometimes tries to keep the scales
balanced between how much he will give and how much he will get.
He is wary that someone might take advantage of him or might ask
too much. And, always, he must protect himself and his sources of
security: "Give what you can. Take what others want to give, just as
long as you aren't obligated or don't lose your independence."

194

THE WORKING WORLD

The Perceptive Personality functions well in any profession or job where his responsiveness to others can be used to advantage, especially in the helping professions and service areas—medicine, nursing, teaching, training; social worker, personnel director, travel agent, beautician, coach, physical therapist, and so on. I should note, however, that many Perceptive women interested in nursing sometimes find it difficult to bear up under the sight of blood or to deal with terminal cases. Their alert perception of the acuteness of suffering is painful to them, and Perceptive nurses have been known to weep along with a crying patient, especially a child.

Because he is so perceptive and so attuned to others, and since he has such a capacity for sensing their problems and needs, the Perceptive Personality usually is a pleasant and effective supervisor— although a little shy of being called the "boss." He is especially effective in working with trainees, particularly problem trainees. His handling of problems normally is low-keyed and unthreatening, his style of helping and supporting subtle and unobtrusive—so much so that his perceptive ways are only gradually appreciated. He may be direct and down to earth in his approach, but he isn't likely to offend. He will offer straightforward advice and a very definite opinion, but he will soften his recommendations by adding, "At least that's my opinion," or, "Anyway, that's how I think I would do it." He leaves room for negotiation or countersuggestions, and he isn't likely to come down hard on a worker who is having problems on the job— or off the job, if he is aware of the situation. More often the Perceptive supervisor will go to great lengths to help the worker under him solve the problem or master the task, or he just might plunge in to do it himself.

The situation reversed doesn't always work as well. The Perceptive Personality tends to have problems with his own supervisor under stressful conditions. Any slight, any lack of recognition, or any harsh criticism might send the Perceptive worker into a slow, smoldering burn. His security might be threatened, and he would feel unappreciated and a bit rejected. He might think—and possibly say—"I'm working my tail off, and you want more." The really troubled Perceptive Personality might finally walk off the job, or he might demand to see the company president to complain about that unjust, depriving Scrooge who runs the section. Or he might, on second thought, go home to sulk and burn for the remainder of the week. He might consider starting his own business—never again does he want to "take all that crap" from an ungrateful, unfair boss—but this, too, is a hazardous lunge into independence that can be self-defeating rather than self-sustaining. Rather than sulk, bitch, or run, the unhappy Perceptive Personality would do better to pause long enough to allow the embers of resentment to cool so that he might possibly understand his supervisor's comments and to respond more constructively to the situation. Constantly lamenting "Nobody cares" doesn't leave much energy for discovering that the boss cares enough to want to discuss the problem.

HOME LIFE

When things are going well enough in the working world, the Perceptive Personality contributes with a great deal of enthusiasm, a sense of duty, and plain hard work. Then he gladly collects his earnings to head for home where he can enjoy the rewards of his work in the company of his family. His real gratification, in fact, is coming home to the love of his spouse and children, and he will do whatever he can to enrich the warmth and contentment and security of his home life—not just for himself, although that is important, but what he wants most of all is what he considers a good life for his children. He wants to raise them well, and to share with them his cherished values—honesty, reverence for the truth and for one's word, loyalty, decency, integrity, fair play.

The Perceptive Personality can experience great stress when one of his children or his spouse becomes seriously ill, yet he can be a great strength to everyone in the crisis. This strength seems to endure as long as the crisis lasts, then some sort of switch-off mechanism turns the Perceptive Personality toward his danger zone: independence. If it was his wife who was sick, he might, for example, continue to make breakfast for himself and the children long after she is up and about and willing to resume her routine, but the vulnerable Perceptive husband doesn't want to take any chances of being dependent or of being deprived again by another bout of illness. If he were reasonably mature and realistic, he would recognize the stress and fear underlying his move toward independence, and would move instead toward interrelating with his wife and trying to meet her needs.

One of my Perceptive patients experienced great fear of deprivation when his wife underwent a mastectomy. He reacted quite well at the time, supporting her after the diagnosis of the malignancy on her breast and throughout her surgery and hospitalization, but as she showed signs of returning to normal life, he became more and more self-sufficient, becoming even somewhat removed from the lives of his children. He took a part-time second job, supposedly to pay off the remaining medical expenses, but really he was trying hard to put himself into a more independent position. Yet as he moved toward independence, he found himself growing lonely and depressed. He didn't want to know of her doctor's long-range prognosis lest it remind him of the seriousness of the crisis just past. Only after he accompanied his wife to the surgeon's office for her follow-up examination did his depression lessen. He began to involve himself again in family life, and the more he did so, the better he felt. He was later able to offer this insight: "I have always dwelled more on what I didn't have rather than on what I did have."

The less secure Perceptive Personality can suffer a sense of abandonment or rejection over short absences of those he loves. A Perceptive woman, for example, felt forlorn when her husband and two teenage sons went away for a three-day fishing trip. She looked so sad and miserable waving goodbye that her husband felt like calling the trip off. But he didn't, remembering how many times he had seen that same sad look on leaving for a business trip only to return to find that she had managed so well. More, she always seemed so independent on his return. But, as he left, it was good that he couldn't read her mind. To herself she was saying, "He cares more about his fishing trip than he does about me." Had she pushed past her feelings of jealousy and rejection, she might have understood that the fishing trip gave her husband a much-needed break from his working routine, that it permitted his sons some time with their father sharing a mutual interest, and that it gave her the time she had been wanting to redecorate the boys' bedroom. She was missing an opportunity.

Major changes in the stability and security of the Perceptive Personality can create stress: the time when his children arrive at independence and seem not to depend on him so much; death or divorce; loss of a job or a well-liked supervisor; relocation; good neighbors, friends, or relatives moving away; the illness of a loved one.

Retirement, however, is no great problem for the Perceptive Personality as long as the prime sources of security—both human and financial—are adequate and available. The Perceptive Personality will continue to enjoy the opportunity to pursue a wide range of interests: traveling, camping, fishing and hunting, the bridge club or poker games, visiting children and grandchildren, reading all those books he had been wanting to read, or just swapping stories and laughing with old friends. Having to give up the family home for a smaller place might be painful, and the death of anyone close to him can be viewed as a painful deprivation—loss of his spouse is terribly debilitating for the less mature Perceptive Personality. His grief, even when disguised by a façade of go-it-alone independence, is enormous and prolonged—unless he is willing to share his sorrow. Here family and friends can be of great help, if he will permit them to enter his loss. One Perceptive woman, for example, seemed to be doing well enough after her husband's death. In time she considered remarriage and sought her son's advice. He was sufficiently impressed by her show of independence that he didn't detect how difficult the situation was for her, and advised against her remarrying. Later he wondered why she seemed so forlorn when she heard his advice. Deep inside, she needed someone. She was terribly grieved and lonely when she didn't have to be.

ALTERNATIVES AND OPTIONS

We have noted that the healthy Perceptive Personality is very warm, outgoing, and likable, so decent and loyal that he makes friends easily, and he keeps them. He is compassionate, attuned to the hardships and ailments, trials and sufferings of others. He will do what he can to remedy their sufferings and sorrows since he can put himself inside their problems. He is generous in crises, and hopes that everyone else will respond in like manner. He would be frustrated if he were unable to help. Above all else, the Perceptive Personality prizes happiness, a good home life, calm and contentment, and security of every sort. He is true to his word, just in his dealings with others, outspoken in his convictions.

But the less secure Perceptive Personality, especially under stress, is vulnerable to feelings of rejection and deprivation. He tends to see his glass as half empty rather than half full. He is not at all surprised that he gets the rock in the beans, the apple with the worm in it. The wishbone never seems to break his way. If he were to find a pearl in his oysters, he would complain to the waiter. He is the Good Samaritan who rushes to help the little old lady being mugged only to have her yell "Rape!" His dog has fleas, and his cat is pregnant, but instead of buying the dog a flea collar and having the cat spayed, he complains about the dog and nags at the cat. When his wife has heard it all for the ninety-ninth time, she goes off to her mother's for the evening. He isn't surprised; he expected that too, so he pops open a beer and turns on the television set to hear comedian Rodney Dangerfield moan his signature line. "I don't get no respect around here." The Perceptive Personality laughs and sighs, "So true, so true."

But on good days, the Perceptive Personality is able to see the silver lining that edges his lead-gray cloud. Give or take his grousing and grumbling when things aren't going well, at least as he perceives them, the Perceptive Personality is resilient; he is so well attuned to his own common sense that he can respond to changes for the better. After all, the beer still has its zing, the television set is working right for a change, and his wife comes home before the program ends. So he puts out his pregnant cat, pats his dog on the head and his wife on the seat, and off they go to bed. All's well that ends well.

So that all life's happenings have a chance to end well, the vulnerable Perceptive Personality needs to understand his own inner dynamics, especially his fear of rejection and deprivation. This fear of rejection is so strong that he attempts independence only to suffer terrible feelings of loneliness and possibly depression. He wants others to make him happy, but he feels no one can do enough for him, so he debates his need for help, and then he wants to do it himself. He contends that he wants to pay his own way, and doesn't want to be obligated. In his worst moments, he feels that nobody cares, that no one will meet his needs. *Everyone* has more than he has. He tends to overlook the gifts and the good times, dwelling instead on old hurts and new privations, and in moments when the negative out-look dominates, he complains mightily and long, driving everyone away. Then he is indeed alone and feeling wretched. All the while the love and concern he so badly wants are usually only a moment's thought away, and by pausing to read the signs of care all around him—instead of the bleakness and privation—he could move away from his fears into the love and security of those who care so much for him. These rich and positive affections are present and available, and when the vulnerable Perceptive Personality considers the many positive options open to him, his once half-empty cup begins to fill to overflowing.

If you are a Perceptive Personality, consider the following:

• Whenever under stress, get involved. Everything you want is present in relationships dear to you, so wrap yourself in friendships and family.

• Rejection is usually your own projection. People aren't rejecting you; you're walking away from them.

• Don't dwell on rejection. True friends should be able to talk over problems.

• There aren't so many pieces to love like so many pieces in a pie. Love grows, thrives, and multiplies as it is shared, so the more you give love, the more it grows, the more you get.

• Beware of your jealousies. They are signals of your tendency to feel deprived or of fear you will be deprived—or that someone is getting more than you are.

• You are the Good Samaritan who does so much for the less fortunate in your environment. But do one more kindness: stay around long enough after you have helped to recognize your contribution. Those you have helped won't ask you for more; they simply want you around. That's how much people like you.

• People are indeed deprived when they aren't permitted to thank someone for helping. Would you deprive them?

• Try to remember the gifts that are given you and the other ways people show interest in and concern for you. At the end of every day, make a list in your mind of all the kindness, the affection, the smiles, the greetings, the gifts, the friendships that others have given you.

• See the larger good and not the small flaws in things that come your way. The grocer doesn't single you out for the rotten apple, and the car dealer didn't save you the lemon. Take the long view of life and the small flaws will fall into perspective.

• Nagging and grousing won't solve problems. Understanding them and working toward corrective solutions will.

• Give up your survival kit and your survival training. Come celebrate life. Get involved with family and friends. Don't just survive. Thrive.

• You draw too many lines, defining just how much you will give or do. You fear that someone will take advantage of you or misuse you or that you might become obligated for the rest of your life. Drawing lines only causes friction or challenges the good will of others. You are setting up what you fear most: rejection.

• Don't overprotect your children. That can be stifling. Don't depend on them for your emotional gratification—like the mother who still expects her thirteen- and fifteen-year-old sons to kiss her good night.

• If you get up every morning to fix the family breakfast, don't be bitchy about it. You are doing it because you want to, not because they demand it. Be honest. You love it, don't you? And you might love it more if you would open your ears to the thank-yous and smiles and happy looks.

• Quit always looking on the dark side of working relationships. Do your best, stay involved, and let the recognition come in its own proper time.

• Give the boss a break. Realize that he has problems too. Let him pick his own time to give you a compliment, not just when you feel he owes you one. Let him surprise you—it's more of a delight that way.

• When you are so busy remembering someone who was kind to you twenty years ago, you are no doubt missing a dozen opportunities for good times right now. Live in the present.

• Your acceptance of support from others, like your sharing of feelings, is either feast or famine. You go along for long periods of time without genuine communication of feelings, then, suddenly, you gorge yourself. Afterward, you go back to your independent ways. Involvement has to be practiced on a daily basis to have a nourishing benefit.

• Nobody can know what you're thinking, or guess your needs, or predict your feelings. You'll just have to speak up.

• Your tendency to hem and haw is an indicator that you are measuring whether or not to get involved, whether you want to make an effort to have your needs met. It's better to adopt the attitude, "What the hell, let's get at it," than to stand there mentally shuffling. Make a commitment, get involved, accept feedback. Learn to be a good listener without wanting some dividend in return.

• Plot your goals, then have the courage—and kindness—to announce them. That way people can know what kind of support to give you—and if you let them know that you want their support, so much the better. But don't get your plans mixed up. Don't let others set your goals. And don't you decide what kind of support they should give you.

• Relationships are less fulfilling than frustrating when they aren't reciprocal and mutual. If you are always giving, that's only a halfway good. If you are always getting, that's still only a halfway good. When you are giving and getting—without taking time out to measure which is which—then the relationship is working. You're sharing. It all begins to flow together. Then who knows who did what and when? And who cares? You did it together. That's the joy of it all.

• You can give without fear of losing some of yourself, but the only way that you will ever know the truth of this reality is to try it. The more you love, the more loving you feel.

• Pessimism is the view from the bottom of the pit. There is a much better view up in the open with people. People are the best cure for pessimism. Take them in regular doses—but double the dose when you're feeling pessimistic.

• Don't spend so much time at work being angry when others need you. Instead, back off from your anger long enough to realize how very much people appreciate your efforts, how very much they appreciate you.

• One hug of a child makes a million diaper changes worthwhile. So every time you change a diaper, get that hug!

• Stop moaning the blues about all the time your husband is away. Don't always be so jealous of his bowling or his golf, or even his time watching the ball game on television. Make the most of your moments together.

• After someone does something for you, don't take out your inspection kit to check if it has been done well enough. You can't measure love by the millimeter or concern by the ounce or feelings by the cup. So don't even try. Instead, reach out and have as much as you want from those who love you.

• Forgive. Forget. Kiss and make up. It's all fun.

• The greatest self-help book in the world is the book of life. Responding to real people in real situations is the sort of self-improvement opportunity that will benefit your life the most.

• Security is portable. Genuine confidence, openness to others, caring, sharing, and feelings are the real sources of your security, and they go where you go.

• Contentment comes with doing for others and with being open to others on a steady give-and-take basis.

• The next time you feel like bitching or nagging at your wife, keep your mouth shut. And the easiest way to keep your mouth shut is by kissing your spouse.

• Don't think so much in concrete terms. That isn't just a box of candy; it's a gift of love. It isn't just a soccer game; it's your child playing his heart out in front of your eyes. And that isn't just a meal you're serving; it's heaping portions of your love.

• Every time that you say, "Leave me alone," think again. You don't need a corner alone in the bedroom for sulking. You need closeness, warmth, caring, people. When you think about it long enough, you might end up saying, "Please don't leave me alone."

• You probably receive more love than you suppose. You just haven't taken the time—or the attitude—to assess how much others love you. You are, as you know, trustworthy, dependable, fair, loyal—all traits that others respect.

• You really ought to appreciate that easy sense of humor that you have. Everyone else does.

• Sex is great—but it isn't the all-purpose measure for how well things are going in your marriage. Nor is it the all-purpose means of experiencing gratification. The more you learn to express your needs and the more you permit others to meet them, the less you will need to depend on sex as a substitute. Then you can enjoy sex for its own sake.

• Quit being so sensitive to slights and snubs, real or imagined. And don't always store them up. Rather, speak up. Don't sulk. Don't smolder. Say it. Now.

• People admire you for being open, honest, and candid. Don't spoil the impression by being less than honest and open and candid about your emotions.

• Beware of being so involved in compassionate concern for the less fortunate across town that you forget or slight those at home who also need your help and your love.

• Griping is a very poor substitute for honest discussion.

• Appreciate what you have rather than feeling deprived of what you would like to have. Think before you demand.

• "If you expect the worst, you'll never be disappointed" really means "If you expect the worst, you'll always be disappointed."

• Stop viewing your compassion as a curse. People aren't out there ready to drain you of all your concern and care. If you are so busy avoiding and dreading involvement, you are going to miss all the good things—and good people—that might come your way. Let the good times happen.

• True companionships are open and ebbing, like the tide. The tide comes in, the tide goes out—it doesn't cling to the shore and just stay there. But you can be so clinging in companionship that it stifles the free flow, the easy rhythm of love and affection. Let it flow.

• Don't pick up other people's problems as a way of avoiding your own problems at home.

• It is not *his* car and *his* bank account or *her* home and *her* child. It is *our* car and *our* bank account and *our* home and *our* child. Because it is *our* love.

• Don't sit home sulking because your husband is away on a business trip and you're missing a party. Go. Have fun. Enjoy.

• Don't always suppose your love and compassion are greater and more giving. Greater than whose? By how much more? Just how do you measure? Really, you can't. So don't try.

• Relish those compliments. Lovely, aren't they?

• The view from the first floor is never as good as it is from the second floor. So when things aren't looking so good, take the next step up.

• Be neither dependent nor independent. Try interdependence—it's very productive and gratifying.

• Whenever you view the glass as half empty, look again. See if it isn't really half full.

• Everyone knows how much you care. Do you know how much they care?

• When in doubt, get involved. And then stay involved.

204

IX

*Do unto others as you
would have them do unto
you.*

THE GOLDEN RULE

The Sensitive

Personality

THE SENSITIVE PERSONALITY is keenly aware of himself, keenly aware of other people, and of the environment around him. He is a reflective, introspective person, highly sensitive to his own moods and moments, feelings and thoughts. But he is equally attuned to the moods and moments, feelings and thoughts of others, and, at the same time, he is curious about and highly observant of everything happening in the world around him. When his feelings about himself harmonize with the feelings of others and the events going on around him, he is a very content and serene person, happy to be alive. He feels one with the world, one with his fellow human beings, and he is quite willing to work diligently to affect and preserve that harmony without and that tranquility within. He is the lover of peace, the maker of peace, the keeper of peace. He wants it for himself, and he wants it for others. Otherwise, there is no true harmony, no real peace—there is only discord and chaos; and the Sensitive Personality—always so sensitive and aware—cannot abide chaos.

If all the world were his, the Sensitive Personality would see to

it that all the trains ran on time, that all energy resources were husbanded, that the foodstuffs of the world were distributed equitably, that all wounds were healed, that every mortgage was paid, that every worker received a fair day's pay for a fair day's work. There would be a chicken in every pot and a car in every garage—not *coq au vin* perhaps and no superchromed gas guzzler; just a nice plump bird and an economical, fuel-conserving, sturdy means of transportation. The Sensitive Personality normally is not interested in frills and fuss; in fact, he dislikes them. He always looks for the sensible, efficient, dependable, purposeful solution to a problem, avoiding the pretentious and the extravagant. Even worse, to him, is the kind of fuzzy thinking that produces pretension and extravagance—those kinds of solutions, he knows, throw the system out of balance to produce waste and want. He is frustrated when the equilibrium is disrupted and outraged at the sight of waste and want—he can't see them without wanting to do something about them. He wants to make all things whole and harmonious. He is the peacemaker.

One could wish for a Sensitive Personality to preside over a court, twelve Sensitive Personalities on every jury, a Sensitive Personality behind every policeman's badge and on every city council. But be glad that they are where they are, distributed throughout our communities, some in high places, others tending shops, baking bread, machining parts, having babies, building bridges. Wherever they are and whatever they are doing, Sensitive Personalities are pursuing equity and justice, working to effect peace and harmony and community.

They come well equipped for the task. Not only are they intensely observant of what is happening around them, and sensitive to other people, they are adept at planning and organizing, ordering and integrating the various elements and opportunities within their competence, within their environment. They produce results. Their goals are usually high, and they are creative in pursuit of their goals, whether studying better ways to care for the aged or devising better traffic signs for the corners in their neighborhoods. They are confident in approaching their objectives, aware that they bring to any task their unique resources of keen observation, organization, a sense of justice, care, concern, curiosity. Still, they are usually comfortable to work with; they are not overtly competitive; they are willing to share; they are normally gentle and friendly. And they have a mellow, warm humor.

The healthy and mature Sensitive Personality is as aware of the characteristics of his style as are his friends and colleagues, although he is too shy and modest to acknowledge them to others or to want them praised. But here is how two Sensitive Personalities, a man and a woman, described their strengths to me:

"I think loyalty is one. I've seen other women I would have liked to date, but I wouldn't. I'm very loyal to my wife."

"Friendship is another strength."

"I think we're fair-minded. You always try to think of the other guy; you try to see his side."

"I always seem to stand up for the underdog."

"A way of backing off, finding a quiet place, and thinking over a problem."

"A sense of humor. That helps a lot. It gets you through."

The more healthy the Sensitive Personality, the more he can use these qualities for his own benefit and for the benefit of others. Those around him note that the Sensitive Personality is also honest, kind, and considerate—but he is so prone to maintaining a low profile that it is possible to miss some of his many productive attributes. He finds deserved praise uncomfortable, and, being sensitive and shy, he hears a compliment as if it were amplified ten times over, and winces. He reacts no differently to criticism—it too is amplified by his sensitive feelings, and he suffers. Yet he is so well-organized and purposeful that he can integrate constructive criticism, even when it hurts. But when he believes that he is right, he is tenacious, and when he believes that he has been criticized wrongly or harshly, he might feel resentment—although possibly he might never voice it. He is capable of maintaining a placid exterior while his feelings are shouting angrily inside.

THE AWARENESS URGE

What is it that prompts the Sensitive Personality to be so observant, so keenly aware, so sensitive? His abiding regard for peace and harmony and his desire to safeguard them. This demands vigilance. "Vigilance" in its Latin root means "watchful," as does the word "aware" in its Old English and Middle English roots. With his constant concern that good order and peace be preserved or constructed, the Sensitive Personality is ever alert, ever watchful. The *urge to be aware*, then, is the Sensitive Personality's essential approach to maintaining peace in his environment, and tranquility within himself and in his relationships with others. Thus his emphasis on observing and being aware of what is going on inside himself as well as in the world outside. And thus his high level of sensitivity; he is a finely tuned instrument measuring his own well-being, the welfare of others, and the good order of his environment. One Sensitive Personality said it so simply: "We like to have everything going smoothly with no ripples."

Here is how a Sensitive friend explained to me how it feels to be so highly aware and sensitive in his everyday life: "You're sensitive in every way—your whole body is sensitive—but mostly your feelings are so acute. I think you feel everything just a little more sharply. When you enjoy something, you enjoy it more, perhaps, than the average person does. If you hear beautiful music, you hear it fully. If you rub your hand over a piece of wooden furniture, you feel everything—the smoothness of the surface, any tiny blemish or nick, even the grain of the wood. If you smell your favorite dish cooking in the kitchen, the aroma is tantalizing. You're excited by the sound of a bird singing or the beauty of a sunset with all its shifting color tones. And when you love somebody, you love that person completely. Your feelings of love are so great. And when you grieve, it's terrible —the loss is heavy, and it lasts a long time. You're very, very sad."

The Sensitive Personality as an inspecting officer in the military could be a terror. He would immediately be able to note any small detail out of order; yet he would be so aware of a frightened recruit's feelings that he might choose to overlook offenses that he felt were trivial. A Sensitive television repairman might be quicker to spot the trouble in your set. A Sensitive teacher would be more likely to catch a student cheating on an examination. A Sensitive music critic might hear a rushed beat or an instrument out of tune—or the exceptionally fine tone of the solo instrumentalist. A Sensitive official might spot a foul more immediately on the football field than the other officials might. A Sensitive machinist told me that his hands were so sensitive he rarely needed a micrometer to gauge the level of tolerance on certain jobs he was familiar with. When quality control ran spot checks, they always found his tolerances well within the range that he said they were. A basketball player, also a Sensitive Personality, found that he could detect subtle foot movements of his opponents that would give away their moves and, typical of the Sensitive Personality, he always shared these keys with teammates.

THE GOLDEN RULE

Why would the Sensitive basketball player so readily share his knowledge with teammates when, by keeping it to himself, he might stand out as the star player? Because he lives out the Golden Rule: "Do unto others as you would have them do unto you." The Sensitive player would appreciate others helping him, so he helps his teammates. The Sensitive Personality has this sense of mutual regard and fair play. It comes with his concern for equilibrium in all relationships as in all of life. He knows how he wants to be treated, and that is his guide in his treatment of others. It is as if he invented the Golden Rule. One Sensitive Personality once told me, with a show of excitement: "I remember when we were kids and the teacher passed out wooden rulers that had the Golden Rule printed on them. I read it and said to myself, 'That's what I want to do. I'm going to remember the Golden Rule.' I remember the good feeling I had. I've always remembered the Golden Rule, and I still think about it."

Again, the Sensitive Personality is finely attuned to his own feelings and the feelings of others and is keenly aware of everything in his environment, good or bad. Thus he might volunteer to work in a local charity; he senses the tragedy of poverty, and responds to it because he wouldn't want to be poor. In much the same way he wouldn't hesitate to be generous to a panhandler; he would not like to be hungry. (The less mature Sensitive Personality, in contrast, might shun the panhandler, suspecting him of being a fraud and a swindler.) Whether soliciting for the Heart Fund, or collecting used clothing for the poor, or circulating a petition for streetlights, the Sensitive Personality willingly gives up a weekend or a day's wage to be of service to others; and when he experiences indifference or callousness toward the plight of the less fortunate, he is shocked and outraged. He supposes that everyone will be as concerned and as responsive, so for that reason too he doesn't hesitate to ask close friends to share the burden. Thus he is a good neighbor, a good friend, a contributing member of his community—the peacemaker.

This same sensitivity to others makes the Sensitive Personality a great friend of children. He thoroughly enjoys their company, and they enjoy his. He can enter their world, delight in their innocence, share their play, meet their needs. He can laugh with them, and he knows so many ways of soothing their troubles, calming their fears, and wiping away their tears. He is a child among children.

So much concern for others, so much vigilance, and so constant a state of keen sensitivity inevitably lead the Sensitive Personality to wanting moments of solitude. He enjoys getting away by himself—a weekend camping, a day fishing, an evening walk around the block. Or he may go quietly into his bedroom, read a book, listen to music, or simply reflect on the day's happenings or the evening news. As one Sensitive Personality described his use of solitude: "When I'm home, I like to lie on the couch with my stereo headphones on and listen to music. Or I go down to my workshop in the basement alone, tinker a bit, smoke my pipe, and turn the stereo on down there. But what I'm really doing is kind of thinking things over, taking a look at how life's going. If the pace has been hectic, then I try to take a weekend off to go up to the farm with my wife and sons. I just sit around and watch everybody and take my family for a walk in the woods. You know, once I'm there I don't want to leave. I really like it there."

Another Sensitive Personality offers this: "My husband works second shift, and when I get home from the office, he's gone. Some nights I wish he were home—too much time alone isn't good—but other nights I'm content. I'll sit and play records or watch television. Sometimes I read detective mysteries, and I even try to write them. I'm happy doing these things by myself. You've got to be by yourself sometimes."

One way or the other, Sensitive Personalities manage to find the time to slip into solitude, and it is a benefit to them. They need the time to integrate all that is happening around them, to sort problems, to seek solutions, to slow the pace, to savor the good feelings of peace and contentedness—or simply to enjoy the splendor of a good earth, a visual feast.

VULNERABILITIES AND CRISES

A healthy Sensitive Personality leisurely strolls the park on a summer evening, alive to the soft breeze, the glimmering lake, the sweet scent of summer, the sounds of crickets and children at play. His spirit is refreshed by the breeze and the moonlight and the fullness of life around him. He and the night and his world are one. Not the unhealthy Sensitive Personality. He dreads the night, a cover for evil. He walks in the shadows of his own fears. He shuns the moonlight and the possibility of any human contact; he curses the darkness, rages against the world around him. Rather than integrate with his environment, he runs from a world that he sees as fearful and fragmented, a place of lost hopes and brooding suspicions. He twists the Golden Rule to mean: "Get them before they get you." He never really knows who "they" might be; "they" might be anyone or everyone. Beware. Never trust. Suspect your neighbor as yourself.

The two individuals, one a healthy Sensitive Personality, the other not, represent the polarity between life viewed as a blessing or a curse, a harmonious whole or fragments in chaos, a place of trust or mistrust, of hope or despair, heaven on earth or hell on earth. The choice, really, is between maturity and immaturity, good emotional health or debilitating illness. But the choice for the troubled Sensitive Personality is difficult. In his better moments he can say, "I can enjoy life and the feeling of being one of God's creations, but there are other times when I shrink within myself." In those times he mistrusts the world as he mistrusts himself, and the more he shrinks into himself, the less he trusts, and the lower he sinks into the slavery of his own fears. "Life's a jungle" is the anthem of his misery. He is oversensitive to any criticism, any slight, or even the smallest abrasions of human exchange. His whole being becomes intensely sensitive, touchy, like an unlanced boil. He can be self-righteous and snide, believing himself the only person with an acceptable point of view or genuine feelings. Yet he is tormented by self-criticism, and he can wilt during disputes with others. He perceives the world as cold and hostile to his sensitive feelings. When that happens, he shuts off all communications and retreats into sullen solitude; he broods; he accuses himself of causing every mishap that happens in his presence: "It's all my fault." He is, he feels, always to blame.

"If anything can go wrong," states Murphy's Law, "it will." The troubled Sensitive Personality believes it, and he or she is the guarantor that something wrong will happen. At a party, someone comments on her new hairstyle: "It really suits your face so well." Oh? What does that mean? So intensely sensitive, she questions the comment, wondering if she isn't being ridiculed. She reads things into it, and then multiplies the suspicion by ten, her evening spoiled. Still, she might smile back; but inside, she is grim and feeling terrible.

The basketball coach jumped all over one of his players who happened to be a Sensitive Personality: "You haven't got it. You're not big enough or quick enough. You never make the big play. You don't hustle." The coach was blowing, as he always did whenever things weren't going right in a tight game, but the Sensitive player, so vulnerable in his feelings, began to get down on himself: "The coach is right. We're losing, and I'm to blame. I guess I'm not pushing myself enough. I'm not helping the team." In his amplified and negative reaction, he forgot that this same coach recruited him, started him, and praised him often. The Sensitive player simply couldn't work his way out of the gloom of his self-criticism and inner hurt. After the game he went off by himself feeling depressed and toying with the idea of giving up his scholarship and college career. Only after he heard his roommate griping about the coach also giving him hell did the Sensitive player begin to put things into perspective. He thought over the whole season. He knew he had worked hard, had carried his share of the load—and he realized too that he was prone to blame himself for other players' mistakes and the coach's wrath. He was able to resume practice the next day, working up a degree of confidence, playing a looser and more spontaneous game. Everything was back in equilibrium.

A troubled Sensitive Personality might tell you, "Don't take any wooden nickels." He might say it with a smile, but he isn't kidding. He means that *he* is the wooden nickel, the counterfeit; don't trust him. Why not? Because he doesn't trust himself. He is the master of self-fulfilling prophecy. Things always seem to go wrong when he expects them to go wrong; in fact, sometimes he gives them a nudge. If the hostile world doesn't attack on his time schedule, he attacks; he sets up some sort of rejection. Then he can kick himself; it's all his fault.

There was this lovely young girl, a Sensitive fifth-grader, who was told by her best friend that boys didn't like girls who were fat. This was her good friend whom she trusted, and she felt this message was meant for her. So she ran home to her mother's full-length mirror, and there she discovered what no one else had ever noticed: she was fat, especially her hips. After that, she no longer liked going to school, and she dreaded meeting the boys in her class. As she approached them, she kept her eyes on her feet, sure that everyone was staring at her hips. Every day she consulted the mirror, and every day her hips swelled before her eyes. As she grew older, the hips grew larger; she hid when she could and wept when she couldn't. She tried every fad diet, and she joined a health club, bumping and pounding her hips till they were blue with bruises. Still, the mirror showed her ugly things: she was a blimp, a balloon, the girl with the blossoming behind. She married and lived unhappily ever after, avoiding the eyes of neighbors and friends, never going to parties, shunning the pool, rarely going out of the house. Didn't everyone notice? Indeed, men noticed, and they looked, and they liked what they saw. But as they looked, she died inside. She was sure that they were looking and laughing at her horrendous hips. And that is the way it was for too long for a very trim, attractive, quite Sensitive woman who weighed a tidy 103 pounds, who was the one and only person who could see those hideous hips that she saw in the mirror. What she observed in the mirror so imperfectly was really the reflection of her intense focus on her overly sensitive feelings. Her inner world was so distorted that she projected it onto the world outside. Reality gave way to her distorted feelings about herself. For many long years she lived a hell that wasn't there.

So it goes for the fragile Sensitive Personality. He walks into a room, glances around, then quickly retreats, sure that all eyes are watching him. If he is sufficiently aware of his fear that others are watching him as intensely as he is prone to watch them, he can develop countermeasures. One Sensitive Personality explains how he handles this fear: "I go over to someone in the room I know, talk to him, buy him a beer. That way I feel less out of place, less aware of strangers."

An overly Sensitive woman is seated in a restaurant only to find the salad fork missing from her place setting. She is sure that the waiter removed it deliberately. There he is, standing two tables away, glaring at her—or so she supposes. A Sensitive Personality is godfather at a baptism, but he shrinks from holding the baby; he might drop him or crush him. He can't trust himself. A Sensitive wife considers hiring a private detective, certain that her husband is having an affair with every woman who frequents his shop. A troubled Sensitive Personality would dearly like to be a mailman working in the open air, but he knows so well that every dog alive has it in for him —and if the dogs don't get him, the pigeons will. To the thin-skinned, super-Sensitive Personality, it's a cruel, cruel world. Things can become so doom-laden that the troubled Sensitive Personality retreats more into himself; and as he cuts himself off from the outside world, he becomes increasingly depressed. His awareness of the outside world is void; his inner world is a fragmented ego slipping into darkness and chaos.

THE NEED TO TRUST

The middle ground, where most Sensitive Personalities find themselves, is typified by an awareness of the environment and a zeal to make it safe, serene, and productive for self and others. There is a keenness of observation, a curiosity, a quiet approach, a need for moments of solitude and reflection, a sensitivity to one's own feelings and the feelings of others. When all these elements are working in harmony and balance, the Sensitive Personality finds life peaceful and plentiful.

But there can be moments of stress that produce gray zones. His equilibrium might slip; he might overload his emphasis on self, others, or the environment. Zeal for a secure and serene environment might prompt him to espouse a rather rigid law-and-order attitude and to develop a sense of self-righteousness. Too intense a curiosity and too keen an awareness of others might lead to suspicion and jealousy in personal relationships and a tendency to look for conspiracy and subversion in political matters. His need for occasional moments of solitude might at times degenerate into moody moments of alienation and estrangement. Then too, he might slip into so much introspection that he becomes terribly critical of himself, his attitudes, and his actions. If he is not careful, he might end up blaming himself for everything wrong around him, a gloomy Atlas shouldering all the blame for the troubles and woes of the world. In moments like these, he tends to let others run over him; he gives in or gives way much too easily. He has trouble communicating; he wishes he were more open, more assertive, more vocal. Once again, he ends up blaming himself too much. He simply doesn't have enough confidence to act otherwise. Inside he becomes angry and sullen, pushing the anger deeper and deeper. The Sensitive Personality can be his own worst enemy. What he ought to do in moments like these is to seek out a good friend to whom he can open up. Rather than keep all his pained feelings locked up inside, better to talk it out. Better to trust.

GROWING UP SENSITIVE

The cluster of traits that distinguish the Sensitive Personality manifest slowly in childhood. He may be a bit more prone to colic as a baby, more sensitive to temperature, in small ways evoking a little more concern from his parents. He might be more afraid of the dark than most children, and he seems to experience more nightmares than other personality styles. This is *not* the child to threaten with the bogeyman or other horrors meant to keep him in line. He is so keenly aware and so imaginative that the imagery can become all too powerful.

The Sensitive child gives and receives affection rather easily, although in the early years, especially between one and two, he can be a one-parent child. He tends to react sensitively to that parent's moods and attitudes, particularly when that parent appears nervous or upset. He may cuddle up to that parent without saying much. He reacts well to other children although he may be a little more shy than the others. He can be stubborn, but he is slow to show temper. He does not appear overly aggressive, and if his friend were to hit him while they were playing, he wouldn't hit back. Already the basic disposition encapsuled in the Golden Rule is at work; he doesn't want to be hit, so he doesn't hit. He may cry, and cry hard, and it might take a parent or another adult to settle his disputes with other children. If, however, his friend were to hit him yet another time he might strike back mightily. The dispute would usually end then and there.

The Sensitive child enjoys being involved in the things his parents are doing. He may show an interest in helping mother in the kitchen, or he might volunteer to set the table. He will watch his father fix the toaster with intense interest, or he might follow him around as he works in the garden, observing everything he does. He will listen attentively as his parents discuss any subject from religion to rising prices. His eagerness to learn and his awareness of the feelings of others prompt parents and other relatives to describe him as "wise beyond his years." The Sensitive child enjoys those moments when he is the center of his parents' attention. Being something of a worrier, he is prone to express fears of what he doesn't like, even before he experiences them. His feelings can be tender and easily hurt, and he likes to be cuddled and loved. And why not? This child so richly benefits from all forms of assurance that he is surrounded by people who are good and generous, that his is a serene and peaceful world, and that he is quite a lovable person.

But there is a danger. The Sensitive child doesn't benefit from syrupy doses of sympathy—understanding and affection, yes; sympathy, no. Sympathy can block his understanding of events, especially those he finds threatening or discomforting.

A Sensitive child of seven, for example, was punished by his mother for something he didn't do, although she thought he did. He wrote his mother an angry note—"I feel like killing myself"—shoved it into her hand, and ran to his room. He expected sympathy—but he didn't get it, and that was good; sympathy would only have reinforced his impression that he had been wronged. Instead, his mother explained why she thought he was responsible and then told him: "I love you, and I care about you. But I'm not going to accept this treatment from you." She didn't punish him for the note, and she didn't show anger. What she did was help him to understand that there was a point of view other than his own. She offered him a reasonable alternative to his locked-in feelings; and she showed that she really did care.

The beginning of school normally presents no serious problems for the Sensitive child unless he encounters a harsh experience such as an accident in the playground. If so, he might run home instead of seeking help at hand. School is an opportunity for the Sensitive child to pursue his usual curiosity, and to utilize his awareness of what is going on around him and his ability to organize and plan well. At times he may be more interested in the teacher who shows interest in him, who displays genuine regard for him, the sort of teacher who is able to create trust in her relationships with him and his fellow students. The child may remember this special teacher with lifelong affection. He will remember fondly all those moments spent in closeness with any adult—parent, teacher, relative, neighbor—who provides him with a tranquil and secure environment. On the other hand, he may be distressed when his favorite teacher is absent or when a well-loved aunt or uncle moves away. At such moments he may be reduced to tears, his small world fragmenting.

What the Sensitive child needs to develop at this age—and all through life—is a sense of trust and confidence in himself, that his reality as a person is less a matter of what happens in the world outside than how he feels about himself. He needs to learn to evaluate his own behavior. Here he can benefit greatly by learning to make constructive use of his moments of solitude and introspection. Valued adults, especially parents and teachers, have the opportunity to assist him—not by imposing their own standards of evaluation but by helping him interpret his own feelings by sharing them. He needs experience in communication, opportunities and encouragement to express his feelings, thoughts, and attitudes. He needs to hear from these valued adults the benefits of his abilities to observe and to organize, to be told that he is intelligent—and it is helpful for him to be encouraged to use these talents fully. But in all of this, the attention should be focused on the child as a valued person. He needs to be aware of *himself;* he is already so keenly aware of everything else.

But beware of overkill. Don't be so concerned that you try too hard, as if the child were a clam and you were trying to pry him out of his shell. He isn't a clam. He is a sensitive and shy child. Wait for appropriate openings and respond to his initiative. When the child wants to open up, be available, but don't rush into his solitude. Intrude, and he might retreat deeper into himself. Never coerce— this only tells the Sensitive child that you feel something is wrong— maybe him? He doesn't hear the message that his math needs improvement, or that he isn't reading well, or that you are only encouraging him to open up. What he perceives is your frustration, and he reads it as finding fault; he must have done something wrong. This feeling lingers for a long time, and he is likely to slip away to his secret haven of safety. As one Sensitive Personality recalls: "I had my own little hiding place where I could shut everyone out. I thought this would keep them away from me so they wouldn't be hurting me any more." Even when the Sensitive child can't physically retreat when his feelings are hurt, he has a talent for hiding his feelings behind a mask of composure. Better to conceal than reveal, he feels.

The bond between the Sensitive child and his parents seems to grow deeper from age seven or eight onward. He is sensitive to their feelings and moods, and is quick to pick up on their interests in music, books, or sports. He may complain when his father is not interested or is too busy to play ball or to work with him, say, in Cub Scouts. He will be sensitive in his reaction to accidents or injuries; he may lose all interest in baseball after a bruising collision at home plate, or she may never again engage in gymnastics after a fractured wrist.

We mentioned earlier the young girl who reacted far too sensitively to a remark from a friend about boys not liking fat girls. Any negative comment from parents, teachers, or coaches may do similar damage. Let a dancing teacher tell a Sensitive child that she is too clumsy to perform well in ballet, or let a father tell a son that he shows little talent for football, and that child may quit abruptly, losing all interest but remembering the remark. And when told that he is not aggressive enough or is a quitter, the child is genuinely confused.

The adult's actions also speak painfully. For example, the coach was warming up his star pitcher for a Little League game, and he threw the nine-year-old a hard curve that jammed the boy's thumb. The boy thought to himself: "Why did he do that to me? I must be a lousy pitcher." He was still blaming himself, intent on quitting, when his mother said to him: "You get back out there and play." This wasn't the best of answers. A better response would have been to listen to him, hear him out, assure him, and counter the hurt by helping him to understand what happened by offering him alternative ways of looking at the coach's act. *Then* she might encourage him to continue playing baseball.

Adults need to listen carefully to what the Sensitive child is trying to communicate—and they need to listen to themselves responding. The parent who pushes the Sensitive child too hard, wanting him "to be like all the other children," may be pushing him in the wrong direction. He can't be like other children; he can only be himself. Negative comments summarily voiced are perceived as accusations of wrongdoing; lack of interest is viewed as a form of rejection. The cutting remark, contradictory evaluations, even small slights, communicate to the Sensitive child that he deserves little respect, that he is a mass of faults, that he is not to be trusted, that he cannot trust others. He finds it increasingly convenient to project his feelings onto the environment: "My Dad sleeps all day; that's why I can't play football." "My dancing teacher gets me all confused, and I can't tell my right foot from my left." Parents and other influencing adults will find it difficult when correcting the child in early and middle grades because of his sensitivity. They may even feel that the child has a hateful or spiteful attitude, but what the Sensitive child is really feeling is a growing mistrust in himself. At times like these, he may revert to a fear of sleeping alone. Others, including peers, may mistake his hurt feelings and his tendency to withdraw as hostility toward them: "Charlie has that chip on his shoulder." No, Charlie has a cross on his shoulders, his own bruised and tender feelings about himself.

The Sensitive parent has a wonderful opportunity to be an interpreter for the Sensitive child whose feelings about himself sometimes are too intense and confused. The parent has the same sensitivity and awareness, the same tendencies to turn inward and to accept blame. More, he has the great advantage of having lived through similar childhood experiences. One mother, a different personality style, kept urging her Sensitive son to be a better student, to be a more socially involved person, to be a star athlete. She also urged the Sensitive father to be more involved in his son's activities, especially in sports. The father's immediate response was to blame himself for those things his wife suggested were missing in their son's life, and he told me, "I guess I haven't been a good enough father." When the mother urged father and son to spend evenings playing baseball together, the father said he supposed he ought to, but the son said he really didn't think so. To that the father responded, "You know, I think he's right." Still, he told me later, he wondered if he shouldn't have gone along with his wife. I told him that what he did was appropriate and that he was being a good father: "What you did was understand your son." This was a welcome insight that continued to be of benefit to both father and son.

A Sensitive mother told me that one Sunday morning she awoke to find her Sensitive daughter standing at the foot of her bed watching her. The girl explained that she was worried that her mother might be dead—she had diabetes, and the daughter worried that she might eat improperly. She feared too that her mother might go blind. Then, reported the mother, "I thought back to the time I was a child, a daughter, and my own pattern of thinking. So I took her and hugged her and let her know I loved her. Remembering my own feelings, I let her know she was a very good, sweet person and that she had done nothing that might cause me to die. I also let her know I very much appreciated her care and concern. After that, she seemed to feel better." Once again, the Sensitive parent was able to foster understanding in the child by sharing feelings and interpreting experiences.

Sensitive Personalities who move through early and middle childhood without developing feelings of mistrust or rejection usually are well liked and accepted, especially when they have shared in group projects and group efforts. If too shy, the Sensitive child might find any number of excuses for not participating, fearful of making mistakes and being at fault if projects failed. And, as at any age, the Sensitive Personality moves into friendships slowly. But, given the opportunity, the Sensitive child does very well in student politics, sports, debating, social and club projects. She may be too shy for the Maypole dance, but permit her to take charge of organizing the dance, and it will go well and smoothly. Ask him to participate in the student council, and he will contribute productively. He will make good use of his planning and organizing abilities on the debating team, helping his team to reach the state finals, and learning along the way that he can speak effectively without his voice quivering. He learns too that a smile wins points, a frozen face does not. He gains confidence.

THE TEEN YEARS

Adolescence reopens the vulnerabilities experienced in childhood: overreaction to slight, harsh criticism, and physical injury. The Sensitive young woman who is stood up for an important date seems to brood for an unduly long time. The Sensitive trumpeter, upbraided by the musical director before the entire 140-piece marching band for blowing a clinker, may put away his horn forever. Peer ridicule—so easily and glibly exchanged in adolescence—can be felt so greatly by the Sensitive teenager that he feels rejected and might turn to alcohol or drugs. Peer acceptance is so important that the very aware Sensitive young person is uncomfortable unless he or she is very much in tune with the current teen fashions. He is so busy working for acceptance that "you can't relax and just be yourself." If heavy wool sweaters are the vogue on campus this year, she will wear the style, even though she itches all day. If weights are the thing, he will spend his afternoons pumping iron, even when he would rather be home reading a good book. The efforts to be part of the peer group are beneficial; they draw the Sensitive teenager out of his passive role of observer. If all goes well, the youngster grows in confidence. A Sensitive woman remembers disliking school until her junior year of high school when she began to be more outgoing and found herself accepted: "I changed. I started liking people more, cutting up, and just having fun. Then I liked my junior and senior years." Parents and teachers can support the emerging Sensitive adolescent by pointing out and supporting his special strengths, appeal, and capability. With all of his awareness and ability to organize data, the Sensitive teenager will make good use of the information.

But, once again, the Sensitive Personality is also capable of misinterpreting the information, especially in a corrective situation. A Sensitive teenager began dating the same young man rather frequently. Her parents became especially concerned when she talked with him on the phone every day at great length. They finally came to the point where they felt it necessary to discuss the excessive telephoning. They didn't try to break up the relationship; they only told her to limit the time spent on the telephone. She didn't hear it that way; she thought they were telling her that she couldn't talk to him at all. She was very upset, feeling her parents were trying to run her life without considering her feelings. After some reflection, she began to hear again what they said, and she agreed with them. More, she realized that they were not being cruel or mean; they were only concerned for her welfare.

Death of a loved grandparent or one parent leaving home through divorce can be shattering for the Sensitive Personality whether in childhood or adolescence. He very well might grieve unduly for that grandparent, or feel rejected by the parent who leaves the home, perhaps even becoming concerned that he was to blame for the breakup of the marriage. He might think it happened because he wasn't a good person. Here he would benefit greatly if he were helped to understand as much as possible the circumstance of the adult business of divorce. He needs to know that both parents care about him and are concerned for his well-being. This, ultimately, is what needs to be the center of his awareness: "What your parents do about their relationship is their decision. But what is really important to you is their love and your understanding. The other things matter less."

MARRIAGE AND COURTSHIP

The Sensitive Personality, so careful in all his relationships, tends to date fewer people than other personality styles. He tends to be attracted to a warm, outgoing, and friendly person, and is most comfortable with someone who is carefree and pleasant yet sufficiently serious about life. A smile is a beacon to the aware Sensitive Personality, a sign of openness and friendliness. "That smile; it could light up the night." "He was very gentle and kind, and he liked to talk to me. He seemed always to make me feel so good. He lifted my spirit." "He is always happy, and he likes other people to be happy. If you have a problem or are upset about something, he'll help in any way he can." Even so, the Sensitive Personality normally takes his time in pursuing the relationship, noting everything positive and negative about the other person's makeup. But once he makes his decision that this is the right person, he gives his all to make the relationship work; his loyalty, his sense of mutuality, his awareness all work for him in establishing that relationship.

Marriage is never approached casually or impetuously. The Sensitive Personality invests heavily, and should the marriage end in divorce, he will have difficulty. He might blame himself, but he also feels rejected. He broods long and bitterly after the separation, unless he is very healthy, and might be so mistrusting thereafter that he shies from marrying again.

The healthy Sensitive Personality arranges a relationship in which he and his spouse share and enjoy mutual interests that contribute to the growth of their marriage. He doesn't compete with his partner; rather, he supports the outgoing and spontaneous style of his spouse. In turn, his partner appreciates his gentle humor, his kindness, his sensitivity toward the other person's needs and feelings. The partner of the Sensitive Personality very well might be the sort of person who recognizes, appreciates, and encourages the strong

222

planning and organizing talents of that style both at home and in his career—and if sufficiently attuned to the Sensitive Personality's need for solitude and reflection, he will not only tolerate this need but encourage it.

The less secure Sensitive Personality might be tormented in marriage by jealousy, his own lack of confidence prompting him to be suspicious, accusing his spouse of infidelity. His spouse benefits by knowing that this climate of suspicion is really the Sensitive partner's excessive awareness and preoccupation with everything going on outside himself—to the detriment of his own positive feelings. The problem is, again, one of sharing and understanding. Rather than respond with indignation and retaliation—however tempting—the spouse might reverse the polarity of the situation by offering calm reassurance while inviting him to consider his feelings as projected self-criticism. The problem is also lessened by mutual giving, especially if the Sensitive partner is able to go beyond the moment of jealousy by reflecting on the larger moments of mutual sharing and tenderness that he values so much. His tendency to slip into solitude is always a hazard when he is troubled. He wallows in his misery, and would benefit more by being open to communication—only that way can he receive any interpretation other than his own negative readings; only through open communication can he hope for sufficient understanding to resolve his jealousy. That way too, he opens himself up to other relationships and social occasions that are otherwise stifled by his mistrust of self and others. The more the Sensitive Personality opens himself to more friendships and social moments, the better his sense of equilibrium between his own feelings and the human environment.

The Sensitive parent tends to be loving and doting, gladly sharing his observations, insights, values, experiences, and interests with his children. He is quite capable of romping and playing freely with younger children, entering fully into their world. Remembering his own childhood, he may try to provide the same experiences that he so much enjoyed and still cherishes—or that he feels he missed. He will make every effort to fashion a stable, serene world for his children. He will take them into the woods on an autumnal day, to the circus and movies, and he will share peanuts and popcorn with them at the ball park, cheering lustily. He will endure piano recitals and Little League games, Girl Scout cookie drives and teacher conferences for the sake of his much-loved children. He will sit with them watching their favorite shows on television, enjoying them as much as the children do—sometimes even more. Whenever possible, he seeks the company of his children and their friends, delighted to share their world.

If the Sensitive parent's own childhood was marred by frequent moves, he will try very hard—even at some sacrifice to professional advancement—to establish a peaceful and rooted home for his family. Again, his priority is always to establish a secure and serene environment, and—following his disposition toward the Golden Rule—he very much wants for his children what he wants for himself.

THE WORKING WORLD

The Sensitive Personality works optimally in a job or professional situation that allows him full exercise of his strengths of perception, awareness, planning, organization, and creative problem-solving. Thus he works effectively in research, engineering, the sciences; inspection, tool-making, highly skilled crafts; commercial art and design; teaching; officiating in sports, law and law enforcement. The latter might be particularly appealing since it utilizes not only his keen awareness, but his sense of fair play and his desire to make the environment a peaceful place. He might tend to be of a rather exact law-and-order mentality, but would not be the head-knocking policeman; he is too fair-minded for that. He wants justice to be done—and he would not want to be responsible for an injustice.

The Sensitive Personality might be attracted to politics because of his tendency to espouse strong values and to have definite opinions and well-informed attitudes. He would be well aware of social needs and would promote social justice and equity. He might, however, find the give and take of campaigning difficult, and criticism and competition in public might sting. And, being normally a private person, he would find his loss of solitude discomforting. Still, for the sake of justice and the welfare of others, he could be attracted to the political arena.

The Sensitive Personality does not make an enthusiastic assembly line worker—there is little opportunity to employ the full range of his curiosity, creativity, and organization. He might find production

224

quotas and close supervision uncomfortable. Where the level of quality in production was low and the attitude of management one of expediency—"Just get the work out"—he would chafe. He not only believes in a good day's work for a good day's pay, he believes too in giving the consumer a decent product at a decent price. Nothing less is acceptable.

Retirement poses few problems for the Sensitive Personality. He might welcome early retirement so that he can pursue some long-desired interest such as teaching, the ministry, or public service—"something I've always wanted to do but couldn't afford to do; but now I'm going to do it." He might involve himself in those areas where he sees injustice, unhappiness, or things that need correction. He might run for city council or volunteer to work with a social agency or support projects for preserving the environment, natural resources, or rare animals threatened by extinction. He would be delighted to work for agencies promoting world peace or food production or health—again, anything that contributes to a wholesome, productive, peaceful world. He is not usually interested in accumulating money—rather he is interested in people and their needs, and he is willing to try to help. He cares.

Other than desiring to be of service to others, the retired Sensitive Personality enjoys travel—anything from a world tour to exploring a historical site in the next county. He might want to indulge his love for the beauty of nature by going off to the mountains or the desert, the river country or the ocean. "There is nothing more appealing than sitting on the beach, feeling the salt air in your face, and hearing the waves hit the sand. That's the most relaxing thing in the world." Wherever, he relishes the solitude and the feeling of being one with all the rich goodness of the earth.

Socially, the Sensitive Personality tends to move in a tight circle of friends whom he has come to know gradually. While he thinks of himself as an open and friendly person—and he is—he is not comfortable in large crowds, especially where attention might be focused on him. He might enjoy playing bridge, attending concerts, sharing a drink and conversation with old friends, or going fishing where the air is clear and clean and sunlight dances on the stream. Otherwise, he is content to read a book, perhaps a good detective novel, and he often enjoys writing. He might mix his love of music with his liking for solitude. A friend of mine with a Sensitive Personality recently took up the guitar, and while she loves it dearly, she finds the lessons and the awkwardness of the beginner something of a challenge to her sensitivity. Still at the "plunk, plunk, plunk" stage, her husband enjoys teasing her, and, she reports: "I get a little upset by his sly remarks." And her shyness surfaces in the group instruction she is taking. When the teacher has each student play a piece individually, my friend feels the strain, which she manages to conceal rather well. "I'm trembling away inside, but outside I'm doing my darndest."

ALTERNATIVES AND OPTIONS

We have seen that the Sensitive Personality is a gentle and kind person who, despite a tendency to be shy, is keenly aware of everything and everybody around him, who desires to respond in a helpful way to the needs of others. He pursues the Golden Rule as a basic disposition toward others and as a guard against disruption and chaos in all parts of the environment. He is the peacemaker. Above all else in life, the Sensitive Personality desires happy and harmonious relationships, especially in marriage. He likes to work in a position that utilizes his skills in observing, organizing, and planning while permitting him to be productive and contributive in a personally satisfying way. He makes friends slowly, and he tends to restrict his friendships to a few; but, as a friend, he is loyal and trusting. And, always, he is a person who wants and works for a peaceful life in which he and his family and friends can enjoy serenity and safety.

These very worthy goals are quite possible and available to the healthy Sensitive Personality. The more he knows his strengths and weaknesses, the more available they are. For the less healthy Sensitive Personality, the same goals are possible, but the struggle to achieve them is much greater. He can try too hard to be helpful and nice, so much so that he doesn't lead his own life. He can be so loyal and sacrificing in his love that he is willing to give up his good feelings about himself to be the person he believes others *apparently* want him to be. He can be so influenced by the environment that he feels responsible for every mishap, and he can assume the blame for every fault and failing; he can be his own worst enemy. He tends to be so aware of the possibilities of hurt and harm that he fears he might cause them to happen—and then he is prone to retreat into solitude

226

as a defense rather than as an opportunity for objective evaluation. He hides. He has emptied himself of all trust and confidence in himself. The solution, then, is to work back into the environment, into human company, into communication and trust. He needs to restore equilibrium within himself and with the world outside him.

If you are a Sensitive Personality, how do you go about this? Consider the following:

• First, don't keep it all inside. Turn it outside by opening up to close friends and family, people you trust.

• Begin by taking small steps—one step at a time. Get to know people. Let friendships grow, however gradual the growth rate. The more you are involved, the more you will learn to trust yourself.

• "Getting involved" means for you the ability to relate to others without being so guarded.

• Stop blaming yourself for every tragedy, major and minor—you really aren't that powerful or that negative an influence. It's only that you magnify and amplify perceptions, and convert flaws and failings in the environment into personal flaws and failings.

• Be more responsible for your inner feelings and less responsive to any slight from the outside.

• Loyalty is a great virtue. Try being loyal to yourself more often.

• Use your capacities of observation and reflection to examine and evaluate those experiences where you have been highly successful in trusting yourself and others. You need to acknowledge these moments positively.

• You tend to depreciate, criticize, and condemn yourself. The next time you hear yourself saying, "It's all my fault," look again. You're projecting. Don't.

• Try a little more tact. You sometimes blurt out snide and inappropriate remarks when you are feeling suspicious of others. Tact comes with trust.

• Use an occasional moment of reflection to tally the good jobs you have done, the kind deeds, the thoughtful gestures. Each night before you go to sleep, you might make it a practice to review the day with its many good moments.

• Don't let shyness rob you of opportunities for communication and interaction. Try the new restaurant you've been wanting to try; go to that party that interests you. The more you try new experiences, the more you mingle with others, the easier it will become. And when you don't go because you fear being a bumbling idiot, you've already bumbled a bit.

• Trust your own wishes, your own feelings, your own hopes. Trust that other people really care about you and your needs. Trust is the first step in growth. Acting on that trust is the second step. Acknowledging your effort is the third step. Feeling good about it is the fourth. Once you've gone that far, each step gets easier.

• People find your shyness and reserve refreshing in this aggressive society. Did you know that?

• Beware of your bitterness. You need to recognize your bitter feelings as anger, especially when you feel rejected. Recognize too that this bitter anger paralyzes you; it interferes with your ability to share care and concern; and the more you show your anger and hurt, the more you provoke rejection. This is that sad way of making your worst fears come true.

• When you are feeling sad and lonely and wanting human company, don't plunge. Sometimes you want to be too friendly too quickly. Friendships can't be made like instant coffee. They are more like wine that needs slow aging. And this is more your style. So take it slowly.

• Don't let your easily embarrassed feelings make a quitter of you. If you would like a new hairstyle or to grow a beard, do it. Sure, people will tease—that is a strange, tribal sign of recognition in our society. It also means people like you. So try that new dress. Take guitar lessons. Wear that new swimsuit. Enjoy.

• You have an engaging, subtle sense of humor. People enjoy it. Use it, but don't push it; and don't back off if you should. Just be yourself: a gentle person of gentle mirth.

• You are creative at work. But, like everyone else, you have your limits. Why invent the wheel every time out? Trust others enough to share in the enterprise; benefit from their contribution. Joint effort and group success will foster a climate of trust. And it will help you avoid that great sense of fatigue you sometimes experience when you face a task to be shared with others.

• You don't need sympathy. You need to understand what is going on around you and within you. Let others help you interpret interactions. That's what friends are for.

• Stop looking on life as a battlefield. What you are experiencing is your own mistrust that sometimes takes a hostile turn. What you really fear is how well you will relate to others. Try trusting enough to find out that you can—and do—relate in so many acceptable ways. Turn the negatives into positives.

• Quit supposing that everyone is watching you. This is your projection of your tendency to be so aware. Besides, since you have become so accustomed to looking at the ground, how can you know if others are watching you? Look up. Look around. Smile.

• Your timing can be unfortunate. You tend to open conversations with your spouse, co-workers, and friends when they are busy with a task. This poor timing invites rejection—which may be what you unconsciously want. It's a little like wearing a "Kick Me" sign. Wait until the other person is available, then have a good exchange.

• Avoid using your curiosity and analytical ability so much that you close off opportunities to interact and be close.

• Avoid hashing over old grievances. This is another ploy for avoiding getting involved with people.

• You can see what you want to see in a mirror. If you feel your image is poor, you'll see a poor image in the mirror. If you want to see a fat man, you'll see a fat man. If you want to see a drab woman, you'll see a drab woman. But you are a person, not an image. The true mirror of your whole self is your ability to trust yourself and others.

Everyone tends to see the world around him in the same way he sees himself. In your case, you view others as you view yourself: mistrusting, open and vulnerable to being rejected. Once you begin to trust yourself, you will discover, suddenly, that the whole world is more trustworthy. The more you trust, the more friendships are open to you.

• Always accept the opportunity to be with children. Relax, play the clown, laugh, enjoy. The more you experience the company of children, the more you will gain in confidence and the better you will interact generally. Remember: an adult is a child who has kept his sense of wonder intact while growing in wisdom and age.

• Stop always observing others. With your creative imagination, you can see what you want to see in others: when you are feeling poorly about yourself and not confident, you see nothing but threats; you see only evidence of your own inadequacies. Let your anger tell you that you are mistrusting not those whom you observe, but yourself.

• Pursue your religious values. They will help you promote a greater sense of trust and will help you see the harmony and equilibrium between you, other people, and the world around you.

• Don't conceal. Open up to others—communicate. Don't hide; you can't run from your own feelings about yourself. And don't try wearing a mask of composure. It is great for playing poker, but is a poor disguise for hiding a troubled self. Don't try to be different persons for different people. Just be yourself.

• Don't hold back the laughter. Laughter is a healthy sign that you are becoming more realistic, more relaxed about yourself. That's healthy. You are learning to trust enough to be happy. So laugh, love, and be happy. You deserve it.

• Peace . . .

X

*I had rather be right than
be President.*

HENRY CLAY

The Determined
Personality

THE DETERMINED PERSONALITY stresses the three R's that constitute the fundamentals of his personality style: right, responsibility, and respect. Always and in everything, he tries to do what is right, to be responsible, and thus to merit the respect of family, friends, and associates. The Determined Personality goes about the business of doing what he believes is right in a quiet, yet tenacious—even stubborn—way; even so, his tenacity is usually softened by his composure and his capacity for empathy. He is a persuasive person, adept at soliciting the support of others in pursuit of his goals, although he will make the effort to be aware of the other person, his feelings, and his needs. The Determined Personality wants to be agreeable, and, more often than not, he is indeed agreeable; abrasive attack and indifference are not his style. He can be competitive, but he goes about it in an unassuming and low-keyed fashion, so understated in his aggression that he is disarming.

There is this too about the Determined Personality: wherever you encounter him, something is happening—but just *what* is happening may not always be so apparent. The action may be so subtle, so obtuse, that you may miss it or its significance. But don't bother to ask the Determined activist what's happening—he might find it difficult to explain, or he might prefer not to tell you. Still, *something* is happening.

Consider the following example.

Negotiations between the local police association and the city council were deadlocked at contract time. The police were prohibited by law from striking, and the council, well aware of the law, was sitting tight, rejecting the association's demands. So what were the police to do? Capitulate—simply give in—or go out on an illegal strike, an alternative that was unacceptable to most of the police officers?

The police did neither. Instead, they chose a rather simple tactic: they enforced the local traffic ordinances rigorously. They ticketed every misparked vehicle, cited even the slightest moving violation, and wrote up every jaywalker, noisy muffler, and broken taillight. All week long, city hall's switchboard glittered and buzzed like a pinball machine; traffic court overflowed; frustrated citizens wrote irate letters to an irate editor who tried vainly to reach the mayor, who was trying vainly to appease his twice-ticketed wife. At the next council meeting, a packed gallery of concerned citizens watched as the council voted to grant the police association its new contract with the major portion of its demands intact.

Not surprisingly, a Determined Personality suggested this no-strike, no-capitulation tactic—and, rather typically, he found the oblique approach, the roundabout strategy, that broke the deadlock to produce victory without wounds. The healthy Determined Personality has the knack of putting together a strategy that can make a difficult situation productive. His approach seems to be governed by a clear vision of goals and values pursued, sometimes openly, sometimes surreptitiously, whether in search of a working contract, uniforms for the girls' hockey team, lights in the park, or a better budget for running the household. He always tries to take a calm approach, to consider both sides of an issue, to work things out in a fair and equitable way. He is willing to consider compromise, if the situation so indicates. Thus the Determined Personality is often cast in the role of mediator or negotiator, even in family disputes; as we saw in the case of the police association's negotiations, he functions well as a catalyst who can make things happen. He also has a respect for authority, even when he disagrees or disputes the actions or position of those in authority. He works to keep opportunity alive, to keep his options open, and, if at all possible, he will try to avoid head-on confrontation and hardnosed stalemates. His preferred tactic is persuasion, gentle and constant; he tries to avoid bloody wounds that leave scars and bitter resentment. However right he believes his views and his position, he is concerned that justice be done. That is his understanding of what it means to be responsible.

THE RIGHTNESS URGE

"The only obligation which I have a right to assume is to do at any time what I think is right." This statement by Henry David Thoreau so well summarizes the essential disposition of the Determined Personality. We call it the *urge to be right,* or the rightness urge. It includes not only the Determined Personality's prevailing concern for being right and doing right, but his respect for all human rights, his own and those of others. The constant intent on doing right and being right and fostering rights supposes a great sense of responsibility, a sense of purpose; and indeed the Determined Personality is concerned that he pursue the right values, the right goals, the right means, the right course of action. All this requires right thinking and right planning, so the Determined Personality goes about the business of doing right in a deliberate manner, maintaining a low profile as much as possible, keeping tight focus on both ends and means, and planning in a way that minimizes any risk that might impede his effort or prevent him from reaching his goal.

But the Determined Personality can be so deliberate and unhurried in the formulation of his strategy that others find it difficult to know what he is about—and he very well might not think it necessary to let them know. The Determined Personality tends to remain undeclared until he is sure of himself, sure that his strategy is right. Thus his style of always wanting to be sure that everything is right before he proceeds is often perplexing to others, even to close friends and supporters. It makes no difference whether he is fixing his carburetor or contemplating a job change, arranging the furniture or buying a house; since he is absorbed in his enterprise, he supposes that everyone should know what he intends by observing what he

233

is doing. But if he is walking through the shopping center, how can you tell if he is going to the auto parts store or to the barber shop? Is he rearranging the furniture or getting ready to give it away? In the event that he is asked what he is doing, he might say, "I thought you knew," or, "Can't you see?" or, "I really didn't think you needed to know." Or, silence. And if you probe further into his thoughts, plans, or actions you will be wasting your time and his. He will only clam up more firmly; even in resisting, he is determined—and there is no way to be more determined than a Determined Personality. Better simply to observe what he is doing, and hope that you can discover what is happening. When he feels the time is right—when his goal is clear, his plan is sure and structured, and he feels that support is needed and available—he will solicit support and invite others to share responsibility. But before then, silence and ferment.

Here is a typical situation. The local school board was considering various ways of trimming its budget for the coming years. One item that board members thought might be reduced significantly was the cost of maintaining the high school marching band past football season, so its budgeted allowance was to be cut in half. But one band member's mother, a Determined Personality, knew that the reduction would eliminate two trips very important to the band's pride: one to compete with other high school bands in the state capital, and one to play at opening-day ceremonies for the major-league baseball team in a nearby city. Even more significant, she felt, were a number of small shows that band members put on each year for residents of the local home for the elderly, the school for retarded children, and children's hospital. These events simply were not allowed for in the budget figures.

A series of ideas came to her, which she sifted and sorted until she was sure that she had the right plan. A band show was scheduled for the children's hospital a week before the next monthly meeting of the school board. Meanwhile, she recruited a task force of other band mothers to: (1) invite the school board president to present the band at the hospital; (2) contact the local newspaper editor, supply him with background information, and ask if he might send a feature writer and photographer to cover the event; and (3) solicit the support of the hospital's public relations director to have the children write and illustrate their own thank-you notes and then send them to the school board.

234

Later that week, a full-page photo feature ran in the paper. Prominent in one of the photographs was the school board president being hugged by two children in hospital gowns. On the evening of the board meeting, some forty delightful, handmade cards from hospitalized children were displayed along the main hall of the office of education building. Outside, fifty uniformed band members serenaded board members as they arrived for the monthly meeting. The band budget was not cut, and, moreover, the board members praised the high school band for bringing credit to the school. The hospital was delighted with the favorable publicity it received; the editor was glad to have the opportunity to run a good human-interest story; and the band members relished the recognition they received from the board—and from their school peers—for being something more than a halftime filler at football games. And one tired but very satisfied Determined mother enjoyed her first full night's sleep in more than a week.

CAPACITY FOR SACRIFICE

The band episode illustrates many of the distinguishing traits of the healthy Determined Personality: pursuit of a definite goal, response to a problem characterized by the structuring of a careful plan of action, silence until the plan is "right," an indirect but constructive approach, a sharing of responsibility on his own terms. The Determined mother did not call a meeting to discuss the problem with other parents; rather, she presented them with a fully developed plan and solicited their cooperation. She did not confront the school board or challenge its authority; she devised a flanking action that threatened no one. Her avoidance of a frontal attack also permitted everyone to share in the fruits of victory.

One trait of the Determined Personality that was utilized but did not show so clearly is the capacity for personal sacrifice. If necessary, if he feels that it will help him achieve his goal, the Determined Personality will deny himself his evening meal, a night's sleep, a day off or a day's pay, just so long as he feels his cause is right—his children's education, campaigning for a candidate for public office, safety standards at the factory, clear air in his town, safe streets, lower priced utilities for the elderly, day care centers for working mothers, his

s dance lessons, whatever he envisions as something of value.
at even tolerate verbal or physical abuse, a less-than-satisfying
ng hours of overtime, few creature comforts—the sacrifice is
table, the pain tolerable, so long as his goal is right.

His friends can't understand why Jerry is always turning down their invitations to bowl and to play poker; they know that he loves them both. Jerry, in his usual pleasant way, always thanks his friends for inviting him, but always adds, "Some other time." What he doesn't tell them is that he spends most of his free time working at the Veterans Administration Center with disabled veterans; and, not surprisingly, most of his friends are unaware that Jerry himself was badly wounded in World War II.

I know a research chemist who quit a very good and well-paying job during the war in Vietnam because he thought it was wrong to help develop chemical weapons for use in a war he believed was morally unjust. Less significant, perhaps, but no less illustrative is the case of a Determined baseball player in college who benched himself because he felt his weak play at second base was hurting the team. In doing so, he hurt his chances for setting a school record in total hits for a season.

VULNERABILITIES AND CRISES

The Determined Personality, as we have seen, is an activist who pursues his goals with determination. He values planning as a way of assuring achievement of his goals. He is deliberate, purposeful, constructive; concerned about people, and capable of self-sacrifice for the sake of others and his goal. He is ethical, fair, and just in his dealings with others and in pursuit of his goal. He is calm, persuasive, unassuming; he values honesty, dignity, integrity. He often communicates more by his presence and what he does than by what he says, often understating what he is about and why. He is rarely frivolous and usually busy pursuing some objective or planning a strategy to attain it. He has a high regard for others, and he prizes their respect. Always, he wants to do right, be right, but it is *his* determination of right that he values.

But while doing right and being right may come naturally, they don't always come easily, and here is where the great strength of the

Determined Personality can develop into a weakness. Too much emphasis on being right can convert determination into stubbornness, rightness into rigidity; planning comes closer to plotting. Under stress, the Determined Personality becomes hesitant, evasive, surreptitious; so unwilling to communicate that he clams up, retreats into silence. He can become so engrossed in being right and developing the plan that he loses sight of the goal. In effect, he can be so caught up in being right that he runs the risk of being wrong.

Remember how important respect is to the Determined Personality, how important action is to him. Frustrate or threaten his likelihood of reaching his goal and he doesn't want to share his objective; you might get in the way of his achieving it. Or he might not want to share his goal because, if he were to make a mistake in plan or procedure, he would feel embarrassed, and that would demolish his sense of self-respect. So, better not to share; better not to declare the goal—and better to rework the plan, the strategy. No matter what, be sure you're right.

Even the healthy Determined Personality can feel the pressure of always having to be right, to be careful in communication, especially when things aren't going so well; but the less confident or immature Determined Personality can feel the pressure in the daily give and take of life. He tends to back off, avoid sharing, deliberate. If he is pushed to open up or follow someone else's plan, he might push back or clam up or go on strike—simply slow down or do nothing. Or he can somatize his grievance and take to bed, his back in spasms, his head aching, or his digestion disputing him. And he can become quite depressed.

Burt is a young machinist who takes pride in his craft, who is always thinking of ways in which he can improve his skills and do a better job. Once, when a very important order was falling behind schedule, he worked two straight shifts to finish the needed parts— and not one part missed inspection. He was particularly pleased when the sales engineer came into the shop to thank him personally. But a new foreman came on the job, and was always pushing Burt to hurry the work, even if that meant lesser quality. The young machinist was upset; he pointed out to the foreman that the high-stress parts he was turning out might pass inspection, but might cause the units they went into to break down under heavy use. "That's someone else's problem," the foreman said; "you just get the stuff out." Burt said nothing more, but every day he asked for a transfer to another department. "I'll see what I can do," the foreman told him; but six weeks later, no transfer had come through, so Burt began reporting to the nurse's station complaining of headaches and eyestrain. Two weeks later, he went on sick leave, the headaches more frequent and more intense. Had he repeated his complaint about quality to the foreman? No. "He knows what I think. If I can't do my work the way I think it's right to do, what's there to say?" Had he gone to personnel about the transfer? "They're just paper pushers." Had he talked to his union steward? "They never do anything." Had he shared his feelings with his wife? "Why should I? What can she do?" About all Burt achieved in being right was being angry. Everything else was going wrong because Burt wouldn't communicate—and all the foreman and his wife could remember of Burt's complaint were his headaches, not his grievance or his request for a transfer.

Molly is a fashion photographer who slowly built a fine reputation with her peers, magazine editors, and advertising agencies. She would like to open her own studio, and has been making plans to do so for three years. She saves her money, scouts possible rental space, updates her portfolio, and plans some more. She is still not sure that the moment is right, her savings sufficient, her contacts ample. Strange, not even her closest friend or her family know of her plans. Why not? "I didn't feel it's necessary to tell them." But the real reason is that she fears that if she told them, they might make suggestions that conflict with her own ideas, might question her plan. Worse is her fear that her plan might not be right; and if she failed, the embarrassment would be enormous. So Molly continues to mull over her scheme of some day opening her own studio. Oh yes, she told her husband, and she is sorry that she did; he keeps encouraging her to make the move. But whenever he does, she retreats into the bedroom, closes the door, and pouts angrily. If only she could share her feelings and fears with her husband and permit him to support her, Molly might have her studio.

FULL OF DETERMINATION

Frank is a road construction worker, married, and determined some day to be a painter—a fine artist working in oils, painting all those

238

wonderful images that his eyes see and his imagination interprets. Meanwhile, life is hard—but bearable—to Frank so long as he can buy paints and canvas and have to himself an occasional clear day with good light to work in. Doing construction work is hard on his hands, but that, Frank feels, is the price he pays.

His wife doesn't take it all that well. When she started going with Frank in high school, he was a solid fullback on the football team, a good student, and one of the more promising young people in the school. He expected to go to college, but she became pregnant, and he married her two weeks before graduation. "I thought it was the only right thing to do," he said. Then she miscarried, and they still have no children after nine years of marriage. Frank feels it wouldn't be responsible to bring children into a difficult situation —and the situation is difficult. His wife believes that Frank could do much better if he would give up his notions about art, but they don't discuss it. Frank gets angry when she talks about money and about taking nice vacations. To him these aren't important and he feels they shouldn't be important to her. He feels right about these issues and won't budge, not considering that his rights have perhaps interfered with hers. "We have our difficulties," he says. "She doesn't even care about shopping right. I can't stand her buying things that aren't on sale. I'm usually calm about it, but after I've said nothing about the prices, she pays twice what she should. She still doesn't shop at the supermarket that has the sale on that week. I get mad. I really blow up." Does he feel guilty about his bursts of anger? "Why should I? By God, I'm right."

Frank is big and strong, so he always seems to get the heavy jobs that involve swinging a pick in the close areas where machinery can't be used, or loading trucks with a shovel where a machine won't manage. He never sloughs off the job: "I always work hard. I always do my job. I hate it, but I feel I shouldn't be there if I'm not going to do the best I can." Why doesn't he ask for a change of jobs? "I have, but it doesn't do much good. I'm their big bull for the heavy work, and they like it that way." Frank isn't the type of person to lean on a shovel handle or sit down on the job: "That's irresponsible. If I can't do my job right, I won't do it at all."

But there are days when the job is so miserable and the conflict at home so depressing that Frank phones in sick. What Frank is suffering is the effect of staying much too long on dead center, not dealing with his miserable home life or his miserable work life.

True, he works hard at his painting, taking night courses at the art institute and working over canvases when he can. He has sacrificed every pleasure and even a few needs—his workshirts and pants have been stitched and restitched, patch on patch—but he has never sold a painting: "That's okay. Vincent van Gogh never sold a painting as long as he lived. But he left his mark on the art world." So Frank keeps on painting, keeps on sacrificing, keeps on hating his job, keeps on struggling with his wife, keeps on insisting, "It's okay as long as I can do my thing. I can't change me. I do the best I can with what I've got."

With his stubbornness and passive aggressiveness conflicting with his ambitions, Frank is trying to be right in the wrong way. He needs to open up, especially to his wife; he needs to see that she too has rights and is entitled to her own notion of what is right for her. If he were less fearful of her possibly blocking his hope of some day working professionally as an artist, he might be able to enlist her support. Now she only resents his goal. Frank also has the option of seeking another job, perhaps one more related to the art field, perhaps as a key-liner in an art studio or as a draftsman in an architectural firm. He is struggling much harder than a struggling artist needs to, sacrificing more than is necessary, especially in his marriage. Frank's chances of reaching his goal—and enjoying the journey—would be enhanced if he were more flexible, more direct, and more communicative. Meanwhile, his silent struggle poses a danger to his dream.

GROWING UP DETERMINED

Nothing in infancy seems to forecast the style of the Determined Personality, unless, perhaps, it be the tendency to need more physical handling. Parents mention the child crying more than the other children, and the crying is usually remedied by holding him. As the child develops, he shows other evidence of enjoying physical closeness and touch, perhaps an early indication of communicating more by his physical attitudes than by verbalizing his feelings. The Determined child often is seen as somewhat shy, yet he enjoys the attention of parents and siblings. He is described usually as a good child but somewhat reserved. He seems to move through the early learning phases—sitting, crawling, walking, toilet training, talking—routinely and well. There is sometimes a hint of rivalry with siblings, especially a younger brother or sister.

The Determined Personality's resolute, insistent style of having things his way can show rather early. One mother told of an incident relating to a visit to the grandparents. The child was told by his grandmother that he couldn't come into the house with the blanket he always carried around, and rather than leave the blanket behind, he chose to stay outside the house throughout the visit. He was only four but quite deliberate in his decision. This was only the first of a long, long series of his going out on strike.

The Determined child enters school with no particular problems and tends to adjust comfortably to the classroom routine. He will do very well in subject areas that interest him, and this may surprise parents who sometimes interpret his resistant responses to their demands as laziness. The Determined child, however, is really behaving consistently. Those things that interest him, especially activities that he initiates, are pursued vigorously. Lisa, age ten, had been receiving excellent grades in spelling, and decided that she would enter the spelling bee. She purchased a study booklet and studied secretly, but it was only when she felt she had a reasonable chance of meeting her goal of staying in at least until the final round that she shared her plan with her parents.

The Determined Personality tends to balk when confronted with chores or activities that are imposed, and the same attitude prevails socially. He tends to get along well with teachers, classmates, relatives, and family friends on the basis of his own determination of their acceptability—their "rightness" in his evaluation. Already he is deciding who and what are right for him. Classmates and neighborhood children who do not seem the right kind of friends are shunned. The Determined child is content to do things that interest him, even if he does them alone, and he is the kind of person who will avoid pranks that are destructive or dishonest. If he makes a promise, he will make every effort to keep it. Those people, adults or children, he doesn't feel he can trust he tries to avoid, and when others do things he believes wrong, he is not afraid to say so. But once he has said it, he tends to clam up and pursue the point no further. What more is there to say? He's right, isn't he?

This desire to be right and do things right shows in all sorts of ways. The Determined youngster likes to be on time. When he thinks he might be late for school or for play, he can get upset. He may insist on wearing certain clothes—a favorite pair of faded jeans, a very tired pair of tennis shoes, for example—perhaps his way of feeling right about himself. He may become irritated when he can't complete a project as well as he would like. Once he has made up his mind to do something a certain way, he won't change; he doesn't like others to interfere with his plans and will easily let them know it. He manages, however, to show considerable respect for his parents and teachers, even when he isn't too happy with their directions.

Throughout childhood and beyond, the Determined Personality explores a wide range of interests. Most Determined children seem to develop an interest in reading, and they also seem to pursue a wide range of individual hobbies—rock collecting, model building, art, crafts, and so on. They follow their interests in a quiet, orderly fashion and are frustrated when others disturb even the physical arrangement of their projects. They also are interested in group activities such as scouting—but only if the organization is of their own choosing. If a parent tried to push a Determined daughter into the Camp Fire Girls, for example, she would balk and back away. All in all, the Determined child is a purposeful, generally happy, and carefree child who is resourceful and who expects much of himself and others.

THE TEEN YEARS

The Determined Personality's pattern of self-direction, pursuit of what he feels is right for him, and deliberate style of choosing friends and interests continues into adolescence. He becomes more skilled at planning the appropriate strategy for achieving his particular goal, whether in scholastic, social, or extracurricular activities. He tends to pursue one thing at a time, doing it well, completing the task, before going on to another activity, and as long as he follows this pattern, he does whatever interests him quite well, much to his own satisfaction. Male or female, the Determined teenager enjoys competition, especially in sports, but his style of play is not the hard-nosed, head-knocking, "get the other guy" way. That wouldn't be right, and if the coach pushed the Determined player to go at the game that way, he would find a way to go on strike. Or he might simply drop off the team. For him, winning isn't everything; the right style of play is.

Honor is another way of being right and doing right, so the Determined high school student would find it difficult to cheat on an examination, even a critical one. As one Determined Personality commented: "I was tempted a few times, but I never cheated. I always thought that if I cheated on a test, I'd be cheating on myself. I wouldn't be learning anything. That wouldn't be honest." But another Determined Personality went to a school that followed the honor system and tells of a principal who spied on students. He and his fellow students felt it was justifiable to steal the exam forms— the principal had already violated the code. So what is right is sometimes relative to the Determined Personality. Who decides? The Determined Personality, of course; he truly believes in his own sense of what is right and wrong. But if it is a matter of keeping his word, the Determined Personality will; that is a personal commitment: "Nothing bothers me more than someone not doing what he says he will do. I always do what I say I'm going to do."

In much the same way, the Determined teenager responds well at home when he or she is treated as a responsible person. Tell her that you trust her, and the Determined teenager doesn't need to be given a curfew on dates. If she says she will be home by twelve-thirty, her parents needn't stay up; she won't sneak in at one-thirty: "That would be betraying a trust." Trust invested in a Determined Personality, adolescent or adult, is a good investment.

The Determined teenager is less likely than other teenagers to experiment with alcohol and drugs or like behavior. It wouldn't be morally right, and the Determined Personality has a sense of morality that goes with his other convictions about what is right and proper. Its development during adolescence is evident in his attitude toward family values. He tends to keep an ear out for parental statements of values relating to religion, social justice, ethical conduct, but he may not assimilate them too easily without having first probed their meaning and value against his own experience. He may not see church as an essential element in behaving religiously, and he might resist pressures to go every Sunday, but if he thought attending church regularly were right for him, he would be positioned in a pew up front, even if no one else were there.

The Determined teenager can be right without being overbearingly righteous. He is selective about his friends, but is very responsible as a friend. One Determined young woman had a friend in high school who developed a serious alcohol problem. She didn't drop her or look the other way: "I went right after her, and eventually I was able to help her get off the stuff. Friendship isn't just being someone's pal. It's being there when somebody needs you." So the Determined Personality makes a good friend, in need or not—you can depend on him. Yet while he values and prizes friendship, he doesn't feel a great need for a large circle of friends or a great deal of socialization.

The Determined teenager is not an open rebel. He may disagree with parental judgments or teacher demands, but as long as he feels authority is being exercised fairly, he will go along with the directives. The Determined adolescent reserves his right to be right. One man tells of a day during high school when the bus arrived at school ten minutes late. There had been a detour necessitated because of a fire. When he entered the classroom, the teacher snapped, "Where have you been? Why haven't you got a note from your advisor?" before he could sit down. "I was so mad I told him, 'Just listen. The bus was late because there was a fire and I couldn't do anything about the fire truck or the traffic.' He got a stunned look on his face, but when he heard what I had to say, he just grunted and went on with the class. It was the only time I ever talked like that to a teacher, but, you know, I felt pretty good about it. I was right and I knew it."

By graduation time, the Determined Personality has begun to show clearly the type of adult he will be: rather deliberate and purposeful, normally hard-working and resourceful, honest and dependable, responsible. He may maintain a low level of verbal communication, yet he is rather predictable and consistent in his behavior. He tends to avoid extremes, preferring to take a middle-of-the-road approach to issues and problems, but only after he has carefully sorted out possible ways of meeting the particular problem. He likes to finish what he begins, and he functions optimally when he takes on tasks one at a time. When he says he will do something, he will do it, but he might not care to tell you the way he will do it. Still, you can trust him to keep his word. He is a doer.

244

THE WORKING WORLD

The Determined Personality will approach his work or career with the expected deliberate style of considering, choosing, and planning. He may have a fairly clear idea of what he wants to do with his life, but he might be hesitant to announce his plan. When asked, he might reply, "I don't know." He wants to make sure that the goal is clear and his plan is right, and he wouldn't want to discuss it lest he be embarrassed by failing to reach his goal.

The Determined Personality will approach his work or career with he can look for a completed product, something concrete and tangible, or at least some conclusive step that says the process is complete. He might not be as attracted to an academic career as he would to work in the practical world. He is the activist who isn't too interested in the speculative and abstract. If he is interested in law, it is the *practice* of law, not so much the theory of constitutional law. If he is a physicist, he will more likely work for some commercial firm than do research in a college or university.

The Determined worker enjoys working with others, but he likes the job that permits him his own defined area of responsibility. He wants to be the one who makes the final decision about his work, and shies from a job assigned to him where he feels less than competent. That wouldn't be responsible. He can be very helpful to a less experienced worker, gladly showing him the skills and processes connected with the job, but he wouldn't do the work for him. That wouldn't be responsible. The Determined worker wants the total working situation to be well-structured and well-defined. Sloppy supervision irritates him, as do low quality standards, poor safety standards, and bad working conditions—and if he feels that a supervisor or management is sanctioning poor working standards, he might passively buck the system. If he thinks his talents are misused, he might take longer coffee breaks, and if he feels he is always the last one chosen for overtime, he might erupt angrily at the foreman. However, he might so understate his grievance that only his anger is memorable.

A seemingly strange attitude on the job: the Determined Personality doesn't particularly like anyone standing over him watching him work. He feels he's a responsible person and doesn't need to be watched: "Just by the way I work, people can tell I'm doing my best." On the other hand, the Determined Personality likes to watch the work someone else is doing for him; the mechanic tuning up his car, the furnace repairman installing a new motor. He's not comfortable when he can't see whether or not they're doing it right.

The Determined Personality might experience some trouble in deciding to make a career or job change, as we saw earlier in the cases of the fashion photographer who wanted to open her own studio and the construction worker who wanted some day to make his livelihood painting. He would want everything well planned, wrapped up in a neat, careful package of right steps. He would probably have a difficult time soliciting other points of view or opinions in the planning process since any differing view or countersuggestion might be perceived as a threat to his own carefully constructed plan. The healthier the individual, the more likely he is to be flexible, thus to benefit from the insight offered by others.

The Determined Personality usually does well operating his own business or working in an area where he personally directs his own functioning—running his own plumbing company, remodeling homes, tending bar, managing a small boutique, or operating an independent consulting service.

No matter what his work assignment, the Determined worker often derives great satisfaction by assuming job-related responsibilities such as being involved actively in union affairs, accepting a position on a safety or incentives committee, serving as chairman of the annual charity fund drive, or such. He enjoys the feeling of responsibility, and the respect he earns is a very large bonus.

COURTSHIP AND MARRIAGE

The kind of person who is attractive to the Determined Personality is someone friendly and considerate, someone who permits the Determined Personality his own counsel in those quiet moments, someone he feels is capable of sharing respect and trust. The Determined Personality might describe that person as rather independent, meaning that he or she won't come between him and his goal, won't ever embarrass him by pointing out his deficiencies. He might also say this person won't burden him unnecessarily with worries and problems that can turn marriage into a pressure cooker. One Determined husband talked of his wife during courtship as "someone who was friendly and fun to be with. She let me do my thing. We could have fun together and apart. But since we've been married, she seems to want to change me into her concept of what a husband ought to be." And he adds, "She isn't going to win that one."

The marriage where there is open sharing, good communication, and mutual regard permits the Determined spouse to be highly productive, to approach family goals and problems in an organized, systematic fashion. He or she gives support and accepts support. The Determined spouse manages to establish an aura of calm in the house and to permeate it with dignity and sturdy values. Parent and children find the Determined Personality a model of purpose and responsibility. Life takes on a quality of stability and constancy. Things go very, very well.

But when communications are restricted, when goals aren't shared, when the Determined partner becomes righter than right, the pressure builds, and relationships become strained. And the strain and the pressure have a way of becoming locked on dead center. The Determined workingman comes home, says, "Hi," nothing else, then heads for the aspirin bottle. His wife tries to open him up, asks how his day went. "She wants to know what I'm thinking. At times like this I subtly get the feeling she's nosy. I don't think she or my mother or anybody needs to know. Other times I think she ought to know without my telling her; and other times I tell her to mind her own business." If she pushes, he balks. If she keeps it up, he blasts away with angry words. But he tells her nothing. Off he goes to bury himself in a book, avoiding her, avoiding his own feelings. His standing directive to his wife is: "Just bring me the real big issues, not the little bitty ones."

One Determined wife confesses that she is always lecturing her husband for "not thinking the right way." What is the right way? "My way." And how does she know she is thinking right? "I'm right."

Any major move in the life of the Determined Personality comes home in a shroud of silence. One young Determined husband was contemplating a job change. He told his wife, then immediately wished he hadn't. She was interested, and she wanted to know more, and he wasn't ready to tell any more. Time passed, and there was no evidence of anything happening except his show of preoccupation: "My wife calls me a delayer. Maybe I am. I just don't take any action. I try to think things out before I do them, but I end up sitting back with nothing happening. Then when she asks me how I'm doing, I feel like she's brow-beating me—so I go out and ride my motorcycle until I calm down." If he could end the strike with his wife, he might find she is much less meddlesome than wanting to support him, whatever his course of action. By sharing his feelings, he might find a healthy release from the pressure bottled up inside of him, and he might find that he is much more able to move off dead center. He really wants to move ahead. By opening up to his wife and sharing his hopes and plans, the goal might become much clearer. Good things might happen.

FAMILY AND HOME LIFE

The Determined spouse might not want to have children until he or she feels life is sufficiently established. It's a matter of being responsible, making sure that everything is right for having and raising children properly. The Determined Personality isn't looking for material things—they aren't that important to him. What he wants is a clear enough reckoning of his goals within and without marriage and his strategy for attaining them. But once he has children, he can settle into parenthood with the same determination and purpose that he brings to whatever he does.

The business of *having* to be right in home life can be demanding. When the children are fussing and feuding, who's right? But remember the Determined Personality's knack for negotiating; he will find a way.

The Determined father observes his teenage son rushing off to work five minutes late and shouts after him, "You're not being responsible!" His wife comes home with her hair freshly tinted, and he has a fit. Why? He would be embarrassed if the neighbors saw her hair that way. It's not right. The Determined wife hears her husband swearing out in the backyard. It's not right; the neighborhood children might hear him. Her oldest son tries to avoid the shower, even after a sweaty game of Peewee football. He's not responsible —and so it goes. The Determined Personality tries always to do what is right, and he always wishes everyone else would. More, he

248

supposes that everyone feels as right as he feels, so sometimes when one of the family or a good friend comments or shares an opinion, the Determined Personality supposes that the other person, like him, is issuing an edict on what is right. And he's wrong. The healthy Determined Personality, when he thinks about it, might laugh, then respond, "How right you are!" Sometimes it's nice to let the other person be right. It cuts down the pressure while letting the feelings flow back and forth.

The Determined Personality, give or take his concern for being right, more often tries to *do* right—and doing right essentially means caring deeply about people. This is why in marriage, in parenthood, in friendship he is able to deal so effectively with people. Despite his reticence in communicating verbally, he says so much in the way he affects others, shows concern for others. He puts the welfare of his family above his own and is capable of much sacrifice and constructive doing for his children. But his active regard for people spreads far beyond his property line. It goes out to anyone and everyone. The only limit to his caring is his awareness of need and his own ability to help.

We know a young Determined woman who, despite her own limited means, took her sister, brother-in-law, and their three children into her apartment when he was out of work. She found her brother-in-law disagreeable and rude, and had never been fond of him, but she took them in: "I was tempted to say no, but I just couldn't do it. I had to let them come." Such is her sense of responsibility. On the other hand, she fully expected her brother-in-law to be responsible, to keep looking for work, and, as insurance, she nightly clipped the want ads from the newspaper and left them for him.

One young man, when he was single, was a member of the local volunteer fire department—his way of fulfilling his sense of responsibility to the community he lived in. Twice since he left the unit, he found his emergency rescue training helpful: once he was able to save a boy who couldn't swim and who had fallen into a neighbor's pool; another time, he splinted a skier's fractured leg on the slopes when the Ski Patrol was nowhere to be found. This young man's attitude was simple: he had the competency in both instances to help; thus it was his responsibility. When he himself was hospitalized for a hernia repair, he was surprised how many people from his office sent flowers and made personal calls. Although he wasn't necessarily their closest friend, he was seen as a respectable, good citizen who could be counted on in a time of need.

The Determined Personality is the kind of a person who is disgusted when he hears people express contempt for someone's poverty or misfortune or background. He is the kind of person who would disobey a law that he felt unjust and oppressive. No doubt the civil rights demonstrations of the sixties were peopled by Determined Personalities; they wouldn't mind jail for the sake of what is right, but they would not take part in a violent demonstration. Violence is useless to the Determined Personality. It's not constructive, responsible, or right.

ALTERNATIVES AND OPTIONS

We have seen how the fully alive and fully mature Determined Personality is always moving toward realizing his vision of life as a purposeful, harmonious whole. He keeps his eyes on his goal, and is always refashioning his strategy for reaching that goal in an open and flexible way. He goes about achieving the goal and organizing his plans calmly and deliberately. What can appear at times as stubbornness may only be his fidelity to the dream, his determination to pursue his goal and all of life in a resolute way, so unhurried that it may annoy more aggressive colleagues and friends. But he is moving ahead, planning, arranging his strategy. He is so dedicated that he is willing to make sacrifices to attain his goal. Those around him, sensitive to his style of communicating through his actions, realize that this sometimes enigmatic person is simply involved—pursuing his chosen goal, fully immersed in his process, acting to make the dream a reality.

Yet in his quest after his goal, the Determined Personality is a man for others. His goal is unselfish. He very much wants to please others, remain open to change, even while keeping a steady pace in pursuit of his goal, and while he doesn't mind competing, he never does so at the expense of others' rights. He wants to win his share of victories, even if only symbolically, but he can accept compromise if that seems the proper course. And when he does win, he knows that he has attained the prize honorably and responsibly—then he

250

can share the sweetness of victory with those around him. He knows how to celebrate—with family, friends, competitors, colleagues, in community.

The less healthy Determined Personality is less likely to share the victory and the celebration. Achievements are fewer. His tendency to restrict verbal communication can degenerate into a battle of silence and an uneasy game of stealth. His seeming calm can be a cloak concealing frustration and anger, and he can become so fixated on the strategy that he loses sight of the goal. He can so fear the embarrassment of failure that he never moves off center. He says little and does less, and is so rigid about being right that he runs the risk of being wrong. He risks little else, fearing miscalculation might wreck the plan, so he tends to mince over the plan detail by detail, all purpose lost. Nothing ventured, nothing gained—but frustration. Dreams become nightmares of struggle and anguish. The intended doer of deeds temporizes, procrastinates, becomes immobile. He can't share. He can't communicate. And after a while, he can't move. All that splendid dedication and sacrifice are buried in a heap of un-executed plans and tired strategies. He is a living monument to lost opportunity.

Transition from immaturity to maturity is largely a process of the Determined Personality identifying his tendencies to restrict com-munication and sharing his goals and strategies with those he lives with and works with—those who are most able to give him support in pursuit of his goals. And, since he has the natural grace of setting goals and making plans, these talents will serve him well in effecting the transition to maturity. Then all things are possible.

If you are a Determined Personality, consider these points:

• Be open. Don't conceal. Reveal. Sharing is the ferment that makes things happen.

• Speak up. Express yourself in more than one or two terse sen-tences. Say what you really mean.

• Getting it right is important, but getting it done is more im-portant. The end result is what counts.

• Temporizing is a terrible temptation. Resist it. Keep moving.

• You can do more of the things you want to do if you quit doing the things you don't have to do. Learn to delegate.

• Don't take your many good works for granted, and don't take the good works of others for granted. Compliment others on their achievements. More, permit others to compliment you on your achievements. You can enjoy the recognition as well as the achievements.

• Consider your attitude toward authority figures—your supervisor, your parents, your union steward. Consider that these people might be very interested in you and your achieving. Work toward closer identification with your job.

• Sometimes we have to work against adversity in achieving our goals. But working against adversity for the thrill of it is nonsense.

• Announce, loud and clear, your goals and your strategy. Make a deliberate effort to say what you are thinking to those persons who would benefit by knowing. That way the plan moves forward. Commitment makes things happen.

• Let people know the principles from which you operate. Saying, "That's just the way it is," explains nothing, and it's irritating and frustrating to those who are interested and involved in your activities.

• Others also have rights, and one of these rights is to know, especially when you have made alliances with significant persons in your life.

• Don't be so critical of others. That suggests that only you have the right way of doing things, which is very pretentious.

• Humility is real when it accepts the total you—the strong, capable person as well as the person with some weaknesses and fears. Being humble doesn't mean self-effacement; it means recognizing—and announcing—your strengths and your successes.

• Dignity is a great prize. But dignity is kept shiny and sparkling in the process of getting things done.

• Try making fewer judgments and more observations. That way you will be more open to other people's observations.

• "By God, I'm right" has been the motto of every tyrant, dictator, and demagogue. Is this the company you want to keep?

• Work more on the settlement and less on the strike.

• Planning the right strategy is the beginning of an action, not the end.

• A retreat, it has been said, is the better part of valor. At least with friends and family, it is a more productive approach than fighting and exploding.

• Review those grand moments when you fully pursued your strategy and reached your goal. If you've been successful in the past, why not again?

• Planning well reduces risk, but there is **no** such thing as a riskless venture.

• Being irritated and irritable both mean you aren't being open.

• Don't be so undeclared that you can't win in the little things in life.

• Don't be so busy accommodating others that you lose sight of what you want to accomplish. Be nice, but keep busy.

• Sometimes you are so secretive you even avoid eye contact. Try looking the other person eye to eye—this could be the opening to better communication.

• A really good plan is hard to tear apart. So set your plan, take it one step at a time, go all the way. Victory!

• Stop hiding, holding back. Assert yourself—without exploding. Take a chance. Strive for the respect you dearly desire. Recognize and appreciate your progress and contributions.

• By keeping your communications open, you also keep your options open and operative, and the feedback is so helpful in keeping the plan alive and working.

• As you recognize your capabilities, so will others.

• Don't sulk. Don't pout. Don't blow up. Any of these negative reactions is an indication that you want to assert yourself. Find a constructive approach, a positive expression, a declaration of your strivings.

• You might ponder this statement attributed to Davy Crockett: "Make sure you're right, then go ahead."

• And this statement of Abraham Lincoln: "I am a slow walker, but I never walk backwards."

• Hanging back from acting on your impulses is another way of freezing your progress toward goals.

• Compete even when you can't see clear victory at the finish line. Not competing is another way of losing.

• Dream dreams of sweet victory. Make plans. Set goals. Share them. *Do* them. Then enjoy the good feeling of moving forward.

• Celebrate your victories. But never alone.

 **XI**

*Sow kindness and you will
reap kindness.*

DOROTHY DAY

The Persistent
Personality

THE PERSISTENT PERSONALITY looks on life as a journey, a pilgrimage. Every day he heads on down the road of life, his hopes high as he puts feet to his faith. Hope and faith in what? That depends very much on the individual Persistent Personality: spouse and family; friend or lover; home and mother; God, government, or the general manager; the state lottery; an oil scheme; a radical cure for cancer; the home team; peace and plenty; the salvation of his soul; salvation for the masses; a day in the sun; a rainbow . . . love. More often than not, the Persistent Personality's quest is expressed in terms of another person or persons in a significant relationship. Life is much richer and more rewarding when there are two for the road. The Persistent Personality doesn't like to travel alone.

When the road is smooth and relationships sure, the Persistent Personality is a genial and gentle person who thrives on the good things in life. He appreciates every moment shared with others, and views life openly and zestfully. Even in bad moments, when the road is rough and rocky, he holds out for the happy ending—such is his faith, hope, and love. He is the believer whose faith just might move

254

mountains. His dreams are grand, sometimes scaled larger than life; but his enthusiasm and devotion to them make them seem plausible and possible. Whatever his prize, his faith is unwavering; he lives that faith, is nourished by it. He trusts mightily, and he persists. His beliefs are sometimes so rich and vibrant that others are caught up in their splendor—or shy away from their grandiosity. No matter. His faith persists as the vital core of his life and his actions.

The mortgage may be due and her bank account overdrawn, but she knows that, somehow, they will manage; they always have, thank God. His team is down 11–0 in the ninth inning with two outs, but he is confident that his heroes can turn it around: "You gotta have faith." Her child may be sick, terribly sick, but her faith and devotion to that child keep hope alive. The Dow-Jones average may be slipping and sliding downward, but he has faith that his stocks' prices will hold. He isn't selling, he's buying. Nine publishers have rejected her manuscript, but she *knows* that she has written the great American novel, so off goes the manuscript to a tenth publisher. Cynics may say that God is dead, but to the Persistent believer, God is alive and acting in his life. Her date is an hour and a half late, but she still has hope—he must have had car trouble; he'll be here any minute.

The mature Persistent Personality is affectionate, large-hearted, and charitable in deed as well as in attitude. He is receptive, open to others, mindful of their needs, responsive. Everyone around him benefits. She is that friend at the office who always bakes a cake on your birthday. He is that good buddy who will lend you ten dollars till payday and then never ask for it back. She is the good neighbor who, when you mention the loveliness of her roses, snips you a dozen. He is the pensioner who can't pass a charitable coin box without emptying his pockets of change, even when it means he has to miss lunch. He is the college student who volunteers to do the grocery shopping for the old people who live in his neighborhood. At home, she is forever busy doing an unexpected kindness for someone: drawing her husband's bath, mending her son's baseball glove, brushing her teenage daughter's hair, singing softly to the baby—her sister's baby. In sum, the healthy Persistent Personality is a person who sees the needs of others and tries to meet them. He truly cares. He wants to share. His job is the simple pleasure of seeing others enjoy what he does, what he gives. And the closer the relationship, the greater his effort to promote the happiness of others.

RELATIONSHIPS ESSENTIAL

The key to understanding the Persistent Personality is the great emphasis he gives to relationships. Relationships are vital and important to all of us. We are all social beings who need and want to share with others. But no other personality style places such consistent and persistent emphasis on relationships as does the Persistent Personality. His basic disposition, his primary orientation, is to establish a close bond with another human being. Within the relationship, he experiences his sense of identity; here he finds his sources of pleasure and joy, his personal enrichment; and the more actively and intimately he participates in that relationship, the greater his sense of purpose in life. Thus the mature and healthy Persistent Personality will fully immerse himself in the relationship, giving, sharing, contributing, enriching in useful ways the substance and quality of the bond.

In a time when alienation and apathy are too evident in our culture, the healthy Persistent Personality has much to teach all of us about the value and dynamics of relationships. We talk of "meaningful relationships," but sometimes too glibly, too easily. The very term "meaningful relationships" notes something of a hunger we have for greater and more gratifying exchanges with those around us. We can be jostled morning and evening in the crowd and deal with customers, co-workers, and clients until we feel numb with all that passing contact with others, yet we experience so much loneliness in our society. Even supposedly significant relationships—marriage, family life, friendships—sometimes hint of shallowness and touch-and-go superficiality. Our human contact is characterized by quantity, not quality.

Every genuine relationship supposes an "I" and a "Thou" that become a "We." Whatever the origins of association, the bond grows and is strengthened through communication and exchange—sharing. There is always a dynamic quality to a relationship: something is happening. There is involvement, a climate of mutual regard and reciprocity. To a greater or lesser degree, each party exercises some freedom of choice within the relationship, and this consent evolves into commitment, which finds its expression in fidelity. A new identity defines roles and what is expected of each other: "I will be your friend, and you will be my friend." "I will be your husband, and you will be my wife." "I will be parent to my children." And with the commitment and role identity come obligations and benefits. Something is given up, something is gained. Nothing really is lost, but something is added: fresh opportunities, shared hopes and expectations, purposes, promises to keep, oneness.

No relationship is ever static. It grows and flourishes, or it dwindles and dies. Those relationships that are real and true and growing have a way of rippling out to touch and enrich the larger community with all its other interconnected relationships. This, in fact, is how community is formed. Again and always, something wonderfully alive and humanly grand is happening. The "We" keeps growing and growing until it encompasses all of life. And, marvelously and productively, as the "We" grows, so grow the "I" and the "Thou" —together.

THE SEARCHING URGE

All of these elements in relationships are well known to the Persistent Personality, consciously or unconsciously, and he desires them all—sometimes perhaps too keenly, too avidly. His emphasis on relationships can be so great that he searches constantly for and within them. We call this the *searching urge* the continuous questing and craving that can affect the Persistent Personality's ability to appreciate and enjoy the existing relationship. Within reasonable and realistic limits, the searching urge can prompt the mature Persistent Personality to work toward bettering and improving his relationships. When he accepts the limits of reality and the relationship, he is content to be discontent.

A certain desire to go farther, to reach higher, to give more is healthy and productive—but only if the individual can still appreciate what already exists in the relationship. This is the measure of progress in his journey through life. An endless, restless quest, filled with vain wishing and hoping, condemns the less mature and less realistic Persistent Personality to wondering and wandering unfulfilled and joylessly. He is never content. He is the pilgrim without progress, leaping out in all directions, looking here, looking there, satisfied with nothing, with no one. He is doomed to greater searching in what seems to him a dry desert of discontent.

The more mature Persistent Personality comes well equipped for his searching. His faith, hope, and devotion work in tandem with his great capacity for loving, caring, and sharing. He is able to recognize opportunities—for doing, for giving, for receiving, for being mindful of what is happening, for appreciating what he has and what he gets, for enjoying what he gives. He is willing to make sacrifices for the sake of others and for the sake of his beliefs, and what he feels he must do, he does. While he might seem shy and timid at times, he can be bold and outgoing in pursuit of any worthwhile opportunity. He is something of a visionary who delights in overcoming the adversities he encounters as he faithfully follows his chosen course. He has a facility for resourceful and reflective thinking that produces tactics to match his vision. He persists in his convictions, holds fast to his commitments. Whenever things have gone his way, he can fully appreciate how well it has all worked out— he feels gratified and grateful that life is so abundantly filled with so many opportunities and joys. And if he is a religious person— as well he might be—he may pause to utter a pilgrim's prayer of thanksgiving to God for all his goodness.

VULNERABILITIES AND CRISES

Appreciation is the measure of how well the Persistent Personality is doing as he moves along in life, interacting with others, pursuing his goals, planning his tactics. When he maintains a realistic approach and is sufficiently appreciative of the give and take, the gains and losses, and is able to keep moving ahead, he is a contented person. He is mature. But when his wishing and wanting blur his vision of all the good things happening, when he fails to appreciate the moment with all its immediate value and promise, he is vulnerable. He is missing the good feelings that ought to be his, that rich sense of appreciation that is its own reward. He doesn't appreciate the old proverb: "A bird in the hand is worth two in the bush." In his fascination for the two in the bush, he permits the bird that he has to escape.

258

Appreciation, for the less mature Persistent Personality, is a two-edged sword. He can fail to appreciate his own efforts and progress, or he can fail to appreciate the efforts and concerns of others. Sometimes he fails to appreciate how much others appreciate him, and sometimes, too, he simply never knows when enough is enough. Then the search goes on—more intense, unsatisfied, and unsatisfying.

A Persistent dentist spends his Christmas holidays in a small rural community that has no dentist. During each annual stay there, he offers his services. The land is poor and the people are poor, so he charges only a dollar per patient, no matter how extensive the work, and he charges only because he doesn't want to hurt their pride. More, he brings with him bundles of used clothing and blankets that he has collected through the fall and winter months from members of his church. When the local newspaper in his own hometown discovered his good works and printed a feature story on the dentist, he was embarrassed, a little crushed. "I don't do it for the publicity," he complained. No, he does it every Christmas simply for the joy of seeing healthy teeth and happy people. That is his focus of appreciation, but what he failed to appreciate was the value of the newspaper story in prompting others to be generous, to share with the less fortunate. Still, his generosity and sacrifice were enormously healthy.

A Persistent young man finds a wallet thick with credit cards. He calls the owner, and while he is waiting for him to retrieve the wallet, he begins to imagine the reward he might get: $5, $25, $50, maybe $100? But when the owner says, "Thank you," and hands him a fresh twenty-dollar bill, he is chagrined. "Next time, I'll use those credit cards to buy myself a fancy stereo and throw the wallet in the sewer." He really didn't appreciate either his kind act or the owner's sincere gratitude. That wasn't so healthy.

A Persistent wife nursed her husband through a long illness during which he needed attention day and night for eight months. Her devotion, perhaps as much as her ministrations, helped him to recover, but when the family commented on her great care and sacrifice, she just shrugged: "Isn't that what a wife is supposed to do?" She didn't appreciate her own monumental effort, and she missed the satisfaction that she should have enjoyed. Sad.

The Persistent bride threw a tantrum when she saw the room in the lodge where they were to honeymoon. It was quite nice, but it wasn't the bridal suite—which wasn't available and which the groom couldn't afford. A tragic beginning.

THE INSATIABLE APPETITE

The less healthy Persistent Personality too can be generous, but without the spontaneity or the pleasure. He can give, but his motive might be selfish; he might want something in return. A young man sends his girlfriend flowers, not so much to please her as to entice her into bed. The less healthy the Persistent Personality is, the more he expects others to meet his needs, satisfy his desires. And he can be very demanding. The Persistent daughter may borrow her mother's charge card to buy a sweater, then return home with two cashmere sweaters and skirts to match; and in her naïveté, her trust that Mother would want her to have all the best of everything, she may be truly surprised when Mother protests. The less healthy Persistent Personality's appetites—for things, for attention, for favors, for special treatment—are endless, insatiable; yet he rarely appreciates what he is given, what he has; he always wants more and more, so much so that his demands often provoke rejection. But he is undeterred. He may withdraw momentarily while he plans and connives new schemes for having his way, but he will return, demanding vigorously. He clings, and his persistence can be suffocating.

The ruses of the unhealthy Persistent Personality are imaginative at times, simply brazen at other times. Whether conscious or unconscious, they are endless. He will feel ill, inadequate, in poor health, helpless—whatever seems to work in eliciting the attention and the pleasure he craves. He can spend the day walking around a pool table, yet claim that he can't stand on his painful legs to work in a factory. He might stay home, shut in his room, expecting his mother to bring him meals, suffering terribly—until it is time again to go off to the pool hall. He may call his doctor at 2 a.m. on any provocation, real or imagined. He might drink six quarts of milk a day and then complain that he is always thirsty and that nobody seems to care. He can be petulant, angry, rebellious, obnoxious unless his demands are met—the sulking child who will hold his breath, blue in the face, until his father gives him his piece of pie. He is so demanding that he can exhaust and drain everyone around him who will submit to his tyranny, yet even so, he may become terribly depressed because he feels so deprived. Even God, he complains, doesn't care enough. When all else fails, he might retreat into fantasy, scheming and dreaming of making a million dollars and having whatever he wants.

What differentiates the healthy from the ill is the Persistent Personality's great emphasis on relationships. The healthy Persistent Personality cherishes the other person for his human value; he seeks to contribute to that person's well-being. The unhealthy Persistent Personality values the other person as a source of gratification; he seeks to gain from that person whatever he desires. The healthy Persistent Personality is the unstinting, selfless, generous donor, especially to those close to him, whereas the unhealthy Persistent Personality is the insatiable, self-centered, demanding recipient, usually from those close to him. This endless appetite is physical as well as emotional. The debilitated Persistent Personality is capable of eating and eating and eating, gorging himself into obesity: "I can never get enough." Or the opposite tactic may also be adopted—he may starve himself into a skeletal bag of bones as a way of increasing the pressure of his demands: "See, you never give me enough."

The polarity between health and ill health in Persistent Personalities takes many extremes. The healthy individual, as we have noted, is generous, capable of much personal sacrifice, appreciative of others and what he has, but the less healthy Persistent Personality can be generous to a fault—profligate, reckless in his spending on others—and on himself. Or he might take the opposite turn, hoarding all that he has. He might be the ragged scavenger who roams through alleys picking through the trash cans; even though he has a substantial bank account, he lives in a bare, one-room apartment. He can't appreciate or be satisfied with the security he has, so he lives like a miser.

The healthy Persistent Personality dreams, but he tests his dreams against reality before he sets them into motion. Not the less healthy Persistent Personality. He is a dreamer who can lose himself in fantasy, dreaming the impossible dream. Or he can use his mental skills and his flights of fancy to contrive a grandiose scheme to make himself—and all who are gullible enough to get caught up in his scheme—rich overnight. And it happens. His enthusiasm, his exuberance, his persuasion are mighty. The first snake oil peddler very well may have been a Persistent huckster who could imagine his miracle medicine curing everything from corns to curvature of the spine.

THE FULLNESS OF FAITH

We noted earlier the great capacity of the Persistent Personality for faith and devotion. But faith and devotion must have objects, and, since the Persistent Personality values relationships so highly, his faith and devotion often find their object in a relationship close at hand: spouse, children, parents, good friend, pastor, employer, supervisor, or all of these. But, on the other hand, it is not surprising that the Persistent Personality might invest his faith in religion, and when he does, he fully involves himself; he fully commits. He senses that the core of every religious impulse is the desire to bring himself into a closer relationship with God and the things that are God's. He yearns for the fullness of faith: to be one with God. He strives for a rich and full prayer life, and is usually responsive to the full range of values espoused by his church or synagogue: fidelity to creed, involvement in worship, attention to rules and rubrics, practices of piety and virtue and morality, participation in the life of the community. He readily engages in good works, within and without the community, ever giving generously and willingly.

The more mature the individual Persistent Personality, the greater his ability to participate and contribute meaningfully, often sacrificing himself and his resources for love of God and neighbor. He brings to religion all his visionary outlook and tactical skills, his enthusiasm and appreciation. He sees all of life and all of creation —the dawn, the sun and moon, the snow in winter, fresh buds on the trees—as signs of God's presence, and he deeply appreciates it all. His prayers are filled with praise and thanksgiving. His faith excites others, and he gladly follows in whatever direction God calls him. For him, God is never an abstract being or a set of theological principles; God is a felt presence. The Persistent Personality senses the immediacy of God and his will, and for that reason he is capable of embracing poverty for the sake of the poor or of caring for the sick or of volunteering for mission work. You may find the Persistent Personality tending the Salvation Army pot at Christmas, teaching Sunday School, washing the feet of old men in a home for the aged. He is the mischievous choir boy who never misses practice but who has been known to launch paper airplanes from the choir loft; yet he is the picture of angelic piety as he sings God's praises.

The Persistent Personality's zeal for religion is a model for others who find faith difficult, prayer dry, service a chore, or virtue beyond reach. His faith and hope and joy are contagious and those around him are moved by his devotion. He is embarrassed if they comment on his faith and good works—he is humble—for he supposes that everyone shares his zeal. Still, he sees himself as God's instrument, and he wants to share what he has, including his faith. The Persistent Personality is a person for others.

Not every Persistent Personality finds religion an object for his faith and devotion. Some react against the stiffness of institutional religion and what they perceive as shallow piety, Sunday-only morality, rigid attitudes. Even so, the Persistent Personality will find other channels for his faith, service, and devotion—in relationships close to home or in the immediate community, in organized labor or in women's rights, in fraternal organizations such as the Elks, Masons, or Shriners. There might also be a tendency to pursue astrology, the occult, spiritualism, or fortune-telling—he might tend to be superstitious—but more often than not, the non-religious Persistent Personality invests his faith and devotion in close relationships. In these relationships, the open and healthy Persistent Personality finds many ways to be useful, purposeful, involved. He sees a need, and he wants to be helpful. He relishes the relationship, acceptance, the sense of mutual appreciation, but most of all he appreciates the opportunity to be of help to others. Often, the Persistent Personality views himself as the real beneficiary of his kindnesses. In giving, he feels, he receives: "You see the happiness that you bring to people. They are giving you so much." In sum, the mature Persistent Personality appreciates what he has, what he does, the relationship itself. And he finds it all very gratifying.

GROWING UP PERSISTENT

The first distinctively Persistent trait may not show in the child until three or four years of age—although his parents may remember him as being keenly interested in early feeding. The Persistent child of three or four might begin to show a bit of an impulsive or mischievous streak: "He'd do anything for attention." This desire for attention—positive or at times negative—persists all through life.

Still, the overall impression suggests a pleasant child, normally outgoing and playful, although sometimes fearful of airplanes or trucks or large animals. And he may panic when parents or parent surrogates are not immediately available.

Certain consistent themes run through the Persistent Personality's recollections of early childhood: (1) trust or fear; (2) faith and hope, or the sense of being left or deserted; and (3) testing the environment with resultant acceptance or correction for his behavior. Examples:

Of trust and acceptance: "I think I was about four when I was watching my mother make oatmeal with raisins and toast for breakfast. She burned them a little, but I didn't complain. I just ate them. I figured that was what was supposed to happen, and I didn't want to hurt Mom's feelings."

Of fear: "When I was supposed to go to kindergarten the first day, I hid under the dining room table. I was shy, and I didn't want to go. I had been there for registration with my mother, and there were a lot of kids. I didn't want to go there without my mother. Golly, I was scared!"

Of hope and faith and fear of desertion: "When I was in the first grade, I came home from school early one day, and Mom wasn't there. The house was locked, so I just sat on my wagon and cried. I remember being hungry and feeling that nobody loved me. Then a neighbor came by, and she took care of me until my mother came home from shopping. She gave me two cookies."

Of testing behavior: "Before I was old enough to go to school, my friend and I found some paint one day, and decided to paint each other all over. Then we decided to paint the dog house. Everything was a mess, but it sure was fun. We got spanked, but it wasn't that bad. I wasn't surprised, really, about the spanking. I knew when we did it that my parents wouldn't like it."

Shyness may mar the Persistent child's entry into school, but after some feelings of apprehension and restraint, he will enter into school activities with enough enthusiasm. He might be somewhat noticeable for his tendency to want to help other children or to be with his special friend. Usually pleasant and quiet, his occasional impish or mischievous behavior may concern the teacher, enough to comment on his report card or to send a note home to his parents. Routine and work that isn't a challenge sometimes evokes a complaint from the Persistent child: "It's boring." But the real cause of his disruptive behavior is his craving for attention—even negative attention. Yet if disciplined in school, his feelings can be deeply wounded, especially if he is fond of the teacher. In fact, his relationship with the teacher strongly influences his total performance in school—he does well when the relationship is good, indifferently or poorly when not. And loss of a well-liked teacher can be painful. Later in life, the Persistent Personality might look back on less pleasant experiences as worse than they were; he might remember it all as having been a deprived child.

But not always. One Persistent Personality recalls more the puckishness than pain: "Really, I was a pretty good kid. But I could be cussed at times, a real imp, practically from the first. I remember it was before Valentine's Day and we were making our Valentine's cards. We were supposed to copy down all the names of our classmates from the blackboard. I thought it was dull, so I did something else. The teacher stepped out of the room and I passed around my paper for all the other kids to write down their own names. The teacher came back in and I got caught. I also caught hell. Another time I was supposed to be helping some other kids learn some words in reading, but it was more fun making up silly words. I got it again. But when I think about it now, I have to laugh. It still gives me a kick to remember the things I did. You know, I think I still might have a trick or two left in me. Even now, I sometimes deliberately do things that are different."

The Persistent child, especially the bright child who has the capability, benefits by being encouraged to do extra work that meets his interests or by being given special responsibilities, especially helping activities such as school safety patrol or grading papers for the teacher. He needs to have his interest directed toward others and the larger environment. But care should be taken that he doesn't become overattached to the teacher lest he find the attachment too special; he might tend to cling. The more mix in his activities and in his human environment, the better.

This child has the potential to be a leader; he can be nimble in putting together imaginative schemes and ideas, he has a capacity for faith in what he is doing—if it genuinely interests him—and his enthusiasm is contagious. Even when he is not a leader, he tends to admire and support those among his peers who are. When he is using the traits of his personality style productively, he is an exuberant child who does well, but when the routine is too predictable, his talents unused, the Persistent child can become easily bored, mischievous, disruptive. And when things are going poorly for him, he can respond with a flare of temper, striking out at the source of his unhappiness, or with somatic complaints such as headaches or stomach aches; or he may silently slip away into fanciful daydreams.

ADOLESCENCE

Around the time the Persistent youngster enters junior high school, the tendency to be a little devilish or mischievous seems to escalate. There is a note of testing and probing in his maneuvers, a little more cunning and conniving. But rarely is it malicious. Rather, it is indulgent. The Persistent youngster still likes attention, even if negative—he enjoys the excitement of getting caught—and he may even be competing for attention with an older sibling. One Persistent woman remembers going around the house in a snug blouse and tight shorts, which upset her religious parents, but she quit wearing them when her older sister moved away from home. Give or take these occasional forays into rebellion, usually more irritating than harmful, the Persistent Personality moves into the adolescent years no more awkwardly than his peers—somewhat more gracefully than some, somewhat less than others. He is still governed largely by his sense of relationships and his feeling of appreciation. A little tolerance is indicated. He really doesn't wish to harm or offend anyone. He just craves a little attention, perhaps a bit more than other young people his age.

Parents may be somewhat perplexed by the Persistent teenager's shift in emphasis from close relationships with them and with teachers to his peer group. At the same time, the Persistent adolescent may begin to shun home responsibilities: "He doesn't seem to want to do any more than he just has to. It wouldn't hurt him to do a little more around here, even if he just kept his room in good shape." If he finds that mother will pick up after him, he will let her, which isn't good for parent or child. Should a mother comment to her Persistent teenager, it may draw little if any response; he obviously isn't appreciating what she is doing for him. He usually won't show any

266

hostility—he shuns open antagonism—but he might turn the mood by telling a joke or by making a whimsical remark that he hopes will make the other person feel good.

The Persistent teenager sometimes tends to take advantage of affection offered him. He benefits from a climate at home and school that insists on definite and consistent adherence to the prevailing standards of parents and teachers. More often than not, the Persistent adolescent still cherishes family values, so parental comments that reflect conformity to these values are normally welcome, such as praise for attending church or joining a church-sponsored youth group or a hospital aid group. He might be pleased to hear that his parents are praying for him and his happiness. Feelings of being loved and appreciated are very important to him, so he benefits from signs and expressions of family love, but he doesn't need coddling or pampering or parental indulgence. They only invite immature clinging and an attitude of being special, the family pet. Pampering might also turn him back toward a childish sense of an all-providing environment, just at the time when he most needs to test the outer environment and his ability to function there.

High school teachers may find themselves commending the Persistent student for his good behavior in following school codes and in displaying proper conduct on campus. This is good since the Persistent Personality is motivated by positive comments; they signal to him that he is appreciated. But even as he is the model student in school, he might be cited for driving at eighty miles an hour down the highway, and this would baffle parents and teachers. His explanation might be: "I don't know. I just felt like driving eighty." The real explanation, of course, is that impetuous desire to test reaction, to offset the dullness of routine, and to gain a little special attention.

Still, the Persistent teenager is seldom in heavy conflict with authority of any kind. He might take up smoking—another instance of a low-level rebellion for testing purposes—but he is rarely the teenager who takes up drugs and alcohol or runs with a group that does. He is still inclined toward constructive activities such as scouting, or he might show a strong interest in writing or other communications skills. He might enjoy sports and other competitive activities, but he is not likely to be the most aggressive or competitive player—although the Persistent teenager might very well be the most spirited and enthusiastic. If he doesn't make the team, he might welcome the opportunity to be the team manager, while he might fantasize himself as a great player, made in the image and likeness of his sports hero.

When life around him isn't going well, the Persistent adolescent might show some signs of confusion, restlessness, or depression. His usual propensity for intense belief and firm opinion might slide into wondering and questioning. This is the searching urge intensified. In today's cultural climate, he might plunge into some religious movement such as the Jesus people or follow the call of the Reverend Sun Myung Moon.

The Persistent Personality seems less prone than other personality styles to pursue sexual curiosity and activity in his preteen years. This attitude may reflect his religious and moral values and his pleasing disposition. He may be a little more tentative than many of his peers in dating, feeling perhaps some apprehension about entering a new kind of relationship, questioning his own expectations and the expectations of the other person. The Persistent Personality is normally cautious and a bit shy in approaching any new relationship, but if the initial experience is found gratifying and sufficiently pleasant, he can enjoy the attention and the acceptance. He might be expected to conform to parental rules about curfew and dating. If sex comes up, he is likely to react according to family attitudes and values—unless he is rebellious toward those values. Otherwise the Persistent Personality's sexual attitudes and interests differ little from other personality styles.

The impetuosity of the Persistent Personality is evident in his interest in clothes and his appearance, sometimes trendy or faddish, perhaps at times a bit garish. His appearance tells a great deal about how he feels about himself: "If you're wearing the right thing and looking good, you get a plus. Things always seem to go well when you look good." Here is a blending, perhaps, of self-appreciation, an attention-getting device, and a bit of faith bordering on superstition. The Persistent athlete might wear the same lucky sweatsocks during every game. He might also wear the same shirt or sweater during exams after scoring well on a test when he first wore that piece of clothing.

Moving away from home or the first trip away from home might be very difficult for the Persistent Personality. He might be the child who lives with his parents long after the other children have moved out. When he does leave home, he may make an initial declaration of independence—he wouldn't want his parents to know how much he misses them—but more often he maintains close contact with home and parents, sometimes exorbitantly. He might depend on his mother to waken him in the morning with a telephone call, and if she invites him over for a meal, he would never refuse, even if it were offered every evening. He wouldn't hesitate to bring along his laundry for mother to wash, and if she should also be a Persistent Personality, she would gladly fix the meals and do the washing, tending still to want to pamper her child. Or, on the other hand, she just might turn the situation around, feeling that it's about time that she be indulged with a little pampering. It can go either way.

COURTSHIP AND MARRIAGE

The Persistent Personality is attracted to the person who responds well to him: "She showed a lot of interest in me." "He was someone who seemed to have a good idea of where he and I would want to go." The Persistent Personality values the appearance of the other person, just as he values his own appearance, but the interest, the sense of appreciation the other person shows, is important. He is attracted, too, to the person who has definite ideas and plans and who would encourage his own hopes and dedication. The danger, however, is that sometimes the Persistent Personality leaps into the relationship all too quickly. He tends to fall in love at first sight. The opposite reaction is also possible; he may probe and test and remain uncommitted, fearful that he might risk losing other productive relationships.

Marriage is a great opportunity for the Persistent Personality to utilize his faith and devotion, his caring and sharing capacity, his willingness to sacrifice for the sake of others. He can be a very considerate and affectionate spouse and parent, his normally mirthful and optimistic attitude prevailing. A Persistent Personality might give up his own educational or career opportunities for the sake of his spouse's career, placing greater value on the relationship, and this devotion would show in countless little gifts of self: "I'm a devoted wife. When my husband wakes up in the morning, I have his juice and toast beside the bed and his bath water running. While he is getting dressed, I'm out there warming up the car." And he is no different: "If she sees something she likes, I'll put in overtime if I have to to get it for her." But in return, the Persistent spouse might expect some show of appreciation—if nothing else, the abiding presence of the other person, which can be burdensome: "When she's not home, I get irritable. I hate to be alone."

The Persistent Personality has no particular sexual problems, but he might too quickly assume responsibility for any seeming difficulty, even if it centers on the role or function of the other person. He may not always appreciate his own adequacy.

Some conflict may arise over the Persistent spouse's continued closeness to parents. He may stop by to visit his mother each day on his way home from work, or she might call her mother every evening. He will remember an unusual number of birthdays and anniversaries in all branches of the family, and he will go about the business of buying gifts intensely: "I knock myself out during the Christmas season trying to find the gift that's just right. I know I spend too much money on Christmas. I first buy for my wife and then for the kids and then for my brothers and sisters, not to mention a few nieces and nephews. But giving gifts is a lot of fun, more fun than receiving them. I really enjoy it."

One Persistent Personality told me that Christmas was something of an agony. This bachelor came from a home where his family, though Christian, frowned on the Santa Claus myth and the Christmas tree: "I always felt odd, different from other kids." Today he still doesn't have his own Christmas tree, even though he shares Christmas around the tree at his brother's house. He might enjoy the spirit of the season and his own generosity more if he could appreciate himself enough to buy that lovely green and scented tree. Maybe then he might appreciate religion too, which he hasn't since his childhood of austere holidays when he was so different from other children.

The Persistent Personality who brings religious values into his marriage and family life uses them to infuse a spirit of solidarity—togetherness—in the home. When he speaks of his beliefs, he can do so with deep feeling and true gladness, but he more often communicates his beliefs by what he does rather than what he says. Religion is an emotional commitment more than an intellectual conviction. As one Persistent parent—and grandparent—commented: "When your

270

children see you reading over scripture, when they see you kneel to pray, when they see you go to church on Sunday and how you treat your neighbor as a brother or sister all week long, they remember. I remember when I was just a little fellow seeing my own grandfather kiss the Bible with real affection after he read from it. I can never forget that." Another Persistent parent recalls a familiar slogan from his childhood that he still puts into practice in his own family: "The family that prays together stays together."

The Persistent parent and child, even when the child has reached adulthood, sometimes might underappreciate the generosity of the other, his need to share and do: "My Mom is the kind of person who is always trying to do things for me; you know, those thoughtful little things. She likes to sew, and she will call me to ask if I would like to see a new piece of material she's just purchased. That means she wants to sew something for me. It took me a long time to realize how much she enjoyed doing that. I was always trying to be independent by saying no, but I realize now that by letting her sew me a skirt, I'm giving to her. The worst thing is to say no, or not to show how much you like it and how nice it looks."

Sometimes, though, the Persistent Personality can do too much for either spouse or children. He can be too giving in a way that burdens others. One Persistent wife told me of always being so considerate and thoughtful that her husband found her threatening—and just too good. The more he resisted her giving ways and her desire for constant togetherness, the more she tried to do. The marriage ended in divorce, a crushing experience for the Persistent Personality. In her next marriage, she switched directions in her search for a happy relationship, going toward the loose and easy side, trying to find a chic lifestyle, a free and casual relationship. That marriage also ended in divorce, mostly because this woman was fighting her own values and inherent characteristics—she simply wasn't moving in a direction that was good or natural for her. More, she really didn't make a commitment after her disappointment in the first marriage. Still, she persisted in the second marriage, hoping, feeling wretched, and when the marriage finally broke up, she was terribly depressed. Even today, though more wary, she is still searching for a relationship in marriage, one that will permit her security and opportunity for sharing and mutual happiness. She will need to accent the word "mutual" lest she run the risk of overpowering still another partner. She will need to learn that others too have a need to do and to give.

The Persistent Personality normally is a tender and attentive parent, loving and caring and enjoying his children. He might find the first pregnancy a bit stressful. But that passes. Illness too—to spouse or children—can provoke stress, and if the illness is severe enough, he might tend to experience a feeling of panic, his security threatened. Still, he would be viewed as a source of strength by everyone else because of his persistence and faith. Only *he* would fail to appreciate his strengths. Death would be an enormous, painful experience for the Persistent Personality. Here again his religious faith might help him through the crisis, although it might be heavily tested. The more he appreciates the sharing he has had and his own trust in God, the better he will pass through this crisis—and all crises.

THE WORKING WORLD

Work and career are meaningful to the Persistent Personality largely on the value assigned to the relationships involved. Recognition and being appreciated are important, but the Persistent worker can be too keyed to his supervisor's reactions and comments, or lack of them. He can easily feel slighted. But if the working environment promotes a spirit of closeness and offers supportive feedback, the Persistent worker feels at one with his work. Once he commits himself to the task, he will pursue it with his customary devotion, searching for ways to do it better, seeking to contribute at the same time to the human environment of his job. When he believes in his employer and the product, when he feels that he is valued as a productive person, he is a devoted employee. Otherwise, he can be a nine-to-five worker, content to meet his quotas but glad to quit when the bell rings, eager to go home where he is more appreciated. His great concern at work might center less on the task than on job security, long-range programs of life and health insurance, and adequate retirement benefits. And he often welcomes early retirement, sometimes even when he is involved and committed to his work. There are so many facets of life he yearns to explore—travel, a wealth of good books, good music, fellowship, sports events, people who need help, good moments alone with the beauty of nature, or just quiet moments for reflection and meditation. The search goes on.

The Persistent careerist does well in almost any professional area where he can invest his devotion, sense of service, and enthusiasm. Farming, the skilled crafts, and the arts appeal to him because he appreciates the productivity of his own hands and mind, and so do others—which also appeals to him. He might enjoy journalism, perhaps sportswriting, which would draw on his enthusiasm and tendency to exalt the heroes of the game. Sales would appeal; here too he can use his devotion and enthusiasm, his communicative ability to persuade and excite. The same capabilities might find good use in teaching; and, of course, religion, either as vocation or avocation, is especially attractive—not only in the ministry, priesthood, or rabbinate, but in religious journalism, religious education, religious music, or social work under charitable auspices. He might shun certain areas such as business or law if he suspects there might be less than ethical or moral standards practiced, and he might quit a position should he find out that the boss is something of a liar or a philanderer or a cheat in his bookkeeping. The Persistent salesman might threaten to quit when his sales manager gives him a list of variable prices on products, not appreciating that the sales manager only follows the dictates of corporate policy, and that the market follows the economic laws of supply and demand. In any relationship —not only business, but marriage, friendship, or religious affiliation —the Persistent Personality is vulnerable to disappointment when others violate his own exacting standards of ethical and moral conduct. He may not appreciate that there are other norms than his own.

The Persistent Personality demonstrates a rather fascinating aspect of his personality style when—as salesman or preacher or teacher—he discovers his ability to persuade and move people. He discovers the feeling of power—power to affect the feelings and faith and lives of others. Here is a heady demonstration of his being accepted, verification of his own faith and enthusiasm, an exhilarating moment of intense involvement with others. This is indeed powerful stuff, and even the Persistent speaker is awed by his impact. And why not? When he is at his peak of persuasion, every mountain seems movable, every dream possible. Anything sounds believable, at least for the moment. Throughout history, conversions, crusades, and conquests of some magnitude have taken place because of this Persistent style of persuasion—for better or for worse.

If the Persistent Personality knows these peak moments, he also experiences pallid moments to match. A Persistent store manager tells me of his great letdown feelings when everything is running smoothly: "When all my customers are satisfied and the sales people are taking good care of business, when there are no complaints or crises, I feel rotten. I feel useless. But during the holiday rush, when this place is a madhouse—my help going crazy trying to handle the customers and the customers are yelling for help—that's when I feel my best. Busy, busy, busy. I love it. I'm functioning all over the store, and I'm feeling great." The moral of the story? Our store manager underappreciates his efficient functioning until even a shoplifter can see how purposeful he is. He loves to operate under pressure and adversity; otherwise, he feels useless, dull, bored.

The Persistent Personality's disposition toward money, like most things in his life, can take opposite directions. He can be prudent, handling it carefully, putting away regular savings for security. The unhealthy version of this thrift is miserliness. On the other hand, the Persistent Personality can be the easy-come, easy-go spender, and if the tendency goes awry, he can be prodigal. It all depends on how he appreciates the fruits of his labor: does he want to enjoy it now or later? He can be, as we have seen, very generous either in helping others or in giving gifts, and he can also be self-indulgent, enjoying the immediate benefits of his earnings—spending on expensive clothing, household luxuries, hobbies, and recreation: "What the heck. I'm working. So what's wrong with a few luxuries? I've earned them." When he has the money available, he is just as likely to rush to the financial rescue of a friend in need. Savings are gratifying. The luxuries are gratifying. Helping a friend is gratifying. The bottom line is the same: appreciation.

ALTERNATIVES AND OPTIONS

The Persistent Personality, as we have seen, is a pilgrim on a seeking, searching journey through life. He is thoughtful, kind, tender, loving, generous. He sees life not only as a continuous search, he also views it as opportunity: to give, to receive, to share, to sacrifice, to be gratified by the many occasions that present themselves for him to bring pleasure and joy to others. Thus he is capable of being a very good friend, spouse, lover, neighbor, parent, a contributing member of the community, and, of course, a pillar of his church or synagogue. He is a person who appreciates what he has and who he is, willing to share it all with those around him. He is a person of great faith, hope, trust, and devotion, and he exploits every opportunity to invest these virtues in relationships. He is ethical and moral, persuasive and enthusiastic, and has the ability to inspire others to reach a little higher, to have faith, to share, to care always. He is, everyone agrees, nice to have around. He is so greatly appreciated, even when he doesn't notice how much people appreciate him. It may be that he is just too busy planning and scheming more ways of developing his rich talents and of being useful to others. The search goes on and on.

The less than mature Persistent Personality is also searching, but in all the wrong directions and in all the wrong ways. He is less prone to contribute to others, being more likely to draw on the environment, even to the point of draining every possible source of gratification—even God. His appetites, emotionally and physically, can be enormous, voracious. He tends to flee reality while clinging tenaciously, holding his donors hostage to his appetites. What is a facile, artful way of thinking and planning for the healthy Persistent Personality is a conniving tool for avoiding all responsibility and for seeking even greater gratification. He dreams and fantasizes schemes of amassing more and more—whatever he craves—and he uses every opportunity to further indulge and gratify himself, pinning all his hopes on others: they must meet his needs, his wants, his appetites. He can be so narcissistic that he is unaware of the environment except as a source of his own desires. When reality threatens his fantasy world, he can strike out angrily, and he can become terribly depressed.

The extremely immature, neurotic Persistent Personality needs professional help, but he benefits too from an environment that has some insight into his problem. The healthy, mature Persistent Personality, of course, can benefit by being aware of his vulnerabilities as well as his strengths. He will find it useful to consider the crises and stresses that he normally meets and contends with. Healthy, however, is relative. Even the healthy Persistent Personality can be stronger in certain characteristic areas while being perhaps a bit more vulnerable in others. Any Persistent individual might find the following recommended alternatives and options helpful:

• On the journey through life, take regular pauses to appreciate all that you are, all that you have, all that you do. Appreciation is the key to enjoying all relationships and the continuous search for greater opportunity to utilize your talents and your faith, devotion, and love.

• Don't wait for others to appreciate you. Appreciate yourself. Make it a habit.

• Get involved. The more you are sharing with others, the more you are being your real self.

• Recognize and enjoy what you have to give. Recognize and enjoy all the people who love and care about you.

• Stop hoping so much; start doing. Stop having twenty-one questions for every possible twenty answers. Put your faith in others and permit them to help you.

• Ask yourself why you give so many gifts. Are you asking for special treatment? Are you unhappy if others don't give to you in return?

• Encourage other people's faith by sharing your own.

• Don't be so easily disappointed in the morals and ethics of others, and don't try to make them over in your own ethical image and likeness.

• Beware of how facilely you find all the shortcuts—pretty sly, but pretty disastrous as a learning technique and as an approach to life.

• If you are bored, that means you're either taking shortcuts or you're not appreciating either yourself or the opportunity at hand.

• Superstition is a shallow expression of faith. A lucky number is less likely to help you through the journey of life than getting on with the journey. Put feet to your hopes.

• Don't underrate your abilities and talents. Don't put yourself down as a way of fishing for feedback. Better to realize yourself how well you are doing.

• Humility is a virtue, but don't interpret it to mean not recognizing and appreciating your other virtues. True humility is knowing yourself, the good and generous self.

• Why do you need special attention?

• Don't feel slighted so easily. This is another form of under-appreciation. Try always to appreciate the circumstances and thinking of the other person.

• Relationships work best when the give and take flow easily in both directions. Let others give and do occasionally.

• Today is a good day for taking inventory of all your assets: your talents, your efficiency, your competence on the job, your generosity toward others, your regard for others, your appreciation of friendships, your productivity.

• It's good sometimes to let yourself sink back in a soft chair to think, evaluate, and appreciate; to make decisions, consider responsibilities, plan for the future. And to relax.

• Quit cherishing those little memories of being spoiled, those hallowed claims of being special: "I've always been the apple of my parents' eyes," or "My parents love to spoil me." You'll discover so much more joy in doing things for yourself. You're no longer a child.

• Other people need attention and concern. Give them equal opportunity, equal time.

• Abraham, whom Jews, Christians, and Moslems all honor as their father in faith, spent his lifetime as a wanderer in response to God's call. He put feet to his faith. This earned him the Biblical title, "friend of God."

• It's nice to dream grand dreams, but life is usually a series of the little things done well. Dream, but then do.

• Don't put other people on pedestals. That is unreal. You can only relate to people at ground level.

• The little things we do—washing dishes, cooking meals, mowing the lawn, taking out the trash—can seem terribly humdrum unless, as one Persistent Personality put it, you "put your heart into it." A bit of gusto converts the blahs into appreciation.

• The best way to get attention is to do things well.

• You need to make solid commitments, not "maybe" commitments.

• Genuine involvement means relating to others by actively participating and sharing with them. It also means pursuing those objects of your faith and devotion and seizing every opportunity to develop your talents.

• The greatest discovery in life comes when you discover your own resourcefulness, your own talents, your own great capacity for loving and doing and sharing.

- Ralph Waldo Emerson said that the only way to have a friend is to be one.
- Dietrich Bonhoeffer, while suffering the harshness of interrogation and prison life in Nazi Germany, wrote to his friends: "Enjoy whatever comes your way."
- The best way to overcome confusion, wondering, and questioning is to *do* something and then appreciate what you have done.
- Don't spend all your time looking for the missing one percent in your life. Appreciate the 99 percent that you have.
- When you're giving more in any relationship, it makes the relationship more enjoyable. Who benefits? You benefit.
- Expect less from others and more from yourself.
- During one of those quiet, reflective moments, ponder how much other people really care for you.
- Life is not a wild-goose chase. It is a journey into opportunity with both feet on the ground. Take a firm first step in the direction of your hopes.
- Admit your mistakes and learn from them, but don't be so aware of other people's mistakes. Take care of your own, and by doing that, you avoid the power struggles.
- Be more flexible. Accept others as they are. Don't try to change them. Don't always fight the system. Get involved.
- You can control those impulses, especially once you realize that they are only devices for gaining attention—too often negative attention.
- Be careful of your anger. It causes you more trouble than any other reaction that you have. More, it prevents you from seizing opportunities and from being appreciated.
- Say "Thank you" more often. And really mean it.
- Faith is more than a virtue. It is your great strength. Invest it wisely. Persisting in faith, whatever its object, is the best way of overcoming your faults and frailties.
- Be objective about your financial and business matters. Try writing down the pros and cons of a money matter on paper, then take a long walk before making a decision.
- Be frugal but not miserly. Be generous but not lavish. Moderation in all things.
- Your impish impetuosity, your impulsive remarks and actions,

278

are self-indulgent. Try a little discipline. Learn to resist. It takes practice. Start now.

• Be open to making commitments. Then watch good things happen.

• Set your goals. Channel your energies wisely. Avoid extremes. Make firm decisions. Then act.

• Do the most that you can each day. Live life one day at a time. Be happy with what you do, what you have, and appreciate each step that you take in the task at hand.

• Be a doer of the word.

• There is an ancient and wise saying: "Pray like everything depended on God; work like everything depended on you."

• Give a little. Share a little. Be cheerful. Be caring. Keep busy.

• Count your blessings.

XII

*I have no other choice
than to follow my own
convictions.*

DAG HAMMARSKJÖLD

The Conscientious

Personality

ONCE, when the nation was young, the American character was represented by the popular image and virtues of the New England Yankee: honest yet shrewd, decent, hard-working and frugal, reliable, reserved, quietly religious, an individual of great common sense, a wit, a person who in saying little said much. That likeness is still with us in the Conscientious Personality.

It's a good likeness, a pleasant image. There is something comfortable in the style and presence of the Conscientious Personality and in his low-keyed, steady approach to life. It wears well in all sorts of situations and circumstances. The Conscientious Personality most often is an attentive and dependable friend, a thoughtful spouse, a tender parent, an efficient and methodical worker. He is characteristically organized, careful, deliberate, thorough, and he tries always to meet his obligations, whether social, occupational, civic, or financial—he wants to do everything properly and well. He tends to be neat and tidy about his person and his environment, developing good habits and maintaining them. He likes to be punctual —if he tells you he will pick you up in front of your house at 6:30, he'll be there, on time, waiting patiently, never tooting his horn.

That's the Conscientious Personality; he goes through life never tooting his horn. Too shy perhaps, or too modest. Or too considerate of others. Or none too sure that he has anything or has done anything worth a toot. But he has, and while he might never speak of his many likable and productive traits, he could well imagine a more orderly existence if everyone possessed a few of these same traits.

What is so apparent in the style of the Conscientious Personality is his constant and sometimes meticulous attention to details. She is the earnest student who turns in an immaculate and comprehensive term paper, ample footnotes embroidering the bottom of each page. She spends hours and hours perusing reference book after reference book, always looking for still another scholarly volume that might add further substance to an already substantial report; she prepares draft after draft and then revises again; she endures the tedium of typing so many pages, all error-free. Everything that could be included has been included—except a little bit of her own thoughts and opinion. In subsequent class discussion of the topic of her paper, she doesn't volunteer a comment, but when called on, she has all the information, all the elaborate details for recitation. Her instructor might wish that the entire class were made up of Conscientious students, but he might wish too that his great researcher would let a little of her own self come through her scholarship.

The Conscientious accountant is the sort who will sift through your records and receipts, scrutinize them thoroughly, and then itemize appropriate entries on your income tax forms. You can be sure that whatever is due you from the Internal Revenue Service is carefully reckoned, but you can be sure too that everything legitimately due the Internal Revenue Service is reckoned. If you would like to stretch the legal limits, then find another accountant. This one, remember, is conscientious.

If you are interested in buying a certain piece of property but have doubts about the title being clear, seek out a Conscientious real-estate lawyer. Whatever doubts you have will be minor compared to the stream of doubts that will run through his mind automatically. He will exhaust all possibilities in trying to locate all past claims to the property—rummage the hall of records, visit the historical archives in the state capital, tour the attics of the last ten owners. He is the kind of person who could turn up the original deed to Manhattan Island.

A word of warning: Never bet with a Conscientious Personality.

He would only bet on a sure thing. Even so, he isn't too inclined to gamble; he doesn't like to take risks. If the talk were of horse racing, he would be more interested in the horses, their past performances, their best times, how well the posted odds conform to statistical probabilities; and if the electronic scoreboard at the ball park flashes a stumper of a question—Who was the last switch-hitter to hit consecutive home runs from alternate sides of the plate in an afternoon game?—watch for a hint of a smile along the lips of the Conscientious fan. He knows. He always knows. He is a walking book of records.

THE DOUBTING URGE

What is it that compels the Conscientious accountant to work so diligently over every tax return, the Conscientious student to research so exhaustively yet never be part of the presentation, the Conscientious real-estate lawyer to probe so deeply? His great need for certainty. He wants so much to approximate perfection, finality, certitude. He tends to identify his own worth with the correctness of a solution to a problem, the completeness of a task, the exhaustion of all options less that one that is beyond all reasonable doubt. *Maybe*. There in that one hint of doubt, however trivial, hangs the Conscientious Personality's sense of his own worth. So the tendency in most situations is to question, examine, and then re-examine all possible data in the pursuit of perfection and certitude.

But one thing only is certain, that certainty eludes us all. Most of us accept this finite limitation with a certain amount of grace. Not the Conscientious Personality—he is driven by the *doubting urge*. This doubting is never concerned simply with a solution to be found or a task to be completed; the doubting is wrapped up in the worth of the Conscientious Personality himself. If the job isn't perfect, *he* isn't perfect. If the outcome is questionable, *he* is questionable. So each fact must be weighed carefully, all the data must be sifted and sorted, all the angles considered, and all the options examined. Not once. Not twice. The process goes on until, hopefully, doubt is eliminated—which isn't possible. The healthy and confident Conscientious Personality knows this, so he goes through the process willing to accept reasonable limitations and reasonable risks. Once may be enough—a very careful, thorough once. Doubt is never fully rooted out, but common sense prevails. But not for the uncertain, less sure Conscientious Personality. The process of weighing, examining, questioning, considering goes on and on because the doubting goes on and on. And the more the Conscientious Personality doubts, the more he feels the need to question; but the more he questions, the more he doubts. The circle is not only vicious but paralyzing.

A certain amount of doubting is normal, necessary, and productive in any human enterprise. All of us are bombarded constantly by data that needs to be sorted, utilized, or discarded. Some of it is useful, some not. Questions are posed to us. Good answers have to be constructed. Many options and angles have to be considered, and different problems demand different approaches, different solutions. The very process of selecting includes challenging and doubting the data at hand. This is the way buildings are built, diseases are identified, scientific discoveries are made, the process through which most learning is accomplished, friends are chosen and relationships are formed. Thus doubting shouldn't be thought of only as a negative process; it is one of the necessary phases of inquiry, and in routine day-to-day living, it helps us enormously in making decisions.

The more careful the sifting and sorting, the more careful our questioning, the better equipped we are to make good decisions. So far, so good, but the Conscientious Personality tends to want to sift and sort and question just a little longer and more carefully than most personality styles, heightening doubt, delaying the decision. This is beneficial just as long as, somewhere in the process, the options narrow, the questioning lessens, and a decision is forthcoming. Sometimes a lingering question and a further consideration of the problem trigger a radical discovery. And in those rarefied moments—as well as in the more routine but necessary moments of doing tax returns, term papers, and title searches—everyone benefits from the contributions of the Conscientious Personality.

VULNERABILITIES AND CRISES

But the less certain, less confident Conscientious Personality sifts and sorts and questions endlessly. Options keep multiplying. Data becomes clutter and confusion abounds. The possibilities are too many, and all the while, the Conscientious Personality is telling himself: "Whoa! Careful. Go slow. Maybe this. Maybe that. Beware of this choice or that choice. Don't take risks. Be certain." What happens? Nothing. All the circuits are overloaded. The unsure Conscientious Personality is so stuffed with options and doubts that his mind is unable to handle a decision, so the decision is deferred. Meanwhile, as the doubting increases, his self-worth diminishes. This sort of doubting is negative and very debilitating. Functioning grinds to a halt. The prevailing consideration is the possibility of making a mistake, committing an error, and the great fear is that error would reduce the already diminished Conscientious Personality to worthlessness, total and complete. So he is frozen in his negative attitude, fearing and feeling shame. Few if any risks are taken; real opportunities are missed. The pure pleasure of having accomplished something—anything—is denied. Still, the doubting lingers and, as any doubting Conscientious Personality who has traveled this negative route knows, the process can be very depressing.

The sifting and sorting, the questioning and considering apply to large concerns and to small matters. The Conscientious Personality, for example, might be considering buying a new home, aware that his present one is cramped, that values are peaking in his neighborhood, and that his equity is ample for upgrading to a newer and larger home. So far, fine. Then he begins to probe a second layer of considerations: available developments, distances to work, shopping centers, church and school; interest rates; available improvements; cost of water and sewage; tax rates. The options escalate. Then there are lesser but still important matters: exterior style, interior colors, garage space, insulation, landscaping, whether or not to have the basement finished, the capacity of the water heater, choice of bathroom fixtures, and so on and so on. Even the healthy Conscientious Personality will feel the burden of so much data to process, and how healthy he is will show in how well he handles each layer of decisions, how positive he feels about his choices, and how comfortable he feels afterward. The less healthy Conscientious Personality may simply decide not to decide, to defer consideration of a new home until some other time. Or he might feel uncomfortable with the notion of changing churches and schools and his route to work. Or he might bog down somewhere in the bathroom, perhaps fussing over the new style of toilet: "Is the seat too high, too low, wide enough? Shouldn't the handle be higher, the tank lower? Or maybe the handle lower

284

and the tank higher? Is the tank's capacity adequate? Or maybe it wastes water. Maybe the flush is too noisy; it might wake up the baby. Maybe the shutoff valve will leak in six months." There and then, his dream of a new home is threatened by the agony of questions and doubts. It happens, but not to the healthy Conscientious Personality. He can manage the many options, the necessary sifting and sorting, even when he feels some strain. He can make productive decisions, and can live with them comfortably. He knows what he has purchased and why. No doubt his family and friends will agree that he has made a good and shrewd purchase. Even he can agree. The less confident Conscientious Personality who made it all the way through the various considerations and attending doubts might purchase the new home only to regret it; this is another way of doubting after the fact. And all the joy is spoiled. Blame it on that newfangled toilet.

WIT AS WISDOM

We note in considering each personality style that humor is usually a sign of good health, and this is particularly evident in the behavior of the Conscientious Personality. Normally reticent in speech, he is at his best when he sees the comic or amusing aspect of a situation. And he usually does, since he usually sees the full range of possibilities and options in any situation, even the ludicrous. His style of humor runs to the pithy, concise comment. His wit is wry, sly, and dry. But there are no barbs attached. He doesn't wound. He can tease, but he doesn't taunt. He loves a playful, practical joke, but nobody gets hurt. And he can laugh at himself, the best antidote to his doubting and questioning of himself.

This playful disposition of the Conscientious Personality is a great social asset. His droll humor makes him a welcome guest at a party, and so long as the human content of the party is comfortable —good friends, familiar faces—he can fulfill all sorts of beneficial functions: the good listener who is attentive and considerate, the guest who spots the hostess's distress and knows how to help, the courteous and conscientious guest who never stays too long or gets too boisterous. But he may need a drink or two to loosen up his restraint—then he sparkles. He loves it; it is a relief from his usually serious stance. But if the occasion is formal or the company unfamiliar, the Conscientious party-goer very well may sit by quietly, say little, and leave as soon as it is comfortable to do so.

The Conscientious Personality is also a great party-giver. Here too all the possibilities are inventoried and responded to—the guest list is a careful mix; the environment reflects a desire to make everyone comfortable and accessible; snacks and hors d'oeuvres are plentiful and well-prepared, and when the trays run low, they are quickly replenished. The Conscientious host or hostess knows what everyone likes to drink and has an ample supply on hand, and there is always late-evening coffee just before the party ends. Everyone enjoys the party so much, even the Conscientious host or hostess, if healthy enough. He knows how to have everything ready long before the party begins. Nothing is left to last-minute haste. Not so for the unsure Conscientious party-giver. He might be so concerned, so anxious about all the possibilities, that he prepares list after list of things to do, food to fix, people to invite. An hour before the guests are due to arrive, he is still checking his list and scampering after items. Everyone may enjoy the party except the Conscientious host. He is too busy scurrying around emptying ashtrays, wondering if he has enough food and drink, if everyone is enjoying himself. If he wakes up in the morning with a headache, it isn't as likely to be from drinking as from spending the whole evening and half the night worrying whether or not everyone enjoyed himself.

While the Conscientious Personality likes the social moment, enjoys giving parties, and relishes a casual evening with friends, he doesn't particularly care for the spontaneous get-together. If you ask him to drop by after the Friday night football game, he very well might decline; he has had Friday night's post-game activities planned for a month. And if he asks you to drop by after the game, he doesn't mean tonight's game; he means two weeks from now; he needs the time to plan the spontaneous.

ORDER AND STRUCTURE

The Conscientious Personality really doesn't care for any sort of surprise or any change. He enjoys the familiar environment, whether at home or at work or in the company of friends. He cherishes routine. He prizes the predictable, and he is predictable; his habits govern the flow of his day's activities, the patterns of his life. From the moment his feet hit the floor in the morning until he tucks them back between the sheets at night, his day, as much as he can determine it, is a steady procession of known rituals and familiar activities. And within this structured existence, he thrives. Freed from having to consider all the options and angles and choices of the small things in life—what to have for breakfast, which is the better route to work, when to take a coffee break, whom to lunch with, when to do the wash, when to begin to prepare dinner—the Conscientious Personality is able to devote his talents and energy quite productively to the task at hand. The Conscientious working wife is the kind of person who can have the children fed and off to school, a full load of wash done, her breakfast dishes back in the cupboard, and herself properly preened and prepared to go to work by 8:30—not just today but every day. She's been doing it that way for the past four years without a hitch. She loves the routine, wouldn't have it any other way, and her way of celebrating the smooth flow of the week is to have lunch every Friday at noon with the girls from the office. They always go to the same restaurant, order the special of the day, and have one martini for openers—and the price of the lunch, martini, and tip are fairly predictable too. She's had it in the budget each week for the past year. It's all part of her planned spontaneity, and she takes great pleasure in every predictable moment. Structure makes the pleasure possible. Take away the structure, and you take away much of the possibility of relaxing and enjoying a friendly Friday lunch.

There is always the danger that order and structure can become rigid or ritualistic. The doubting Conscientious Personality can't go to bed at night without first checking to see if the cat is out, if the doors are locked, if the television is off and unplugged, if the light is out in the basement, if the thermostat has been turned down to 60 degrees, if the alarm clock has been set for 6:30. Ten minutes after sliding into bed, he may wonder suddenly if he might not have missed the basement light, so he jumps out of bed and runs to the basement. And once he doubts any one of the items on his checklist, he feels he must go through the entire roster again. Should he not be able to sleep on returning to bed, he might suppose that the reason is that he didn't put his right foot into bed first as he did last night, so he gets out of bed to enter it again according to the rubrics of last night's ritual.

One doubting Conscientious Personality may be driving at night when, suddenly, he pulls the car over to the side of the road and gets out to check if both headlights are working. Another individual may be so concerned about proper bowel function that she must always go to the bathroom at exactly the same time every morning with no one around. Every weekend and holiday she is constipated; everyone is home, so her ritual is disturbed. Another Conscientious Personality can't sit down to write letters to family and friends without her dictionary at her elbow. She constantly checks her spelling, even the spelling of familiar words. She has to be sure.

THE CONSCIENTIOUS CONSCIENCE

The words "conscience" and "conscious" have the same Latin root, derived from the word "to know." The main problem for the Conscientious Personality is that he knows too much—he is so conscious of all facets of a situation, all the angles, all the considerations, all the options and opportunities, and always he wants to make the right choice, the right decision, to be correct and, as much as possible, perfect. Yet he is plagued by doubts—if he is feeling a bit on the negative side, his doubting reduces his sense of worth—so he tries especially hard to be careful and to be exact in all things. He is in danger of becoming scrupulous. Of all the personality styles, the Conscientious Personality has the greatest problem with scruples, not only in moral matters but in everyday matters of no moral consequence.

The Conscientious Personality is a frugal person, but with scruples he becomes austere. He denies himself pleasure, feeling it would be wrong to spend money to enjoy himself. Or he has defined limits: he may have learned as a child that one scoop of ice cream is an ample treat; any more is gluttonous; so even at age forty, despite a comfortable income, he may still limit himself to a single scoop of ice cream. And he may insist that his children respect the same limit. He may have been rewarded with a rare movie when he was young, so he only permits himself a night at the cinema when he feels good about himself, which, with his negative feelings, may not be too often. He never wants to be guilty of pampering himself. That would fill him with shame.

When it comes to morality, the scruples can be devastating, immobilizing. The scrupulous Conscientious Personality might find himself staring at an attractive woman: "Did I have a desire for her? No, I didn't. I don't think I did. Maybe I did." Flooded with shame, he doesn't dare look in her direction again. If the attractive young woman were Conscientious and scrupulous, she might fear that tight clothing would be a source of temptation for her boyfriend, so on dates she wears loose and bulky clothing. The young Conscientious worker may feel that he has robbed his employer because he took a day's sick leave. The Conscientious child might fear he has lost God's friendship because he missed his prayers before going to bed. The situations may seem inconsequential to others, but to the scrupulous Conscientious Personality, they are causes of torment and shame. What is more, the troubled individual may spend so much time and effort avoiding moments of temptation and moral dangers that he does little else. As Hamlet remarked, "Thus conscience does make cowards of us all."

Because of this dominance of negative feelings about himself and his worth, the troubled Conscientious Personality has a difficult time enjoying any of the usual pleasures of life. He feels he doesn't deserve fun or pleasure or good feelings. He makes a monumental effort to keep his emotions in check, and, of course, his talent for doubting is a guarantee that his good feelings won't surface too often. Besides, he believes that others are more deserving than he is, so he denies his opportunities for fun and pleasure, wearing an emotional hair shirt, doing penance for sins that he has never committed, hardly able to do the good that he desires for avoiding the good times that he fears. It's hell.

DECISIONS, DECISIONS, DECISIONS

If temptations and evil are to be shunned, then decisions come close to being the root of all evil. Remember, the Conscientious Personality is capable of seeing all sides of the question, all possible alternatives, all angles of the problem. He always wants to come up with the completely correct solution or answer; his worth depends on it. So he wants to check out all his options—he can't afford to be wrong. Therefore decisions come slowly and painfully—and sometimes not at all for the heavily doubting, uncertain Conscientious Personality.

He temporizes; he vacillates: "Maybe I should cut the lawn today. No, it might be too damp still from yesterday's rain; it might clog up the mower. But if I don't cut it today, I might not have time tomorrow. No, I'd better have the blade sharpened first. It's thrashing and not cutting. But my wife might need the car to go shopping this afternoon, so I can't get the blade sharpened. I'll cut the lawn with the old hand mower. No, my back is giving me fits. Can't do that. I'll borrow my neighbor's mower. No, he might need it. Maybe I should go ahead with my dull blade. No, that's no good. Anyway, I should fix the bag attachment first, but it's missing a screw, and I'll have to run down to the hardware store. Maybe I ought to check to see how damp the lawn is." Before he can come to the right decision—any decision—the sun has set and the grass hasn't been touched. Now he can spend the rest of the evening considering undesirable qualities about himself.

The young Conscientious careerist decides that he ought to make a decision about taking a position with another firm. He knows he doesn't particularly like change, and he also knows that he has good advancement opportunities with his present firm. But he can't be sure about that advancement until next month when management reviews candidates for two positions opening up in his division. He is healthy, so he does an exercise in studying the possible sequences of opportunity within his present job, the other possible candidates for promotion, his awareness of management attitudes and criteria within the selection process. He also makes a study of the company that is offering him a position, its recent growth record, and the market potential that might affect its future growth. He phones a friend who sells to that company to gather what information he can about its management personnel and attitudes. As he gathers all the pros and cons on both sides of the question, he is aware that he can doubt too much and fear risking too easily. He tells himself: "This isn't the Last Judgment. Let the facts, not the maybe's, speak. Both opportunities are good, and if this decision doesn't work out, other opportunities will come along. Choose." And he does. Weighing all considerations, including an awareness of how he feels about change of location and his enjoyment of the work he is doing, he decides to remain with his present employer. The foreseeable advantages are better, but the great benefit in his choice is that he realizes this decision isn't eternal and immutable. He doesn't have to live with it forever. He knows this is the best decision he can make, given the information he has. It is a comfortable decision—and very healthy.

GROWING UP CONSCIENTIOUS

The Conscientious child is normally contented and rather quiet. He is not particularly demanding and has few problems with feeding and toilet training. He is receptive to parental direction, although prone to remember brusque correction all too well. He benefits greatly from a warm and affectionate environment that fosters his sense of self-worth.

As he develops, the Conscientious child enjoys toys that permit tinkering and taking them apart and putting them back together again; later he will show an interest in building things and seeing how they work. His play with other children, including his brothers and sisters, is no more and no less boisterous than his peers', although he isn't given to emotional displays. He doesn't like to upset anyone, and he worries when it happens. He is thoughtful of others, putting their pleasure above his own.

The Conscientious child enters school with little difficulty; he can be expected to enter into the routine rather easily, and he responds well to authority. Teachers are usually fond of the Conscientious child; he wants to please. The danger is that the Conscientious child is too easily ignored; he makes so few demands, even for attention. He is willing to work hard; he wants to do everything correctly and well; but he tends to go along with what the other person decides is good for him, even how he feels about himself. He may think his drawing poorly done until the child next to him says, "Gee, that's a pretty cow." Then he wonders, "Do I like it, or don't I like it?" In a case like this, the teacher gets the tie vote. Then too, if he misses a day of school because of sickness, he may wonder: "Did I get sick just so I could stay out of school? No, I didn't do that. Or did I?"

The Conscientious child of a friend was working in the first reading group in second grade when a new teacher took over the class. Not familiar with the grouping or the reading skills of the children, she shuffled the class, assigning this Conscientious child to a lower reading group. The child said nothing. He worked hard to do all the required work, then quietly moved into the circle of the first reading group. The teacher watched, noting that the child worked quite capably with the top readers. She realized what had happened and accepted the situation, permitting the child to remain with the upper group. Here is an example of the Conscientious Personality's subtle handling of a difficult situation. He didn't defy or challenge: he moved toward an acceptable solution peacefully and purposefully.

The Conscientious child does particularly well not only in the classroom but in any structured situation such as Girl or Boy Scouts, choir, gymnastics, or band. He seems to enjoy collecting as a hobby—rocks, stamps, coins, and the like—because of the detail and the orderliness of the activity. If he is engaged in organized sports, he may show some doubt about his ability if he isn't picked in the first several selections of players, but it would be rare if he wasn't picked early. Even as a child his athletic efforts are recognized because he is competitive and likes to win—he especially likes to compete with his own recent performance. In whatever he is doing, the Conscientious child may show signs of frustration when he isn't able to do things as well as he might like. He is rather exacting. He tends to daydream and to "think way too much," as one Conscientious Personality remembers, analyzing and considering the many aspects of those interests that appeal to him.

ADOLESCENCE

Things go rather well for the Conscientious youngster until puberty. Sometime in the junior high years, he comes to realize that there are so many matters involved in growing up that invite consideration and decision: What kind of person am I? What is sex all about? How well am I doing as a student? What kind of people are my friends? These are never easy questions for a thoughtful young person, but they place heavy demands on the Conscientious adolescent. No longer is it enough to accept answers from parents and teachers, answers that earlier were simple and adequate and acceptable; now he is beginning to see for himself the multiple angles and options in life. He begins to spend more time reflectively analyzing who he is and what he wants to do, but the danger is that he might spend more time analyzing than he spends doing. He tends to withdraw more into himself thinking things through, or at least trying to. This is when the doubting urge begins to dampen his confidence and bring into question how well his worth matches his desire to do all things as perfectly as possible. He wants to minimize the risk of making mistakes, of making poor choices. He temporizes while he considers all options: "Should I try out for the football team? Or should I try wrestling? Or basketball? Or should I be studying harder? Should I try out as cheerleader? Maybe I'm not good-looking enough, not popular enough. Maybe I won't like it. Then again . . ."

The Conscientious teenager is usually included in whatever the activity because he does things so well. When troubled, however, he often misses out on much of the excitement because he can't make up his mind what is the best crowd to join, what sports to participate in, what else is important. In the end, he does little. One Conscientious Personality remembers going out for baseball only because his best friend went out, and he wanted to be with him. Another Conscientious Personality missed freshman football because he couldn't decide whether he really wanted to play the game. But he did go out for practice in his sophomore year. Unlike the returning players, he didn't have a uniform, so he practiced for three days without equipment before deciding that he wasn't going to make it. The coach called the next day to find out why he had quit. He mentioned first a hay fever reaction to rolling around on the grass and then his feeling that he wasn't going to make the roster since he hadn't been issued equipment. The coach told him it would only be a day or so before he would have his uniform, but the young man said no, quietly thanking the coach. Why wouldn't he return to practice? He had already made his decision, and that was tough enough. He didn't want to go through the agony of remaking it. But, as often happens to the Conscientious Personality in the aftermath of missing an opportunity, he regretted not rejoining the team: "I can pretty well date my confidence beginning to sag from that time."

These teen years are critical to the developing Conscientious Personality as he faces decisions. He needs to be encouraged during these years to push past the doubting, to reduce the data, to take reasonable risks, and most of all, he needs to know that most of the decisions he makes at this time are transitional, and don't commit him for life. He must learn to function as well as he can without demanding perfection of himself. The best path through all the doubting is to seek the simplest and most direct approach to the problem at hand, and then do it without looking backward.

The Conscientious teenager who learns to move ahead begins to show his strengths slowly and very subtly. He is something of a late bloomer, and only in hindsight do contemporaries look back to recall his admirable qualities. She didn't make cheerleader in her freshman year—she didn't even go out for anything but volleyball until her junior year—but sometime during the fall of her senior year, people began to notice that parties were more fun when she was present. She was the one who came up with the float theme that won the grand prize in the Thanksgiving Day parade; and she was the staffer who wouldn't let the school newspaper die of dullness; almost single-handedly she put out an April Fool issue that fractured the faculty while breaking up the student body. Until then, she hadn't had her first date, but she was asked to the senior prom. Everyone wondered where she had been all through high school. Late bloomer? Yes, but a full bloomer. No doubt about it.

Parents, teachers, and other adult authorities should take care in their criticism of the Conscientious teenager. He is always so critical of himself that adult criticism only reinforces his own negative feelings about his worth. A better approach is to give him positive support for decisions and accomplishments, even when they aren't much more than a good effort. What counts is the effort—his having acted in a moment of opportunity, his having taken risks. When he seeks reassurance, support his activities as much as possible, and, above all, don't encourage his long lapses into silent doubting. Invite him into family and school happenings. Beware of overanalyzing his problems as he tends to overanalyze them, because this only increases his opportunity for doubt by increasing the data available for processing. He needs *less* data, not more. Encourage the simpler solution, the more direct approach, and encourage him to decide *more* and to analyze *less*. Support his decisions—by accentuating the positive, much of the opportunity for the negative is eliminated. Once committed, the Conscientious Personality does work vigorously to achieve his goal. He has the courage of his convictions.

COURTSHIP, MARRIAGE, AND FAMILY LIFE

All of us are attracted to someone who is physically appealing, but the Conscientious Personality seems especially aware of physical attractiveness. The male tends to find a woman who is not only good-looking but petite, and the female finds a man who is tall and handsome. Popularity in the peer group is also appealing, as a decision has thus already been made on that person's attractiveness. One Conscientious wife recalls: "All the other girls on campus were after him—or at least I thought they were—so when he asked me for a date, I thought, 'Wow!' " Beyond a moment's vacillation, so typical of the Conscientious Personality, she realized that here indeed was a desirable prospect. Then that beautiful Conscientious way of seeing all the angles worked in her favor. She was able to go beyond his good looks to consider all his other qualities and potential as husband, father, companion, provider, appreciating all of the positive traits. More, he saw in her those quiet, steady ways and her gift of seeing the humorous side of any situation. And he found her quiet moments comfortable and undemanding.

The Conscientious Personality can prolong courtship by working very hard to reach a decision on marriage. There are so many factors to consider, such a definite commitment to make, and marriage, however carefully approached, is a plunge into the unknown. The Conscientious Personality will consider all the negative fears as well as the positive hopes. If healthy, he or she will put greater stress on the positive side and move toward a decision and a commitment. The less healthy Conscientious Personality can be so ridden with doubt and uncertainty, so concerned that this be the perfect union, he is unable to decide. And while the process is such hard work for the Conscientious Personality, the other person may see it only as procrastination. This can be very trying for both parties, and the Conscientious Personality may doubt too long, missing the opportunity and later regretting his indecision. Sometimes not deciding is the greater risk.

Once the Conscientious Personality commits, he or she will work very hard to make marriage a success. His planning and sense of purpose are productive, and his ability to consider the various sides of any situation make compromise possible. He is considerate, thoughtful, and attentive. Yet, whether male or female, the Conscientious Personality tends to accept rather traditional roles for both parties. The male is viewed as the breadwinner, head of the family, head of the household; the woman is the homemaker, mother, and wife. He may bend a bit on the definition of roles, but the tendency is to continue to cling to his conservative values. Male or female, the Conscientious spouse will want to maintain a neat and orderly house; clutter only invites confusion and unnecessary things to consider. Budgets will be planned and maintained rather vigorously, and habits and routine will be established. Initially in marriage, the Conscientious partner may try to maintain lists of things to do, schedules to keep. It isn't a good idea, as it reduces flexibility; it prevents any spark of spontaneity. And it only points to things undone, like an accusing finger, becoming an exacting exercise in futility and negative feelings.

Major decisions in marriage may come slowly, with much deliberation: to have children, how many children, purchasing and furnishing a home, relocation, job change. Any significant change may bring on vacillation and elaborate consideration of data before a decision. The young wife who has begun a promising career in journalism may want to begin a family, but: "Is it a good time? Maybe I should wait. But I might have a more difficult pregnancy when I'm five years older. Can we live without my income? Would I be a responsible mother? I might miss my job. My mother says being pregnant is awful. But I want to be a mother. My mother has varicose veins—I might get varicose veins. Will my husband still love me with varicose veins? Maybe I should wait. But I want a baby now." The longer she takes to make a decision, the more negative she feels about herself, and she becomes edgy and quiet, although she sometimes finds fault with her husband. She is struggling to control her emotions, letting up only long enough for those short bursts of anger, which provoke feelings of shame and further doubt. If she could break through her doubting and controlling long enough to discuss her feelings with her husband fully, he might give her the assurance and support she needs to make a proper decision. That would be a far more productive course.

No doubt our worrisome Conscientious woman would make a good mother. She is, after all, conscientious, and she would be both responsible and responsive, concerned about and committed to her children, just as long as the decision to be a parent were truly her own. Lingering doubts might reduce her job and effectiveness as a mother. Otherwise, she would be the kind of parent who would structure a calm and orderly home life for herself, her husband, and her children. The values she could be expected to promote would be conservative and traditional: the practice of religion, an accent on family sharing and doing things together, definite rules about homework and school activities and hours away from home; she would promote her children's interests in music, hobbies, and physical activities whether in organized sports or as a personal discipline; she would encourage her husband's career, although along cautious lines, not wanting to take too many chances or to invite too many moves. She might herself join the church choir or volunteer to teach Sunday school. She might like occasionally to have a small party for friends or to visit with family, to attend class reunions or lunch over the holidays with one or two sorority sisters from college days. She has an abiding regard for her roots and tends them lovingly.

As a father, the Conscientious Personality is no different. He promotes sturdy values and an established routine for family life, welcoming the evening meal as a moment when everyone is gathered together to share dinner and each other's company. He can sit there quietly, enjoying the interplay among his children, occasionally making some quick, pithy, even playful comment, issuing a word of correction if the banter gets too noisy or if someone displays rudeness or bad manners. Often a look from a Conscientious parent is enough. His tastes at the table run toward simple, nourishing fare—meat and potatoes and two vegetables, chicken every Sunday. And when he takes the family out to eat at a restaurant, his choice of place and menu will also reflect his emphasis on a nourishing meal without frills— and without too much of a strain on the budget.

Male or female, the Conscientious Personality is usually an involved, loving, tender parent, and children are good for the Conscientious Personality. It's difficult to doubt your worth when a child is perched on your lap, hugging and kissing you, and it's difficult to be too structured when interacting with children. They act and react spontaneously, inviting spontaneous response. The Conscientious parent can always use the practice.

THE WORKING WORLD

The Conscientious Personality obtains much gratification from his work. By doing what he feels he does well, he grows in confidence, and he particularly enjoys any form of enterprise that permits him to finish what he starts, pursuing his own methodical, planned approach. He works well with others as part of a team, but likes to feel that he has command over his responsibilities. He can be aggressive, not so much in open competition with peers but in pursuit of excellence and improvement in his working efficiency. The Conscientious worker doesn't like his routine disrupted, and doesn't appreciate fellow workers who want to chat and play games during working hours. He is the American work ethic personified. He is on the job when the whistle blows in the morning, and has done a full day's work when it comes time to quit for the day. He takes great pride in his competence and productivity, yet he is not the person who takes his job home with him—not if he is healthy. He knows he has worked hard, done a decent day's work, and then some. If he doesn't receive an expected raise, or if he feels that he has been passed over for promotion, he may begin to question and examine all the possible reasons why not. Or if he has a rather exacting job, where a high degree of skill is mandatory, he may question his competence and be too concerned over occasional mistakes—and then he might carry his doubting home with him.

The Conscientious careerist finds his approach to work and his organizing skills applicable in most fields, although he might not enjoy a position involving extended traveling, living out of hotel rooms, and being away from home. The Conscientious engineer would come up with six different solutions to a problem while his colleagues struggle with one; he will know every facet of the problem and consider all the options. She would be the teacher who introduces a dozen techniques in teaching a routine subject, or the executive secretary who so well structures procedures in the office that her presence is considered indispensable. He would be the internist who, not satisfied with a preliminary diagnosis, would run tests until his identification of the malady was reasonably certain. He would be the legislator who could always be found doing his homework on a bill or the executive whose attention to detail and careful consideration of both sides of an argument would make him a masterful negotiator in labor relations. He might be the salesman who thoroughly knows his product, how it is made, and how it functions, who has answers to questions that the customers might never ask. Yet he would himself have strong sales resistance; if buying a car, he wouldn't appreciate being introduced to thirteen different models with a choice of twenty-four colors and ninety-two options—that simply would be too much data to process. And few salesmen would enjoy him as a customer; he would have too many questions to ask.

How well the Conscientious careerist or worker enjoys retirement depends largely on how active he has been outside the job. If he closely identified with his work, it might be difficult to make the transition: the structure, the routine, the habits, the productivity would be missed. But if he had substantial interests and hobbies beyond the job, he could adjust quite well to retirement. If he has tended a small garden in the backyard, he might pursue it more avidly, expanding those long and tidy rows of carrots and onions and radishes. He enjoys keeping physically fit and active and has most always had an active exercise program, so he might rework the landscaping around the house, or buy a bicycle, or enjoy long walks in the woods, finding simple pleasure in the steady rhythm of his stride, the sun in his face, the beauty of nature all around him. And he would relish the relaxed mood, free from hassle and decision-making, to give more time to old friends, to read a good book, or maybe to travel.

ALTERNATIVES AND OPTIONS

The Conscientious Personality, we have seen, is a person whose approach to life is methodical, painstaking, and purposeful. He enjoys routine and structure, and is reliable and dependable. He is quiet, avoids clutter and hassle, tries to inject order and efficiency into whatever he does. He puts great emphasis on excellence in performances of a task, certainty, and predictability, so much so that at times he is overconcerned with perfection. He equates his own worth with the correctness of any decision; so he considers all options and possibilities, all sides of an argument, every approach to a problem that might be taken. He often becomes so concerned with the possibility of making a mistake that he hesitates to make a decision, tending to doubt himself, and the longer he continues in the doubting, the more he doubts his own worth. He becomes reticent, withdrawing into silence, controlling his emotions, denying himself good feelings and the satisfaction of acting decisively and enjoying the fruits of his decisions. When feeling unsure and uncertain, he is prone to continue his doubting even after a decision has been made and acted upon, thus continuing his negative feelings about his own worth. He is capable of agonizing scruples and great frustration. While he is a person of convictions, he finds it difficult to declare and act on these convictions. He views any commitment as irrevocable, final. He broods over mistakes made.

Rather than brood and doubt continuously, rather than remain uncommitted and indecisive, the uncertain Conscientious Personality might consider these options:

• Perfection is an illusion. Deal with reality. Your best effort is usually more than adequate.

• Avoid long periods of silence and emotional isolation. Speak; express your feelings whenever you have the opening. And since you are so able to see all the options, creating openings should be no problem.

• Don't look back. That first doubt can spoil your pleasure in having acted decisively.

• Eliminate the negative by accentuating the positive.

• More and more, it ought to be apparent that only death and taxes are certain.

• Try doing something spontaneously, even if you have to plan it.

• Spend more time with children. They resist structure, and they invite the playful spirit in you. And it's always safe to do impromptu things with children.

• You don't have to be perfect to be worthwhile. You only have to be yourself.

• People love that wry wit of yours. Let it loose—it's a great social asset. It can be the antidote to your negative attitudes, your doubting urge.

• Go out and buy yourself a double-dip ice cream cone. Or a new dress. Or a new sports shirt. You're worth it.

• Accept more responsibility. Reach out and seek it. Test and extend your talents and capabilities. You are always much more successful and enterprising than you give yourself credit for.

• If negative attitudes are a habit, then positive attitudes can be a habit too.

• No decision is etched in stone. If you can go through the door once, you can back off and do it again. A decision that isn't productive can be renegotiated, and you do well in negotiations.

• Don't invite others to make your decisions for you. They are *your* decisions because it is *your* life.

• Be willing to take more risks.

• Throw away all those lists that you make of things to do. No one can do everything. You only feel bad when you review the list and see what you haven't done. You never see what you have done.

• Be willing to make a mistake. Making mistakes is one very effective way of learning.

• Scruples are a curse. More, all the agonizing over what you *might* have done wrong keeps you from doing anything right.

• Try to break those solemn rituals—getting into bed only one way, muttering little formulas to yourself when facing a decision—or fearing a mistake or doing something wrong. The magic is in positive actions that follow firm decisions.

• Stop pointing out your faults. People aren't interested. They want to know the good news about your successes and joys.

• Don't make a decision and then invite others to criticize it. They will.

• There is nothing wrong in doing something for fun and pleasure. In fact, there is something very right and healthy about permitting yourself pleasure. It means that you recognize your worth.

• Keep the conversation going. When you break off from interaction—with a friend, the boss, your spouse—it usually means there is something important you ought to discuss, something you feel strongly about. Keep talking.

• Try risking a little more affection. Really, there's little risk, just opportunity for feeling good about yourself and for making others feel good too.

• Tell yourself: "Make a decision, then do it. Most decisions come off well enough that I can quit worrying. The odds are in my favor."

• Feeling negative? Deliberately choose to do something positive.

• Doubting only makes a necessary choice more difficult. So if you have it to do, do it. Dump the doubting.

• Think happy thoughts. They take far less energy than unhappy thoughts.

• There is far more certainty in a calculated risk than in doing nothing.

• Before running through all those options and angles and maybe's, tell yourself: "I'm doing great." Then don't question your answer.

• Test the courage of your convictions. Act on them. Make a commitment.

• Obey that impulse, just this once. The earth won't shake, but you might find that a little spontaneity in life is nice, even necessary.

• Not everything has to be precise, concise, and exact. Try being a little more free, frolicky, and fluid.

• Communicate more. You need the feedback. You need to hear the good thoughts and good feelings that friends, family, and colleagues have for you.

• Enjoy that party. You deserve it. Have fun.

• Shame is so often a sham. You do penance for things you have never done wrong. The best way not to suffer the shame is to do something positive.

• Confess your virtues, not your vices.

• Start a project. Finish it. Allow yourself the joy that comes with a job well done.

• Use a familiar environment as your framework for flexibility and freedom. There lies the challenge that you can enjoy.

• Plan a luncheon date. The budget isn't sacred, but your involvement with friends, your need to break out, your need for communication and laughter are very, very important. You're worth a little bulge in the budget.

• You have to let that humor of yours work for you. If you could bottle it, you'd be rich. But you are rich; you just haven't recognized your currency in terms of your friends, your family, your human worth.

• Ever and always: Accentuate the positive.

*The glory of God is man
fully alive.*

IRENAEUS

Epilogue: Choosing to Be Yourself

THE TWELVE STYLES of personality, each so rich in its strengths and opportunities, together contribute to human life and the human spirit. How much and how well these strengths are used to advantage, either individually or cooperatively, is largely a matter of choice, commitment, and conscious effort.

Simply knowing *about* your personality style isn't enough. You have to do something with that knowledge. There are no magic formulas, no easy shortcuts, for overcoming old habits and solving new problems. Significant change never comes easily; you have to leave behind old securities and defenses; you have to face new challenges. Sometimes change is uncomfortable, threatening, and even a little painful. It's new, it's difficult. That's why you have to choose to change. That's why you have to make a commitment to change. Then comes the effort. Potential remains only potential—a possibility—until you do something to make it a reality. That takes knowledge, yes; but it also demands doing. Each alternative and option offered at the end of the chapter on your personality style is a concrete suggestion that is realistic and possible. Each is a step that can help you to grow as a person, meet new challenges and opportunities, act and interact more productively, develop more fully your capabilities, and generally be more fully alive, happier, and more fully yourself.

How do you go about it?

First, be sure that you have identified your style. Read through all twelve styles before making a final judgment. If you aren't reasonably sure, go back over the chapter that seems to describe your usual attitudes and behavioral patterns. If still not sure, read through other chapters that seem close. Don't make the judgment too quickly. Check the descriptions until the spark of recognition hits and then holds.

Be honest. There is the temptation sometimes to want to be someone or something that you aren't and can't be. You may want very much to be like an admired parent, a successful friend, or a dynamic supervisor or working associate of another style. Don't try to imitate. It won't work for you unless you are the same style. Trying to behave in the style of another personality can only create tensions, stress, and new problems. So be yourself—find your own style. It is the only one that will be comfortable, the only one that will work for you.

Be aware. Be conscious of your strengths *and* your vulnerabilities, your prevailing patterns of attitude and behavior, your alternatives and options. Always try to be aware of what you are doing and, as much as possible, why. Be alert to your feelings. Make mental notes. As much as you can, be attentive to those situations in which your style characteristics, both positive and negative, most often affect your performance, your feelings about yourself, and your way of interacting with others. Try to be conscious of opportunities that match well with your strengths. Be alert to stress situations and actual feelings of stress. That way, you will be better prepared to alter usual responses that haven't in the past been too productive for you.

Avoid negative assumptions. The essential element of any personality style can be a strength or a weakness, depending on your use of it. When you recognize that element working in your attitudes and actions, be careful you don't automatically assume it is functioning negatively. Don't back away when it just might be working constructively to aid you in meeting problems or interacting. If, for example, you are an Ambitious Personality and realize suddenly that you are competing, don't immediately assume that this is wrong or inappropriate. It could be, but then again it might be quite appropriate. It depends on the circumstances and your feelings; *you* have to decide—only you are inside the situation. Just remember that the essence of your personality style is a strong, driving disposition. You can't avoid it; it is always there, but you shouldn't be shy of it; it is one of the greatest assets you have.

Don't expect too much too soon. Change takes time. Don't try to alter your whole makeup—you can't—and don't try to alter your less desirable coping mechanisms all at once. That's much like making New Year's resolutions and expecting to keep them all. You developed your habitual attitudes and reactions over a lifetime, and so correcting them will take time, perseverance, patience, and a bit of optimism. Take things one at a time, one step at a time. Build one small success on another, and recognize successful change when it happens. Appreciate progress. Pat yourself on the back, and then move ahead to the next step. And keep in mind that what you are changing are those things you don't like about yourself, that stunt your development, that blur your vision of goals and opportunities, and keep you from being content and happy.

Good emotional health is not perfection. Health and maturity are composed of many different characteristic moments and responses. Good health does not mean that in every instance you respond uniformly to stress or opportunity. One day may bring a better series of responses than another, and you may use one factor in your style more aptly than another. One is strong, another is so-so. An Influencing Personality, for example, may be healthy enough and realistic enough to enjoy the small pleasures of life. He doesn't expect every moment to be "grand and glorious," and he has learned to be open and flexible within the family circle. Still, he has some difficulty on the job refraining from expecting perfection of himself, and, on occasion, he tends to want to control everything relating to his work situation. Overall, we can say he is a healthy Influencing Personality, even though he needs to work on his job attitudes. In sum, what we call health is fractional: it is a general measurement of how well we handle ourselves according to the norms of growth. If we handle most situations well, know our weaknesses, and keep moving ahead, then we're healthy. We generally win more than we lose. So if you are doing well across the board, give or take a bad day or minor faults under stress, give yourself credit for generally good health and maturity. But keep working where you see the need.

Don't overanalyze. Be aware of what you are doing and feeling. Some reflection is beneficial, but extended analysis threatens to become counterproductive. It is so easy to slip into rationalization, making excuses for not changing or for accepting the status quo. You could use the time better in acting directly on the situation that prompts analysis. Beware of the sort of mental gymnastics that only stiffen your defenses and hinder your moving ahead flexibly.

Act rather than react. Reaction too often is defensive. You become so busy dealing with the attitudes and values of others that you forsake your own. Go ahead and do what you believe is right. Do be open to feedback; the responses of others with whom you interact are important and helpful, useful measurements of how well you are handling relationships. But always waiting for responses or reacting to those responses where your own initiative is indicated gives too much power to others. Don't be subservient or dependent always on what others think of you or say to you. Trust yourself. You have to be responsible for what you do, so do it. Act.

Be constructive. How you reflect on your experience is important. Many of us have the negative habit of always finding fault as we reflect on our experiences. The question too often is: "What did I do wrong?" The question should be: "What did I do right?" Don't pass over the many good things you do, the many problems you solve, the new experiences you risk. Recognize the day-to-day, positive successes that you have. They can be more important to your growth than the rare moments of grand victory. Success in life is the accumulation of many, many small gains.

Appreciate your efforts. Remember, there is no such thing as a 100-percent success or a perfect achievement. And there is no such thing as the perfect moment for making the effort. In life, you win some, and you lose some, but whether you win or lose, appreciate having tried. The effort itself has to be appreciated. Having tried often is 90 percent of the victory. Not having tried is 100 percent a failure. When things aren't going well, we tend to forget how hard we tried. The effort is what counts.

Learn from your mistakes. Don't agonize over error. We learn by doing, and if you aren't making an occasional mistake, you aren't doing much of anything. Each new experience involves some risk— the risk of failing, the risk of making a mistake—and the greater the promise of the enterprise, the greater the risk. But if the venture is reasonable and possible, then the risk is reasonable. And if the effort is an honest effort, then any mistake made is an honest mistake—and a learning opportunity. Few mistakes end up disastrous, unless we fail to learn from those mistakes.

Be humble. True humility is not self-effacing. We sometimes confuse humility with humiliation. True humility is nothing more than being honest with yourself. Growing demands that you know yourself as much as possible—the good, the bad, and the beautiful—which requires intellectual and emotional honesty. Then you can recognize and accept the good that you do as well as face failures when they happen. Humility—honesty with yourself—is the prerequisite of personal growth.

Enjoy yourself. The full fruit of knowing yourself is enjoying being yourself. In my practice, those individuals who have come to know their personality styles, and have worked with them, have all exhibited the same response: the joy and excitement that comes with self-discovery. Knowing and working with your personality style, its essential determinant, and its strengths have a liberating effect. Once you know yourself and what you can expect of yourself, you are a truly free person, free to be what you can be, free to interact with others and with the environment at large. And with that growth in knowledge of self and others comes a greater sense of confidence as you move through life. You know that you will still encounter stress and problems, some bad days and disappointments, but by knowing yourself, you are better equipped to handle these moments. Nothing is changed in your motor skills, intelligence, aptitudes, and other individual factors in your total makeup, but competent knowledge of your personality style permits you to channel and use your qualities constructively and purposefully, in your attitudes toward yourself and in your relationships with others. Know yourself. Enjoy yourself. Enjoy the health, the freedom, and productivity that come through knowing yourself and being yourself.

TO BE HUMAN

What does it mean to be human? There is no single answer. But try this: to be fully alive to your own human potential, to realize as much of it as you can. It means always doing your best at whatever you're doing—doing but not overdoing or underdoing, just doing your decent best.

To exist as a human being means to coexist with every other human being, recognizing and liking the family resemblance, feeling kinship. It means living consciously and conscientiously with your neighbor, whether next door or half a world away. It means being aware, caring, sharing, loving. More, it means dwelling sensitively with the whole of life on planet Earth, with the air we breathe in common and the water we share, with the plants of the earth, with all the other creatures great and small who share the same air and water and fruits of the earth. It means taking what you need but leaving what others need. To be human is to know when enough is enough.

The Jewish people have a greeting that says it all: *Shalom*—peace. The word means much more that the absence of hostility. It means sufficiency, harmony, freedom from evil and harm, enough, contentment. This ancient greeting—*Shalom*—runs like a thread through both Hebrew and Christian scriptures, and it has its equivalent in the writings of all the great religions.

To be human means to have faith—to believe in being human, to plunge into human activity with reasonable expectations of yourself and others and not to be too disappointed when you fail or when others fail you. Faith means always being willing to try because you believe you are capable and that others are capable too. To be human means to hope—to trust that all that is decent and good in life is attainable, if not just now, then in some other moment; if not for you, then for your children. To hope means to accept the bad days with the good, the bitter with the sweet, the less with the more, to be glad for the light, and to try always not to curse the darkness.

THE HIDDEN DIMENSION

Mankind has developed rapidly and advanced so remarkably because of our enormously flexible response to environmental opportunity and our varied basic, biological, genetic predispositions. It is not that man has accommodated so well to changing environmental factors so much as that he has remained adaptable through the course of evolution. He did not grow the longest tusks or the most powerful jaws or the greatest speed or the toughest hide. These are all highly specialized adaptations to meet specific environmental pressures. When the pressures change, these specific adjustments can be—and have been—detrimental to further adaptation, and thus so many species have perished. Not man and his ancestors. Rather, by remaining flexible and open, while always remaining somewhat vulnerable, mankind as a species has evolved, increased in numbers, and responded to opportunities offered by the environment with remarkable success. The excesses of the past century, it could be argued, demonstrate all too well mankind's response capability when presented with environmental opportunities. But the same argument could be used persuasively to demonstrate that mankind is quite capable of meeting the challenge of correcting his own excesses.

Consider: man is marvelously equipped biologically to perform varied and complex tasks. But his mental equipment is far more impressive: intelligence that permits him to organize and process information and to conceptualize, creativity, memory, aptitudes and interests, a seemingly insatiable curiosity, and discipline in investigation to match it. The various sciences that study the evolution of man credit much of the rapid growth of human ingenuity to the comparatively rapid growth in size and function of the human brain. They point not only to brain mass but to development of massive fissures and folds of the cortex as making possible the many complex functions we call the mental processes. These processes are what make it possible for man to respond so variably and successfully to environmental opportunity. Each encounter between man and his environment is an experience that he stores in his memory complete with its components and outcome. As his experiences increase and multiply, man is able to recall previous experiences in ways that facilitate and enhance the successful outcome of succeeding experiences. Thus, through his experiences and his memory of those experiences, man is increasingly well equipped to meet new challenges and opportunities posed by his environment. And more rapidly. He is increasingly able to respond to more complex and varied opportunities until he not only can manipulate and control more and more of his environment; he is capable of creating new environments.

But there are definite limitations to the human brain's development in terms of size. The question is: can the rapid mastery of man's environment and the relative speed of his evolutionary progress be attributed solely to an increase in brain mass and surface of the brain's cortex? Possibly, but let me offer another possibility. Man's capabilities were greatly enhanced and expanded by the availability of multiple personality styles. Rather than assume that all the capabilities of the human species were invested in more or less equal portions in every member of the species, let us assume some diversification and specialization made possible by twelve separate personality styles. To simplify the situation greatly, a twelve-way division of basic human strengths and traits meant a division of labor and specialization that could meet different challenges posed by the environment. That we presently conduct human enterprise in this cooperative manner, whether in launching a manned space vehicle or playing a game of football, only supports the theory. We define a goal; we break down the tasks required to accomplish that goal, and we assign specific tasks to those who demonstrate special aptitudes for those tasks. Otherwise, everyone involved would have to be equally competent, or equally incompetent. Everyone would have to be a jack-of-all-trades but master of none. Little would be accomplished well. But through diversification and specialization, not everyone has to be an astronaut *and* a fuel chemist *and* a rocket engineer *and* an electronic specialist—or a quarterback, pulling guard, and middle linebacker. If we did everything that way, if tasks were assigned indiscriminately to all participants, the rocket would never leave the pad, nor the team the huddle.

This diversification and specialization, made possible by multiple personality styles, greatly increases the range of human enterprise both in the number of opportunities that can be met and in the time required to complete the tasks involved. However we lacked consciousness of personality-style options and however rudimentary their implementation in mankind's evolutionary past, it seems reasonable to speculate that they were utilized to advantage and were responsible at least in part for man's rapid progress. If a central axiom in evolutionary theory is that the fittest survive, why not that the fittest assume the tasks best matched to their strengths? If we can assume that multiple personality styles were available to channel mankind's various capabilities, it would help greatly to explain how mankind was able to respond so flexibly and efficiently and productively to the increasingly complex opportunities offered by the environment.

GIFTS TO BE SHARED

Each of us and all of us are more gifted than we know. This is the significance of multiple personality styles. Each of us does not have to be a miniature replica of all that is potentially human. By being less, each of us can be more, but only if we learn to share the gifts. Knowledge of the twelve styles of personality, and conscious application of that knowledge, make the strengths of each style more available to all of us. Until now, for lack of knowledge of the strengths and opportunities of all twelve styles, we have used these gifts randomly and sometimes counterproductively. More, we have made very unreal and impossible demands of each other and of ourselves. We expected the other person to be made in our own image and likeness. We didn't always appreciate the differences; in fact, we sometimes resented them, feared them, even attacked them, and we sometimes used these great gifts to cancel out or destroy the gifts of the other.

Now we know better, so we ought to be able to behave much better toward each other. Our strengths complement each other, benefit each other; opportunities become more accessible, more exciting; and when we pool our strengths with mutual awareness and regard, when we share the opportunities and the excitement, something much greater than the expected outcome is realized: something like *Shalom.* But when we pool our weaknesses and vulnerabilities, our ignorance and our fears, something dark and tragic begins to happen. Humanity begins to fragment toward chaos.

Integrate. The word is so important to good health and to all human enterprise. Life is a process of integration—or fragmentation. The choice has to be ours. Integration means bringing together all the components of our being—our physical resources, our intellectual capabilities, our limitations, our hopes, our feelings, our joys and our sorrows, our successes and our failures, our sense of self. Integration is also the process of bringing everything within our environment, as much as possible, into a mutually productive relationship. Integration means wholeness; it means being fully alive.

The right response to the massive problems that face us as the family of man is not anguish and lament. As with the individual, action is far more productive than reaction, but proper awareness of the situation and the options is a necessary prelude—and no single action will provide the right solution. The answer supposes a conscious, continuous series of many constructive and reinforcing solutions in all areas of human enterprise. That means that we are all involved. Or should be.

The obvious and urgent lesson to be learned from the concept of personality style is that we become more human when we truly know each other, when we work to complement and supplement each other's strengths, when we share each other's burdens and meet each other's needs. Our human capabilities are so distributed among the twelve personality styles that each of us can be fully human and fully alive only when he shares and cooperates with his fellow men.

Scientists have classified man as the species *Homo sapiens*—"wise man"—and modern man, the sole surviving subspecies, as *Homo sapiens sapiens*—"wise, wise man." Whether he is or not is now his choice . . . collectively.

Appendix: A Brief History
of Personality Study

HIPPOCRATES, that wise physician of ancient Greece, had a notion. He thought he could distinguish four distinct types of personality, each corresponding to the four "humors"—fluids—of the human body. A sluggish or "phlegmatic" temperament he identified with phlegm. An irritable or "choleric" temperament was attributed to yellow fluids. Black bile prompted gloomy or "melancholic" personalities, and the cheerful or "sanguine" personality was attributed to the blood. Hippocrates' theory endured for many centuries, and even today we often use his terms to describe the moods of others. In recent years a number of highly creditable research psychologists have tried to differentiate types of personalities on the basis of physiological characteristics but with little more success than Hippocrates.

While the ancient Greeks gave us the first concepts of personality, the root word *persona* is Latin, and it means "mask," the kind that actors in Greek and Roman dramas wore to suggest the characters and emotions that were being portrayed. The mask revealed the role, the person. But it was Sigmund Freud, just before the turn of this century, who really probed behind the mask to reveal significant in-

313

sights into the human personality. Freud, the Austrian founder of psychoanalysis, proposed a structure of the personality made up of *id,* an irrational and uninhibited source of psychic energy, impulses, and aggression; *ego,* the cognitive portion of the personality that differentiated the id and reality and inhibited the id; and *superego,* the learned system of self-control that replaced parental control in adulthood and determined moral and ethical behavior. Freud also proposed that the personality functioned on three distinct levels—*conscious, preconscious,* and *unconscious.* The id functioned only at the unconscious level while the ego and superego functioned at the conscious and preconscious levels as well as the unconscious level. Freud's greatest contribution—if one can be singled out as such—was his theory of human development. He said that every human being beginning at birth passed through consecutive stages that he termed *oral, anal, phallic,* and *genital.* The first three stages occurred from birth until about six, followed by a *latency period* that lasted until puberty when the adolescent entered the *genital* stage. Freud contended that the adult personality was shaped largely by the experiences of the child as he passed through these various stages.

Freud's remarkable insights and theories prompted explosive developments in the study of personality. Carl Jung, Freud's once-close friend and collaborator, introduced the concept of personality divided between *introversion,* interest in the inner world of self, and *extroversion,* interest in other people and the outside world. Jung believed that the healthy personality was balanced between introversion and extroversion, and a less healthy personality was dominated by one or the other.

Alfred Adler, another of Freud's disciples who broke with his mentor, was interested in the way the individual functioned in society. He postulated that the personality's basic striving was for perfection and superiority. Personal frustration and failure produced an *inferiority complex*—a term still in vogue in popular but not professional jargon. Of more value in contemporary personality study is another term that Adler introduced: *life style.* By this he meant the pervading way each individual viewed himself and life as a whole.

Ivan Pavlov, the Russian physiologist, discovered a link between the autonomic nervous system and environmental stimuli, which he called *conditioned reflex.* Pavlov believed that conditioning explained much, if not all, of human behavior, including mental activity. The individual is the sum of his conditioning by environmental stimuli.

Since Pavlov, focus in personality theory has polarized between the behaviorists, championed by B. F. Skinner, who believe that there is no entity we can call a personality but only the total organism's response to his environment, and the humanistic and subjective movements, typified by Abraham Maslow and Carl Rogers, who view the individual as positively good and capable of influencing his own behavior. On the one hand, the environment is viewed as the determinant; on the other, the person is seen acting in his environment, normally growing toward fulfillment according to his capabilities.

Of great popular as well as professional interest recently has been the structure of personality introduced by Eric Berne and popularized in his book entitled *Games People Play*. Berne's concept is that the personality has a structure populated by three coexisting organs that manifest themselves in three distinct ego states, popularly labeled *parent, adult,* and *child*. Any one of these stages may respond to any given social stimulus, and the response is healthy or not depending on how appropriate it is to the proper function of the ego state responding.

Significant to the current study of personality is the contribution of Erik Erikson, psychoanalyst and leading spokesman for modern ego psychology, which views the individual as being in a state of flux, constantly influenced by his adaptation to life's experiences. The personality is constantly developing. Erikson proposed a theory of human development reminiscent of Freud's, but extending through all of human life. Called by Erikson the *Eight Ages of Man,* the theory structures progressive opportunities for growth or development—also called crises—in which the individual learns to resolve conflict in ways that are either healthy or unhealthy, positive or negative.

In *stage one,* the infant learns to *trust* or *mistrust* himself and his environment in the nurturing relationship with his mother. The next crisis—or opportunity—of childhood comes in *stage two* when the infant passes through the anal-muscular stage during which he learns *initiative,* delight in his own person and his encounters with and *doubt. Stage three* occurs during the preschool years. The child learns *initiative,* delight in his own person and his encounters with the social environment, or *guilt,* depending on whether he receives approval or not. *Industry versus inferiority* is the crisis of *stage four* facing the child as he begins his schooling. He must learn the tools of his culture and the accompanying sense of his own competency or he is likely to consider himself mediocre or inadequate.

Stage five, adolescence, brings on the probing, questioning, questing crisis of *identity versus role confusion* in which the challenge is to integrate the various identifications and skills learned in childhood with new social roles and an emerging sexual identity. Once identity has been accepted, the young adult faces *stage six, intimacy versus isolation.* He must commit himself to affiliations and close relationships involving sharing and mutuality, or he is in danger of remaining apart, avoiding intimacy. *Stage seven* is the crisis of *generativity versus stagnation.* Generativity is the physical capability of producing offspring and the willingness to guide and to give, to truly care. The opposite is self-indulgence and apathy. Old age poses the crisis of *stage eight, ego integrity versus despair.* If one can reflect on the past and accept the good with the bad and see his life as having been worthwhile, this person has achieved ego integrity. If he looks back with regret, if he fears death, he knows only despair.

Was Hippocrates so wrong? Yes. And no. His linking personality to body fluids certainly has no credibility, but his perception that so many personalities were remarkably alike is attractive even today. Sigmund Freud's concept of a structure of the human personality was a working theory that gave birth to enormously productive work in psychoanalysis and so much of psychotherapy as practiced today according to various disciplines. B. F. Skinner and his fellow behaviorists continue to challenge psychologists and psychiatrists to examine the environmental influences that affect human behavior. The humanists urge us to work with patients on an intimate and optimistic basis, always conscious of the relationship between therapist and patient. Erikson greatly expanded Freud's developmental concept to a much fuller vision of human opportunity through the various stages of life. But the work of these pioneers is a challenge to academicians and practitioners to go beyond the wealth of literature and experience, to keep probing, to dig deeper, in search of still greater understanding of the human personality and its potential. Personality, like everything human, is an invitation to know more so that human life can be lived fully.

The fields of psychology and psychiatry are still young sciences. My colleagues and I delve as deeply into the human personality as our knowledge permits, recognizing that our skills so often are more art than science. And the art demands that we work at a very intimate level with the individual. We don't always have the depth and range of knowledge that we would like to work more widely and effectively with our patients. The process is limited—despite the research and the many discoveries in personality studies made in less than a century. The human personality is still largely a mystery. Many more insights and many more tools are needed.

Like so many other innovations in psychology, my concept of personality styles emerged from a problem presented to me by a patient—one of those minor moments that nag like a puzzle with a part missing. This patient told me a dream that kept recurring from time to time. For a long time I simply couldn't interpret it. Meanwhile, another patient related the same dream with only minor variations of detail. Then another patient told me essentially the same dream. And another. Even though I still didn't understand the dream, I thought it interesting and exciting that so many individuals of differing circumstances and backgrounds share the same recurring dream. Why?

Another question: Why, in hearing many detailed histories of patients, do you hear so many similar expressions of attitudes, fears, wishes, ways of handling stress and opportunities and failures? And why so often do they express themselves in such similar terms? Coincidences? Not likely, not when the similarities are so consistent and extend beyond a few incidences. Still another question: Why do Freud's and Erikson's theories of growth through stages seem so applicable to some children and not to others? Why do some children experience toilet training with classic conflict yet others, in quite similar environments, go through like experiences with no problems whatsoever? Why do some children raised permissively grow into rigid, demanding adults?

Along with members of my staff, I began sifting through the histories of patients sharing the same problems and strengths for other likenesses. We correlated marked attitudes and behavior patterns that showed similarities. We recorded significant wishes, recollections of early childhood, life-changing events, and so on. We compared ways of handling stress, feelings about others, approaches to opportunity. We sifted and sorted data and then returned to our patients for more information. Slowly, marvelously, the shape and form of similar patterns emerged. Together with psychiatric personnel of local hospitals, I and my staff began to plot first one clearly recognizable style, then another and another, adding another style whenever it became fully apparent. We tested the concept of personality styles again and again, refining, amending, correcting, clarifying until the norms and structure of the twelve styles came into clear focus. We went far beyond pathology to the strengths and operant values of each style. We wanted to construct a profile of each style functioning in varying environments and faced with normal opportunities and stresses. In sum, we wanted to know just how each style demonstrated good health. We felt that the greatest benefits the concept of personality styles could offer the practitioners of psychotherapy—but more, the public at large—were profiles of healthy and productive human beings living and relating at optimal levels, enriching the environment while being fully aware of and content with being themselves.